Beneath the surface

International Library of Sociology

Founded by Karl Mannheim
Editor: John Rex, University of Warwick

Arbor Scientiae
Arbor Vitae

A catalogue of the books available in the **International Library of Sociology** and other series of Social Science books published by Routledge & Kegan Paul will be found at the end of this volume.

Beneath the surface

An account of three styles of sociological research

Colin Fletcher
Department of Sociology, University College, Cardiff

Routledge & Kegan Paul
London and Boston

*First published in 1974
by Routledge & Kegan Paul Ltd
Broadway House, 68–74 Carter Lane,
London EC4V 5EL and
9 Park Street,
Boston, Mass. 02108, USA
Set in Monotype Times Roman
and printed in Great Britain by
Unwin Brothers Limited
The Gresham Press
Old Woking, Surrey
© Colin Fletcher 1974*

*ISBN 0 7100 7978 8 (c)
ISBN 0 7100 7979 6 (p)
Library of Congress Catalog Card No. 74–81995*

For Lyn and Dai bach
and those that are to come

Contents

Figures and tables

Acknowledgments

The Editorial Board of *Sociological Review* have given their permission for the paper 'Men in the middle: a reformulation of the thesis' to be reprinted.

Professor M. Stacey made the data available for the secondary analysis which can be found in Chapter 9. Mrs G. G. Eaton recoded this data and discussed the interpretation.

The typing was largely done by Mrs M. Jones and kindly completed by Mrs J. Keenoy.

Introduction

Sociology is characterized by its polemical and pedagogic practice. There is a tradition of spirited argument and gifted teaching. Sociological facts are polemical in themselves, levelling mankind, likening races and looking for social nature. And beyond this, sociology has proved a quarrelsome discipline as if it gained strength from internal divisions and its feuds with academic neighbours.

When I came to sociology (for that is what it felt like) there were balmy days indeed. Growth all around, one hundred apparent theories, lots of research everywhere. And heading this army was the right to judge; as if the necessity to pronounce on day-to-day affairs. I thought to be a sociologist within days of my first term's study.

It has, however, not proved to be that easy. As I was qualifying there was an accelerating separation of teaching and research. When I qualified the choice was to be either teacher or researcher. I chose the latter. I thought to provide the facts for my fellow teachers. I imagined I would be at the pioneering edge.

In a sense I was. Certainly a fluency in 'methods' or 'statistics' baffles the majority, but somehow my expertise was not appreciated by teachers. Nevertheless I continued to develop my wits and made my little offerings 'from the field'. I soon found that I was completely alone in my field. I had become an expert.

I was then amazed by methods textbooks. They were invariably presenting a formula for research. This formula looked ridiculously easy. Yet in 'doing' research I was having biting difficulty. Again I ploughed on through the quantitative method. Yet at the end of three projects despite my enthusiasm, good faith and flowing funds, I was thoroughly disheartened.

I returned to methods textbooks and was attracted by the gentle arts of the qualitative method. There was lean humour, depth – a definite style you might say – and I tried to be an expert once more.

Meanwhile my conscience and awareness had been slightly stirred by the events outside the office. And these events were beginning to affect life in the office too. So as a personal exercise I engaged in the method of critique – feeling that it was time for me to 'lay it on my brothers'.

So this monograph is an account of a research career. I have written giving examples and experience of the three methods in which I have engaged. Beneath the surface of research is how you get to do the study and what its method means to you. My approach has been to give the surface and then peel it back and expose the researcher – the back-room boy who seems to be out of favour with the subject's teachers. My intention has been to write for researchers, to record a little of what we say at conferences and to distinguish the researcher from the vested interests that have separated him from teachers. Perhaps this remark makes one thing clear from the outset: I prefer the approach of the critique.

I also have a broader concern for sociology. Every responsible sociologist must deplore the wasted effort of bellowing in his colleague's ear and whispering in public places. When those in our midst say there is no theory, who challenges them? When it is said that a particular method is 'best', how can anyone argue? Is it really true that social structures are quantifiable; or that micro-relations emerge through their symbolic interactions; or that critical sociology is the new left's hatchet at the base of the establishment? And why are these caricatures current at all?

It must be more than an unwillingness for public debate. It must be an unknowingness: a fear that theory is as baseless as method is meaningless. It must be a fear that sociology has the future of a mongol: the grinning perpetual child that dies on chronological maturity.

My immodest hope is to write of research in such a way that this fear is seen as only partially appropriate and that polemics and pedagogy may come closer as a consequence.

This book is not an integral work. It was written as chapters and is meant to be read as such. I give examples, write analytically about theories of method and assess their workings. The assessments are the most readable but I hope that other chapters prove rewarding for the reader's efforts.

Finally I should say that many, better writers have visited these fields before me. In fact it is peculiar how little each generation discovers and how much they are forced to reproduce. In one sense this book is self-indulgent; my examples of the methods are taken from my own work. And so I close this introduction with a note of caution. I have tried to compose an ordinary book from commonplace thoughts. My sole aim has been to express myself with honest clarity.

part one

The quantitative method

My introduction to quantitative sociology

Finding my feet in sociological research meant following my mentors' paths. I knew I was supposed to study industry and I also knew I was supposed to work out my own problem. But it was only part of my course so it was not supposed to take a long time. This meant that I did not have to have a theory, or a complex problem or a lot of respondents. I was just expected to go away and do it. Nevertheless I hung around the department with sheaves of schemes until no one would listen to my latest idea. I retired to a quiet office one dinner time and wrote an interview schedule. That was it. The theory could wait because I now needed data. I chose the firm to go to from a register and stalled my way through a conversation with its personnel manager. When the fieldwork was completed he gave me a job for six weeks doing a study for him.

My next mentor wanted a replication done as part of a PhD course. We barely knew each other. He was not really a sociologist. So I studied the university in which I was working, with a concept that my supervisor had suggested. Again it was not supposed to take long. It was only an exercise in doing research. The actual time needed, though, was doubled by fiddling about avoiding the repetitious clerical detail that mounted up around the nascent thinker.

An introduction to part one

Two examples of quantitative sociological work are given. The first exhibits the eclectic nature of measurement instruments and the 'stumbling upon facts' when the results are in. For its part, the second attempts a replication but produces interesting results that 'do not work'. And so whilst the first concentrates upon results the second is more an exercise in technique. Both chapters show how much can be done with very little real information.

1 Men in the middle: a reformulation of the thesis

It could be said that the crucial impact of the social sciences on the world at large is one of demystification. Many common-sense theses have crumbled on scrutiny. Yet some myths have been advanced by the social sciences themselves. One such myth is the 'man in the middle' thesis for industrial supervisors. It is one of sociology's most dramatic tales.

Industrial supervisors, classically foremen, are men in the middle (Roethlisberger, 1943). Wedged between workers and management, they represent both to each other and neither to themselves. Supervisors are constantly torn by competing demands and loyalties. They have come up from the ranks but are not part of management. Nevertheless they are the voice of the front office that is heard on the shop floor. These strains are exacerbated by the continuous whittling away of their power and status by management and machine. The supervisor is robbed of the capacity to withstand the strain of his position. The middle is simply no-man's-land and supervisors sustain the scars of industrial conflict.

Such a thesis is monolithic. It argues that all men in all supervisory positions in all firms experience the same kind and same degree of chronic stress. The evidence to date, of course, fails to support the thesis. This evidence, however, has primarily been concerned with predicating the stress of the position upon conflicts of its role, the prime example being supervisor-worker conflict. Goldthorpe (1959) examined the history of coal-getting and found that the three main methods varied in their emphasis on the supervisor being in a 'service' or 'boss' relationship with his workers: the greater the emphasis on the supervisor as 'boss', the greater the conflict. This makes the work technology an intervening factor in supervisor stress. Woodward (1958) considered variations in technology at an inter-firm level and thought that the supervisor-worker relationship was good in process industries but deteriorated through unit- to mass-production firms. Yanousas (1964) meanwhile was wholly sceptical of such variations on a theme of stress. His data suggested that, for American supervisors at least, there were very slight 'man in the middle' sensations.

A research project was undertaken to examine the parts of the thesis in detail and to try out the utility of an alternative formulation of the conflicts. Three factors were to be considered: stratification, differentiation and identification (Fletcher, 1972).

Stratification refers to the fact that in many industries there are a number of levels of supervision; the simple manager-foreman-worker pattern is confined to small firms. What variations, if any, could be traced to differences in level? Is being a senior foreman more or less or the same as being a foreman when it comes to the severity of conflict experienced? Differentiation refers to the complex division of labour even within a particular technology: there are many types of tasks involved in any product. What variations, if any, could be traced to differences in task? And did different departments – manufacturing and assembly – differ significantly? Identification refers to the variations in social beliefs and backgrounds of the supervisors themselves. It is most unlikely that supervisors are either all one type of person or purely passive recipients of demands. What types, if any, could be found in the group of supervisors studied and what significance could this have for variations in conflict? All variations, whatever the factor, were determined by the operationalization of conflict and the approach used has not been explicitly employed before.

The 'man in the middle' thesis suggests that the supervisor's real conflict is with 'the system'. For every decision he makes there is a 'workers' side' and a 'management's side' and regardless of which he takes he is punished by the 'side' that is slighted. This implies that a supervisor is not necessarily at odds with either worker or management as such, but rather at odds with what he has to do. Each decision forces him back out on to the tightrope. In brief, intra-role conflict not inter-role conflict could be the keynote of supervisory stress.

Such a global statement almost denies validation, and the scope of the reported project is not the substance of more than a suggestion for the reformulation of the thesis. Nevertheless the data are suggestive: the conceptualization of conflict is related to the factors of stratification, differentiation and identification. The 'man in the middle' thesis could be 'a colossus with feet of clay'.

The research setting: the factory and its supervisors

Frazers is a unit-production factory on Merseyside. It is part of a world-wide, American-owned network which has 60 per cent of its specialist market. There is a large measure of interdependence between the 'national' companies. Exchange of parts and knowledge is purported to be free and universal. However, standardization of procedures is the biggest tangible manifestation of this interdependence. The choice of a unit-production factory was intended to put the greatest test on the thesis (Goldthorpe *et al.*, 1967).

Eleven years prior to the study the firm moved from a London site. Since then it has doubled in size to its present 1,500 employees (July 1966). Just over half of these employees were on the shop floor and twenty-six men supervised them, of whom twenty-two were in charge of day-shift production. The night shift was excluded because it was skeletal and responsible for mopping-up operations as directed by the written instructions of the day-shift supervisors. There were four departments: two each for the manufacture and assembly of two products. A department was supervised by senior foremen, some foremen, some assistant foremen, and some working chargehands. The structure of the supervision was not symmetrical; nearly two-thirds of the labour force worked on one kind of unit.

All twenty-two supervisors were interviewed in the summer of 1966 with a schedule that took between $1\frac{1}{2}$ and 3 hours to complete. The 'conflict with the system' measurement took about half the time and the other half was spent on wide-ranging data collection starting with biographical details, continuing with questions on formal and informal interaction and concluding with opinions on supervision.

The research criterion: the measurement and magnitude of supervisor conflict

It has been suggested that the core conflict in supervision is with 'the system'. The root cause of this conflict is the prevalence of hierarchical control over a job which ideally needs a 'free hand'. The supervisor is the 'master and victim of double talk' (Roethlisberger, 1945), largely because he does not make the decisions for which he is responsible. In simple terms, supervisors' conflict is contingent upon the degree to which their decisions are bureaucratized. Bureaucratization entails important additional elements: decisions are procedures, they are impersonal and standardized. The supervisor feels the 'system' as the coalescence of the impersonal and standardized procedures that he must follow and the responsibility he holds for their outcomes without the authority to alter their course.

But for all the victims and beneficiaries of bureaucracy its presence is that of an octopus. Crozier (1964) notes that one of the

5

most frequent uses of the term 'bureaucracy' is that of sheer abuse. The pervasiveness of the phenomenon tends to encourage identical condemnation from most people. This means that conflict with the system could be a 'blanket reaction' if sought in general terms. So in order to encourage discrimination, a measure was developed to which this conflict could be adduced. Conflict was said to be present when a supervisor would like to see a change in the procedure for dealing with a number of problems. The measurement was a simple count of the number of discrepancies between what is done and what the supervisor would like to be done in selected areas. Thus the measure is the product of the juxtaposition of two notions: decision procedures and critical problems – or crises – for supervisors.

The procedures index was developed by conceiving of a decision as a process (March *et al.*, 1958); that is, as a behaviour which has a series of interdependent stages. The stages are not necessarily enacted in every decision, but they will be recognized as relevant. The index of a decision procedure is: (1) stating a problem: spotting and defining it; (2) reference activity: 'searches' to estimate its extent and complexity and possibly experimenting with some alternatives; (3) making a decision; (4) communicating a decision; (5) enforcing a decision. This measure gives five 'counts' for congruency or dissent for each decision.

Of course a great deal depends on what the questions contain – the situations to which they refer. Decision situations were selected that depended particularly on legal authority – that is, where the supervisor acts as a manager by virtue of his position – rather than situations of rational authority where he acts as a technical adviser by virtue of his specialized knowledge. This distinction between rational and legal authority is based upon Weber's original formulation and proved valuable in a laboratory study of supervision (Evan and Zelditch, 1961). In essence the decisions used entail 'critical incidents'. Fundamentally then, for a supervisor, a critical incident is a decision involving an act of management and a part of the art of administration. Six such decisions were determined – three referring to the supervision of men: when dealing with lateness, poor work and allocating work; the other three referring to the supervision of work: rearranging work patterns, handling supplies and planning overtime. Moreover, these decisions could be said to be part of all supervisors' responsibilities and thus allow direct comparison between the many specialist supervisors.

The supervisors were asked to explain how decisions were made in each critical area and to follow the five stages of procedure as the recall framework. Then they were asked for a recent example of this sort of decision. This exemplification had three purposes. First, it filled out their general statements with detail with which they could be discussed. Second, it acted as a check on the general account and gave an opportunity for correction. Third, it 'heightened perception' by asking the supervisor to role-play prior to the preference questions.

The supervisor's attention having, hopefully, been focused on the procedures and problems of a decision area, each stage was gone through again to seek the extent of conflict with current practice. These views were sought by a format as unbiased as possible. For all questions the phrasing was: 'This part deals with your preferences about decisions. I would like you to consider the problem of . . . and tell me whether or not you would prefer to change:

1 a the problem statement
   b (if yes) in what way?
2   . . . .'

and so on, through problem-reference and decision-making, communication and enforcement.

In this way a score was available for each supervisor on:

1 how many stages of each decision process he would change;
2 how many stages of all decision processes he would change;
3 the direction in which he would change stages and decisions.

Thus a score was obtained on whether he wished to decrease the system's sway over him or decrease his own load of responsibility.

Overall scores were also available for all supervisors and it should be noted that seventy-eight preferences for change were recorded (11·6 per cent). The general conflict with the system was small. Of course this is not necessarily an accurate depiction of the situation; the critical incidents chosen need not have been the biggest crises supervisors faced, and there could be more accurate means of tapping such a conflict. The overall low level of conflict is, however, of considerable analytical importance. There was not an atmosphere of conflict with the system on Frazers' shop floor: it was not a revolutionary situation. Nevertheless there was some conflict and those expressing more conflict could be different from general non-conflictful supervisors in important ways.

The research findings: the contingencies of conflict – stratification and differentiation

It is possible that there are at least three factors at work in the expression of supervisors' conflict which are caused by having the experience of being the 'man in the middle'. The factors merit systematic disentanglement and consideration. They differ in complexity as well as perspective. Stratification and differentiation

7

are facets of the shop-floor structure and are, at a simple analytical level, relatively straightforward. Identification, however, is based on the biographies of the supervisors and cannot be stated in too simple and analytical terms. Consequently the broader 'system perspectives' will be taken first and then the more involved 'actor perspectives'. The attempt to account for the findings from these perspectives is withheld until the concluding discussion.

First, stratification – the significance of differing levels of supervision – can be examined. There were five senior foremen (two were in the same department) and seventeen foremen, yet the number and direction of preferences for change were very similar (see Table 1.1).

TABLE 1.1   *Stratification and conflict*

| | | Number of preferences expressed | | |
Level	Number of respondents	More control	Less control	Total
Senior foremen	5	28	9	37
Foremen	17	27	14	41

$$\chi^2 = 47 \cdot 92 \qquad p \text{ is less than } 0 \cdot 01*$$

However, senior foremen were significantly more critical of current procedures than foremen. And to this extent they wanted significantly more control than did the foremen.

Second, differentiation – the significance of different tasks in the process of production – can be related to supervisor conflict with the system. The respective scores of the manufacturing and assembly sections of the same process were compared. There were the same number of supervisors in each department when assistant foremen were also included in the interviewing. Nevertheless the departmental structures varied: assembly had two senior foremen, two foremen and four assistant foremen, while the manufacturing department had a much more orthodox structure of one senior foreman, four foremen and three assistant foremen. The inclusion of the assistant foremen meant that all the full-time supervisory staff were interviewed and it was possible to compare the two departments fully (see Table 1.2).

*All the tables given were subjected to Yates's correction as there were less than 30 respondents, but the data is given as original values to save confusion. The acceptance level was set at $0 \cdot 05$, where, with one degree of freedom, the χ^2 value is $3 \cdot 841$. It will be evident that some values are also greater than the $0 \cdot 01$ value of $6 \cdot 635$.

At first the findings seem confused. The assembly department's supervisors sought nearly twice as much change as their machine-shop colleagues, yet their prime wish was for more system, more 'procedure', more 'guidance': in brief, a tighter bureaucracy. Conversely the machine-shop supervisors wanted more 'say', more

TABLE 1.2   *Differentiation and conflict*

Departments	Number of respondents	Number of preferences expressed		Total
		More control	Less control	
Assembly	8	7	34	41
Machine shops	8	23	4	27

$$\chi^2 = 48 \cdot 02 \qquad p \text{ is less than } 0 \cdot 01$$

'control', particularly with supply and disciplining defects problems. Differentiation could play a part here. The machine shops were the only department to make the same thing twice. Lathe operators would produce 1,000 to 5,000 standardized parts which would be assembled in individual and highly varied units. In effect, though assembly's supply and defects problems could be massive, they were infrequent: a few units could keep a shop occupied for a week. Moreover, assembly supervisors could walk over and talk to their 'suppliers'. The problems for machine-shop supervisors were considerable: a myriad specialist, outside suppliers to be chased and all materials required in considerable bulk to keep the lathes operating. As for discipline over defects, a 'thou' out on a tolerance could hold up a virtually complete unit for weeks until a fresh supply of materials had been ordered and delivered. And their suppliers had to be contacted and reminded by telephone and letter. In brief, assembly epitomizes the unit technology, whilst machine shops have some of the characteristics of large-batch production. Assembly supervisors sought a decrease in the 'uncertainty' and an increase in the range and application of procedures. The machine shops sought the opposite: an increase in autonomy to deal with the more frequent and difficult problems they faced.

The research findings: the contingencies of conflict – identification

Identification refers to the beliefs and backgrounds of the supervisors. In this paper it is a term that refers to one process rather than one dimension – the process of conceiving of one's self and

9

one's role and considering the consequences of the relationship between them. The term tries to highlight the ways in which a man's biography plays a part in his current concerns and what sort of self-conception he holds. Thus whilst stratification and differentiation are variables of the structure of supervision, identification involves variables about supervisors within this structure. Moreover, the establishment of types of supervisor was a process in itself.

First the correlation matrix was examined. It showed that some 'personal' factors were correlated with wanting change and wanting more control. The greater the age the less the orientation to change $(-0 \cdot 47)$ and the less the orientation to more control $(-0 \cdot 45)$, whilst seeking change correlated with criticism of management communication $(0 \cdot 45)$ and the number of supervisory jobs held since joining the firm $(0 \cdot 46)$. These correlations were suggestive but did not imply any consistent 'more change' and 'more control' trends apart from a relationship with age. The two other correlates were not associated with both orientations. Further analysis could suggest whether the supervisors were all of one piece or if there were few correlations because of a multiplicity of types.

Many measures are usually incorporated in the study of occupational types. Here these measures are phrased with reference to the supervisors studied. Are they burgesses or spiralists in terms of how long they had worked for Frazers, the number of promotions, and whether or not they came from London? What do they think of the foreman's position? Are they friendly with other foremen? And what of their views of management, their immediate boss (the works manager) and management communication generally? What people are troublesome in their jobs: the operators or the management or both? What education have they received: did they leave school at 15, or did they carry on to study for ONCs and HNCs?

The final stage of the process was to divide the supervisors into two major groups, one of which contained a special sub-group. The equal numbers in the groups was fortuitous, the division being on the basis of the preference for change – or conflict with the system – frequency distribution. The groups were:

Conservatives (0–4 preferences for change)
Radicals (more than 4 preferences for change)
Sub-group revolutionaries (more than 10 preferences for change and hence seeking to change at least three of the existing decision procedures)

The names of the groups were derived from the numerical and real meaning of the scores; no political or pejorative implications should be drawn from them. (Table 1.3 gives the means for each group.)

TABLE 1.3   *The derivation and distribution of empirical types of supervisor by the mean scores for preferences for change*

	Conservatives	Radicals	Revolutionaries	Total
Mean	2·09	8·638	12·25	5·225
Number in cell	11	11	(5)	22

Each of the factors mentioned already, and a few refinements, were re-examined to seek significant differences between the two major groups and to look for possible trends when the revolutionaries were separated from the radicals. Table 1.4 shows the differences and similarities found.

Conservatives were older, less educated, longer serving, less careerist and more sociable with other supervisors than radicals. Revolutionaries were more extreme: much younger, more educated, relatively isolated, selective about a small number of friends (many of whom were junior executives) and fundamentally critical of management. Revolutionaries were different from the wider group of radicals whose social life was closer to conservatives. For radicals there was more friendship or sociability in and away from work and it was more likely to be departmentally based. Radicals' background characteristics show less meteoric careers and less of the new technological management approach. In a sense it could be said that whilst radicals appear to reflect on management practice from a foreman's point of view, revolutionaries consider themselves practising managers. This puts their criticism of management in a context and reinforces the non-ideological use of terms to describe the groups. Revolutionaries were not anti-management but pro-managerialism. Their preferences for change were to counteract inefficiencies they clearly saw. From their career so far they had reason to believe that they would go far. Revolutionaries' self-conceptions were as managers rather than as foremen and from this perspective they criticized the front office, their peers and those who serviced their productive activity.

The process of secondary analysis thus began with the correlates of seeking more control and of seeking less control, which were then revised as conservatives, radicals and revolutionaries. The final stage did not establish mutually exclusive types, though the two extremes of conservatives and revolutionaries were consistently different. Radicals differ in kind from both conservatives and revolutionaries. Their friendship patterns are 'conservative' whilst their attitudes are 'revolutionary'. These refinements have specified contents and are empirically verified. (Cf. Coates and Pellegrin, 1957.)

TABLE 1.4 *The differences and similarities between empirical types of supervisors in terms of their careers, plant activities and plant attitudes**

Characteristics	Conservatives	Radicals	Revolutionaries
A. Career			
1 Average age (years)	48·1	41	37
2 Average number of jobs at Frazers	1·81	3·09	4·25
3 Average years of company service	19·5	13·72	10·3
4 Educated beyond ONC	No	Yes	Yes
5 Ex-London employees	Yes	Yes	No
B. Activities with other supervisors			
1 Consider them sociable	Yes	Yes	No
2 Meet each other outside the plant	Yes	Yes	No
3 Friends amongst the supervisors			
a. within their own department	Yes	Yes	No
b. in other departments	No	Yes	Yes
C. Plant attitudes			
1 Critical of senior management	No	Yes	Yes
2 'Foremen's problems are with . . .'	Operators	Management	Management

Discussion

It is difficult to argue anything loudly from a small study with rather insubstantial measures and tests. But it is possible to point to the implications of the results.

*The procedure for analysing the values was as follows: the overall mean was calculated for each 'predictor' and compared with the mean for each group and tested by χ^2. Then each group was dichotomized in terms of whether the constituent supervisors' scores were above or below the overall mean. These dichotomous values were aggregated for each group and further tested by χ^2. There are problems when using χ^2 with such a small number. Moreover, Seigal (1956, p. 46) instructs that χ^2 should not be used when 20 per cent of the expected frequencies are smaller than 5, or when any expected frequency is smaller than 1. These conditions were observed.

There were men in the middle. Yet there was no simple pattern in the findings. The results show hierarchical, departmental and individual variations on a rather faint theme. Conflict with the system, as it was operationalized, was not rife. Instead, there was an overall acceptance of the *status quo* in decision-making, even if there were general grumbles about supervisors' problematics. However, where such conflict was present, patterns could be traced.

The key factor would seem to be that for these supervisors conflict increased with their proximity to management. The closer to the executive by position or by identity, then the greater the conflict. Proximity by position means that senior foremen are higher, and in this sense nearer, the source of the decisions affecting the shop floor, namely the works manager. Proximity by identity means that the supervisor feels closer to management and is clearer about mistakes which they might make and of ways of avoiding making them. These two proximities have considerable theoretical significance.

Classically, the man in the middle has workers and managers 'on either side'. But when there are *men* in the middle, a structure of supervision, then those in direct confrontation experience greater conflict: (1) senior foremen were more critical than foremen, and (2) senior foremen wanted more control than foremen. There is a difference in kind between senior foremen and works manager and a difference in degree between senior foremen and foremen. The position of senior foreman is, for the most part, the end of a career structure and the edge of the shop floor. The combination of the occupational limit and the operational limit puts the position of senior foreman on a 'critical level' (Lockwood, 1964). To the extent that the senior foreman is exposed, the foreman is protected.

Departmental variations also have theoretical significance. Technological theorists such as Woodward (1958, pp. 29–30) have appeared to argue that unit-production systems are largely dissimilar from those of mass production and that there are continuous and significant differences in supervisory relationships. Yet (3) the assembly department was more critical than the manufacturing department and (4) the manufacturing department sought more control than the assembly department. There were elements of large-batch and even mass production in the manufacturing department. The implications of these elements seem to be considerable. Unit production need not be as unitary as it is sometimes thought.

However, perhaps the empirical types of supervisor (in terms of conflict with the system) merit most attention. (5) Re-analysis of the conflict responses and use of χ^2 contingency tests suggested three types of supervisors that were called conservatives, radicals and revolutionaries. But there could be a wider significance for the empirical types. First, in background: there is the suggestion of 'generations'; of the old and the new, of pre-war and post-war kinds of supervisor. Second, there is the role of informal interaction between and within the types. There could be less interaction because there is more experience of conflict: the radicals could be uneasy about their job and the revolutionaries could be at odds with it. Conversely, informal interaction could mediate and moderate the impact of conflictful conditions: situations were taken in which there could be crises of authority. Thus 'sociation' with and 'isolation' from peers could be, in part, both cause and effect of the degree of conflict with the system. Third, the attitudes of the various supervisors give strong indications of different self-conceptions. Those more critical of current procedure saw their problems originating in inappropriate management. They tended to see themselves as miscomprehended and even slighted. On the other hand, conservatives tended to see 'worker demands' rather than 'management wishes' as the root of their problems. These phrases have connotations of the 'foreman self-conception' and were frequently used by the appropriate 'type' of supervisor. Taking all three groups of features, the findings could suggest the more critical supervisors were a more recent generation of 'privatized' (Goldthorpe and Lockwood, 1963) aspirant managers whilst the less critical were more parochial, more sociable and less ambitious foremen. Conflict with the system varied with the extent to which the supervisor saw himself as a manager with management problems or as a foreman with operative problems; as an executive over production or as a 'producer' in touch with the executive.

On this examination the 'man in the middle' thesis is refined rather than refuted. Supervisors do experience some conflict when faced with decision procedures involving 'legal' authority; that is, bureaucratized activity based on the authority of their position. The thesis could be more useful, however, if it entailed a notion of 'men in the middle'. Frazers' supervisors' conflict varied with their stratification, differentiation and identification.

2 Latent identities amongst lecturers at a technological university

Gouldner's (1957, 1 and 2) theory of identification is based on a distinction between manifest and latent identities (1, p. 284):

> It is necessary to distinguish, then, between those social identities of group members which are consensually regarded as relevant to them in a given setting and those which group members define as being irrelevant, inappropriate to consider, or illegitimate to take into account. The former can be called the *manifest* social identities, the latter, the *latent* social identities. Let us be clear that 'social identities', manifest or latent, are not synonymous with the concept of social status. Social identities have to do with the way in which an individual is in fact *perceived* and classified by others in terms of a system of culturally standardized categories.

Such an identity is acquired by being located, categorized and then typed by others and, realizing this, the actors 'mobilize their beliefs concerning it' (1, p. 294).

Cosmopolitanism is one such identity. It is a characteristic of professional people. Gouldner 'derived' the concept, and its polar opposite of localism, from three previous studies.

> These three cases suggested the importance of three variables for analyzing latent identities in organizations: (1) loyalty to the employing organization, (2) commitment to specialized or professional skills, and (3) reference group orientations. Considerations of space do not permit this to be developed here, but each of these studies also found role-playing patterns polar to those discussed. This led us to hypothesize that two latent organizational identities could be found. These were:
> 1 *Cosmopolitans:* those low on loyalty to the employing

15

organization, high on commitment to specialized role skills, and likely to use an outer reference group orientation

2 *Locals:* those high on loyalty to the employing organization, low on commitment to specialized role skills, and likely to use an inner reference group orientation [or see Table 2.1].

TABLE 2.1   *The dimensions of cosmopolitanism-localism after Gouldner*

Latent identity	Commitment to professional skills	Loyalty to the organization	Reference group
Cosmopolitan	High	Low	Outer
Local	Low	High	Inner

Whatever the form of the identity, the theory held that it would be organizationally and socially significant; that it would be associated with the inter- and intra-personal behaviours of the identity-holders. Gouldner's study took two organizational variables, the degree of influence and the degree of participation; one intra-personal variable; the degree of 'rule tropism' ('the degree to which members feel inclined to solve group problems using . . . formal rules' (1, p. 299); and one inter-personal variable, the degree of identity homophily (the degree to which similar identities had more sociable interaction). Cosmos (to which cosmopolitanism will be abbreviated in this text) was to be tested as a variable and then its predictive power was to be scrutinized. If the theory held, then each of these variables would vary with the latent identities of the actors studied.

Here is a scheme of considerable thought and vigour. The theory of identity is one of socialization by a peer group into a set of values which though not organizationally prescribed or recognized, could exert considerable influence within the organization's and actor's behaviour. Local-cosmo dimensions would seem of importance in the identities of professionals in organizations.

The cosmopolitanism thesis: a comparison of findings

The procedures and findings of Gouldner's and my own studies will be given and compared. Usually tables hold the measures and their values; they supplement the text. They also show the extent to which the study is a replication (Fletcher, 1969b).

The original study focused on Coop College. This was a small liberal arts, liberally constituted college in a small mid-western town. The replication took place in Civic College, a medium size, rapidly growing technological university, sited near the centre of a city of over a million people. Both colleges had a plan 'under which students have alternating periods of regular institution and work experience away from the campus' (Gouldner, op. cit., 1, p. 292). Apart from the plan, they are practically polar opposites on the continuum from the groves of academe to noise of industrial involvement (see Table 2.2). One Civic respondent wrote, 'If your researches relate exclusively to this establishment it should be recorded that I am an Arts graduate teaching an arts subject and am, to that extent, a fish out of water.'

TABLE 2.2 *A comparison of the available characteristics of Civic and Coop colleges*

Characteristic	Coop	Civic
1 Size	'Small'	'Medium'
Students	1,000	2,300
Staff	130	205
	(faculty)	(lecturers)
2 Education patterns	Liberal arts	Technological
Lecturers: Engineering		84
Science		87
Arts		34
3 Town size	5,000	1,115,080
4 Nationality	American	British

Coop's researchers interviewed every faculty member and had only five refusals. At Civic I sent questionnaires to all at the lecturer level. For whilst Coop's study was interested in surveying variations in identity in depth, Civic's replication was interested in retesting these developed variations. In 1954 'one hundred and twenty-five interviews, with teaching, research, and administrative personnel, were secured, providing a nearly complete census of the faculty then on the campus' (Gouldner, op. cit., 1, p. 293). Civic was less complete; all 205 lecturers were sent questionnaires and 76 were completed and returned in the winter of 1966. A 36 per cent response rate is not the substance of generalizations either to the lecturers or to Civic College. A practical result is that sociometric analyses are impossible. Moreover, it is also feasible that the response pattern is biased. A χ^2 test on the age distributions of the universe and sample indicated that age groups were represented in appropriate proportions. In these terms, Civic's study is smaller and shallower.

The prime aim in our replication was to have a minimum of four items per variable and items that were operable in Civic College.

Problems of language and experience were encountered. American and English means of expression are not identical and, where necessary, modifications were made. Some Coop items were peculiar to the college and to the college in 1954. These items were rejected

TABLE 2.3   *Commitment to professional skills scales*

Item no.	Coop's scale	Civic scale
		(5-point scales of agree-disagree throughout)
1	What college degrees do you hold? (5-point scale from Ph.D. to none)	I wish more students here had a genuine love of ideas and scholarship. (17)
2	Faculty members should have their loads lightened to make more time available for private research, writing or other work in their field. (5-point scale from agree-disagree)	Members of staff should have their teaching loads lightened to make more time available for private research, writing or work in their field.
3	If I saw no opportunity to do my own personal research here, I would find my job less satisfying. (5-point scale from agree-disagree)	If I saw no opportunity to do my own personal research here, I would find my job less satisfying.
4	A weighted coefficient representing the number of books and articles published by the respondent.	Courses which attempt to integrate several disciplines tend to become watered-down and superficial. (6)
5		It is only understandable that the teaching staff should be more friendly with each other than with the administrators.
6		In our modern world knowledge must be practical to be meaningful. (12)
Guttman coefficient of reproducibility	85·8%	90·11%

and replaced from Coop's wider questionnaire. Once or twice items did not connote the dimension in any direct sense and these too were dropped. All these alterations and rejections were necessary but they have substantially changed the originals.

Each Civic scale is given in its scaling order. The numbers in brackets give the position that these replacement items had in Coop's schedule (Gouldner, op. cit., 1, pp. 270–80).

Taking a measure of cosmopolitanism

Gouldner defined cosmo as a composite measure of scores on three sub-dimensions. Each sub-dimension is examined and then the hypothetical link between them is examined. Throughout measures and findings are juxtaposed so there is a heavy reliance on the tables. This allows space to record why particular items and analyses were modified. The Civic commitment to the professional skills scale contains much modification.

The assumption behind both sets of indices is clearly that commitment to professional skills is a keenness for professional activities and a rejection of conditions or ideas that detract from them. In brief, a demarcation and vocation. (See Table 2.3.) Coop's items 1 and 4 were rejected. Amount of education (item 1) could be causal rather than contingent and we treat it as an independent variable. Amount of publications (item 4) could not be reliably recorded by questionnaire as respondents could vary between those who only wrote down the number of books and those who put down every paper and book review. Accordingly, four items were selected from Gouldner's schedule that approach commitment from a variety of perspectives and, like Coop's items, had an acceptable scale coefficient.

Loyalty to the organization is the most emotionally charged sub-dimension. To manifest that one is not loyal to the employer is to expose oneself to risk. Measures of loyalty are predominantly made less explosive by using the notion of propensity to leave for 'objectively' better employment. (See Table 2.4.) Coop's item 2 seemed too devious; loyalists could be less likely to criticize working conditions but they could be more inclined to criticize their salaries if they feel they are making the college their life's interest and receiving a pittance. Items 3 and 4 seem reference-group orientations rather than loyalty. The replacements make propensity to leave the central feature of loyalty to the organization.

Orientations to a group are a matter of kind rather than degree and the reference-group definition used at Coop means that the actor must refer to colleagues either inside the college or inside the profession and hence beyond the college. The combined force of

TABLE 2.4 *Loyalty to the organization scales*

Item no.	Coop's scale	Civic's scale
1	Would you leave Coop if you were offered a job at Harvard or Princeton? (At a lower salary, at the same salary, at a higher salary, would not leave, no answer)	Were you ever a student at Civic? (Yes, No)
2	Although there are probably reasons for this, it is too bad that salaries at Coop are so low. (5-point scale of agree-disagree)	Barring unforeseen circumstances, do you expect to remain at Civic permanently? (67) (Yes, Not sure, No)
3	It is unfortunate, but true, that there are really few people with whom one can share his professional interests here. (5-point scale of agree-disagree)	Supposing a young friend of yours has just completed graduate training in your field. He has been offered positions of equal rank in London, Birmingham and Civic Universities; which would you advise him to take? (88) (Please rank your choices.)
4	About how many faculty members do you feel you know well? (1–5; 5–10; 10 or more)	Would you leave Civic if you were offered a post at Cambridge? (Lower salary, same salary, higher salary, not leave)
Guttman coefficient of reproducibility	89·8%	90·75%

commitment to professional skills and organizational loyalty eliminates the possibility of being an isolate. (See Table 2.5.)

There were too few items in Coop's scale for reliability. Moreover, where a dimension proposes differences in kind it would seem preferable to pattern its items to cover both poles rather than to assume that not having one attribute necessarily means possessing the other. 'Inner-reference group' is approached through the comparative item 1 and the leading question of item 3, whilst 'outer-reference group' is assumed to be, *as a group*, fundamentally through professional association interaction (items 2 and 4). The radical nature of revision is also conditioned by Coop's items 1 and 3 being inapplicable at Civic.

In sum, Coop items were replicated when it was possible. Nevertheless the majority of items had to be modified or replaced. Primarily, there were demands to adapt content to the respondent's

TABLE 2.5   *Inner-outer reference-group scales*

Item no.	Coop's scale	Civic's scale
1	Criticism of the (college) AAUP chapter on the grounds that it is influenced by an outside organization is not justified. (5-point scale of agree-disagree)	I get most of my intellectual stimulation from: (colleagues at Civic; professional colleagues elsewhere; books and periodicals)
2	I get most of my intellectual stimulation from: (rank options: colleagues at Coop; other professional associates elsewhere; periodicals, books and other publications)	How many of your professional association's meetings have you attended in the last two years? (0–5; 6–10; 11–15; more than 15) (113)
3	By and large what effects have the many recent investigations of communism had on the (college) campus? (No effect whatsoever; not much effect; inhibited free speech somewhat; created marked inhibitions)	Even though they are very competent, somehow or other one gets very little intellectual stimulation from colleagues here. (114) (5-point scale of agree-disagree)
4		How many papers, if any, have you read at these professional meetings in the last two years? (Number)
Guttman coefficient of reproducibility	86·7%	91·05%

frame of reference. Secondarily, our replication rejected those items which could have connoted mixed or different identity dimensions and selected replacements from Coop's schedule. This second criterion was tested by Guttman scaling procedure and Civic's scales had consistently higher and more acceptable coefficients of reproducibility. The sub-dimensions of cosmos scaled.

The next stage was to test whether or not they were sub-dimensions of the same variable.

Are the three established scales related? Gouldner tested for this by examining extreme scorers' emphases on each sub-dimension. All the predicted tendencies 'were significant on the Chi Square test at better than 0·05 level' (Gouldner, op. cit., 1, p. 294 n.). So too were Coop's values. A second test was then to construct a 'scale of scales'. This involved subjecting all scores on all three scales to a single application of the Guttman procedure. 'The resulting scale had a coefficient of reproducibility of 91·4% and yielded four categories' (ibid., p. 294). Coop's scale of scales had a coefficient of reproducibility of 88 per cent and by Guttman's rule should be rejected as being below 90 per cent. To reject a putative scale for 2 per cent error seems pedantic. However, points can be made that would support rejection. First, there was a large reduction of the variance by using a single value for each index; that is, by dichotomizing scores at the mean. Second, Guttman procedure is lenient on error as it takes no account of how far out an 'error score' occurs. Third, two items were responsible for a high proportion of the errors, and they were the two reference-group items that sought orientations on colleagues as intellectual stimulation. This suggested that reference-group sentiments need not necessarily be part of cosmos so the intercorrelations of scale scores were sought in the hope of providing some guidance on whether or not to reject Coop's scale of scales. (See Table 2.6.)

TABLE 2.6 *The intercorrelations of Civic's cosmopolitanism scales scores*

	Commitment to scales	Reference group	Loyalty to Civic
Reference group	0·30		
Loyalty to Civic	0·29	0·16	
Total score	0·80	0·65	0·66

Where $n = 76$ and $(N - 2)$ is 74, an r must be 0·23 to be significant at 0·05 level and 0·29 to be significant at 0·01 level.

The intercorrelations do give guidance, for whilst commitment is significantly related with loyalty and reference group, the relationship between the latter two is less certain; less loyalty to the organization does not necessarily mean that the academic has an outer-reference group. And though the intercorrelations of sub-scales is high it masks this weak link, especially as each sub-scale forms a part of that total. Commitment to professional skills and loyalty, then, can be regarded as one dimension, or cosmos. Reference-group orientations are more conditional in the sense that a high commitment does mean an outer-reference group but a high loyalty need not mean an inner-reference group and vice versa. We have here in Coop's findings an indication either of multi-dimensionality of a single variable or of two variables that are related in a complicated form.

The correlates of cosmopolitanism

At this stage it was possible for the Coop researchers to say, 'From the analysis above it seemed we had succeeded in distinguishing two

TABLE 2.7   *Measures of influence*

Item no.	Coop's items	Civic's scale
	Which of the following decisions are you in on?	In which of the following decisions are you involved?
1	Deciding on the tenure of faculty members	Deciding on the academic content of courses
2	Making faculty and administrative appointments	Deciding on the course and examination programming
3	Deciding on curriculum and organizational change	Deciding on broad educational objectives
4	Deciding on student tenure, for example, dismissal or suspension	Deciding on the selection of prospective students
5	Deciding upon the allocation of college funds	Deciding on the allocation of funds
6	Deciding who assembly speakers should be	Deciding on visiting lecturers
7	Deciding upon the selection of prospective students	Deciding on student suspension/dismissal
8	Deciding course and examination schedules	Deciding on the promotion of assistant lecturers
9	Deciding 'community government' structure	Making appointments of members of staff
10	Deciding broad educational objectives	
Guttman coefficient of reproducibility	Not given	91·77%

latent identities, cosmos and local, and had begun to confirm empirically some of their predicted characteristics' (Gouldner, op. cit., 1, p. 296). The Civic study was a little less successful. Consequently, considering whether or not 'being a cosmo or local made a difference in organizationally relevant behaviour of the person' is a little more tentative. More guarded, too, because less was studied. In fact only the formal variables of influence and participation were examined. Coop and Civic approaches to influence were very similar, being defined by items entailing involvement in decisions. (See Table 2.7.)

The Coop analysis involved dichotomizing the influence distribution and correlating with cosmos and locals. The difference lacked statistical significance 'though they do exhibit a tendency for influence to increase steadily as one moves from cosmos to locals – until, that is, the extreme locals who manifest a sharp decline in influence' (ibid., p. 298). And here occurs the first suggestion that there may be different sorts of cosmos and locals.

In Civic study it was felt that dichotomizing the distribution was too lenient on the potential variance. At the same time, naturally, we wished to be able to relate all indices to the scale scores on the identity dimensions. Consequently, the indices were subjected to Guttman scaling with the resulting coefficient of reproducibility of $91 \cdot 77$ per cent. Accordingly, it is possible to claim that a single score is sufficient representation of influence as the indices seem to be measuring the same entity. The correlation of this scale score with the other scale scores is given after the next few paragraphs on participation.

As before, the Coop procedure opens the discussion (ibid., 1, p. 298):

> Where there is room for choice, the degree of participation
> which an individual manifests in a group is a significant item
> in organizational analysis. In order to determine whether
> participation varied among cosmos and locals a 'degree of
> participation' index was constructed.

Civic's procedure was the selecting of five sorts of functions which academic staff can attend voluntarily. (See Table 2.8.)

Similar criticisms can be levelled at the treatment of participation as at that of the handling of influence. First, using a total score requires empirical justification. Second, the scoring has a hefty bias against 'occasionals' – simply that two 'regulars' are worth six 'occasionals' – which seriously alters one's conception of participation. Third, the cut-off point, if six points, is a crude handling of the data – as crude as calling two 'regular' activities out of a possible five high participation.

TABLE 2.8   *Measures of participation*

Item no.	Civic's scale	Coop method (p. 298)
	Please check off your participation in the following activities:	A 'degree of participation' index was constructed in the following manner. The respondents answered the question: 'Here is a list of community activities (councils, committees etc.)'.
1	Faculty meetings	
2	Senior common room meetings	
3	Inaugural lectures	
4	Academic assemblies	
5	Degree congregations (Frequently, occasionally, never: throughout)	Check those in which you participated during the year.
		Respondent was also to indicate whether this participation was 'regular' or 'occasional'. Weightings were assigned by multiplying each 'regular' activity checked by 3 and each 'occasional' one by 1; the individual's total participation score was then added. 'High' means that the respondent's participation score was more than 6 points, while 'low' participation means 5 or fewer points.
Guttman coefficient of reproducibility	93·68%	Not given

Coop's findings with influence and participation were weak and inconclusive. When the influence distribution was dichotomized and correlated with four cosmo categories, the differences lacked statistical significance though they did exhibit 'a tendency for influence to increase steadily as one moves from cosmos to locals – until, that is, the extreme locals who manifest a sharp decline in influence' (ibid.). The dichotomized participation scores also failed to illustrate a trend over three cosmo categories for 'extreme locals tend to participate more than extreme cosmos, though the inter-mediate participates more than either' (Table 2.5).

Civic's analysis had produced five acceptable scales and one possible cosmo scale, so the correlation coefficients were sought between these six measures. (See Table 2.9.)

TABLE 2.9 *The intercorrelation of Civic's scales*

	Commitment	Reference group	Loyalty	Total	Participation
Participation	—0·02	—0·11	0·13	—0·01	
Influence	—0·08	—0·06	—0·04	—0·10	0·12

The correlations shown in Table 2.9 are very weak. Only the relationship between participation and loyalty to the employing organization suggests itself with any confidence. Most noticeable, too, is the correlation between the total score and influence and participation – in the case of the latter all suggestion of relationship is lost in a comparison with the sub-dimensions. Influence and participation, too, are only weakly associated with the implication that 'formal behaviour' is rather more disparate than was thought. But if cosmos does not prove a useful predictive tool there is still the possibility of accounting for it by using the actor's background and these factors would have prominence if types of cosmo and local could be established.

Gouldner was one of the first sociologists to use factor analytic techniques (ibid., 2, pp. 444, 445): he realized that neither cosmopolitans nor locals were likely to be one piece; there might be different kinds of cosmopolitans as well as different kinds of locals.

Returning to the raw data . . with the centroid method of extraction and the Quartrimax system of rotation, six orthogonal and unidimensional factors were produced. The factor matrix . . . suggests that our factors have a 'compelling' structure, that is, that there is relatively little overlap in the items that go into the six factors and that they therefore lend themselves to fairly ready interpretations. In interpretation of the factors attention has been given to the strength of the factor loadings of the component items and the question of whether any item was peculiar to a given factor or overlapped with others. The interpretation was also based on the theoretical considerations presented.

Coop's findings using factor analysis proved less compelling.

Two such analyses were made; one of all the 'orientation' variables (all the indices on the three scaled dimensions), the other of these variables and the activities indices taken together. Three graphs were drawn for each analysis, plotting the first three factors against each other. The first three factors in each analysis are not strong; the orientations PCA extracting 44·92 per cent and the combined PCA extracting 38·57 per cent of the variance collectively. The loading for each of the variables, too, does not suggest meaningful clusters. The orientations PCA, in fact, offered no axes at all and rotation was pointless. The 'combined' PCA distinguished between orientations and activities (Factor I against Factor II), orientations and influence and participation (Factor I against Factor III), making Factor I orientations, Factor II influence, and Factor III participation.

Simply, then, the factor analyses confirmed the scaling procedure's findings. The scales or dimensions have empirical value; but when used together their value is negligible. The factors were the scales. This means that in order to discuss Coop's 'factor profiles' the Civic data will have to yield scale-score profiles.

A close inspection of the written description of Coop's factor profiles indicates that two scales are particularly important. The key variable is commitment to professional skill. Such commitment is balanced against the degree of loyalty to the organization and the more specific object of this loyalty. In effect, whilst commitment to skill always remains at a general level, the qualifications suggest that loyalty to the organization may be a generalization of a more focused loyalty. And the titles given to them by Gouldner carry strong implications of the objects to which their loyalties were directed. (See Table 2.10.)

These varieties suggest the scores on two scales could be re-analysed in Civic's data to see if less sophisticated types could be determined. There are points for and against this step. The immediate objection being that scale-score profiles are just too simple to afford a comparison. Much of the weight of this criticism lies in the fact that within the scale-score types there is no 'informal' data. If Gouldner's thesis is to be accepted then informal relations are as important as crude identities in this refinement. Yet there are some bases for comparison. The specific loyalties are readily available.

The development of Civic's profiles involves trichotomizing commitment and loyalty-scale scores for each respondent and allocating him to one of the then nine alternative groups. The trichotomy is rooted in the mean and standard deviation values for each scale score. 'High' loyalty is recorded for each case where a score is more than one-half a standard deviation above the mean. Conversely, 'low' loyalty is a score more than one-half the standard

TABLE 2.10 *The types of cosmopolitans and locals from Coop's factor loadings*

Empirical type	Commitment to professional skills	Loyalty to the organization	Specific object of loyalty (highest item loading on factor)
Locals			
Dedicated	low	high	values of the organization
True bureaucrat	low	high	town and community
Homeguard	low	high	department or faculty
Elders	low	high	relationships in the college
Cosmopolitans			
Outsiders	high	low	profession: its association and standing
Empire-builders	high	high	department

deviation below the mean. By definition, medium loyalty is less than one-half the standard deviation above or below the mean. The same rule applies to the trichotomizing of commitment to professional skill. This gave nine empirical groups which could differentiate between the objects of loyalty in Civic's terms. Cosmos items could be reprocessed that afforded objectification, making two sorts of analyses possible. First, all nine groups could be examined for trends, that is, for example, the lower the loyalty and the greater the commitment then the more the outsider values. Second, the mean scores of each group on each item could be used to see if they consistently rank the selected groups and are in this sense compelling. This ranking, a more stringent conception of the analytical groups than was felt necessary in Coop's results, are generalizable to Civic, so this procedure would form a more confident basis of acceptance.

The development of this technique was to no avail. As with Coop's participation and cosmo relationship, the middle categories consistently disturbed trends, and the spread of values within each type militated against the use of the mean as if it were a mode – and in that sense a 'typical value'. When the mean was used for ranking 'empire-builders' were true to form in that they gave the highest values on department and colleagues at Civic. But 'outsiders', however, gave second highest values on Civic's ethic, their department, and they were second most likely to be 'old boys' of the college. The most consistent group were the 'uncommitted' who, also true to form, were uninclined towards department, college values and colleagues. Coop's factor profiles could not be traced in Civic College.

Coop's types were not examined causally. Instead, the complexities of factor matrices and factor loadings were given for each latent identity. In effect, all variables play a part in the picture though some seemed especially important for a particular type. The lack of 'success' in replication means that I had to regress to an older method of analysis: to the matrices of correlations.

The predictors selected are those indices of life which blanket a range of variously related factors. When sought in the questionnaire they constituted four simple questions:

1 How long have you been at Civic?
2 How many, if any, years of industrial experience have you had?
3 What professional qualifications do you hold?
4 What is your date of birth?

The first three questions very slightly probe the educational attainment and organizational service common to most studies of professionalism and loyalties. The second question is intended to consider the central component of a technological university: to be half-servant and half-master of industry. Age covers a multitude of sins. These predictors can be employed to re-examine both the cosmo sub-dimensions and the scale profiles.

Age and length of industrial service indicated consistent differences in the profile cells whilst Civic service, academic and professional qualifications offer no discrimination. The greater the age and the longer the industrial service, then the greater the likelihood of localism ($p = 0.05$). Perhaps the greatest shock is the lack of association between academic attainments and academic values; the locals have higher means and more extreme scores than the cosmopolitans. Empire-builders and locals include PhDs but outsiders do not. Significantly, too, age and industrial experience were the most consistently associated with the five scale scores. (See Table 2.11.)

Two coefficients between Civic's scales and predictors achieved levels of acceptability:

1 The longer the industrial service the less commitment to professional skills ($p = 0.01$).
2 The longer the industrial service the greater the localism ($p = 0.05$).

Three coefficients give indications of weak relationships using a cut-off point of 0.15.

1 The longer the service at Civic the less the commitment to professional skills.

29

2 The longer the service at Civic the greater the participation.

3 The greater the age the less the commitment to professional skills.

As in the scaling analysis, cosmos does not prove either a strong criterion or a strong predictor if seen as a unitary concept. Commitment to professional skills, however, is its strongest sub-dimension; though its predictive capacity was slight it could be dependent on the lecturer's age and years of industrial service.

TABLE 2.11   *The intercorrelations of Civic's scales and predictors*

	Length of Civic service	Length of industrial service	Degree of academic qualification	Degree of 'vocational' qualification	Age
Commitment to skills	−0·16	−0·31	0·02	−0·13	−0·21
Reference group	−0·00	−0·03	0·09	−0·09	−0·00
Loyalty to the organization	−0·03	−0·14	−0·01	−0·02	−0·11
Scales total	−0·10	−0·26	0·10	−0·13	−0·20
Participation	−0·21	−0·10	−0·03	0·04	0·05
Influence	−0·04	0·06	−0·00	0·09	0·07

The next section attempts to see what resolutions are possible from these findings and, where possible, to indicate the general principles that come into play.

The cosmopolitanism thesis reviewed

Replication casts doubt, not damnation. As Whitehead remarked, science develops by standing on the founding fathers' shoulders and not by walking on their faces. Consequently, this résumé takes the queries raised in order to consider the possibilities. Of particular interest are the refinements that could be made to facilitate further study. What, then, are the fruits of the thesis; its concept and theory and range of applicability?

Coop's cosmos sub-dimensions were scales, but though commitment to professional skills and loyalty to the organization were related, reference-group orientations were not significantly related to this loyalty. Neither the cosmos scale nor its sub-dimensions were related to the formal variables of influence and participation – the predicted consequences for the organization. The factor-analytic types of cosmos and local could not be traced with the data that was available and used. Only the uncommitted were consistently uncommitted and this group did not appear in Coop's findings. Age and length of industrial service indicated some strength in the commitment and loyalty scales when the former were used as predictors. But a combined loyalty type, the empire-builders, and a non-loyal type, the uncommitted, prevent age and industrial experience being used as general predictors. If cosmos is to be seen as a unitary concept, then it would be preferable to consider it as the juxtaposition of the degree of commitment and the degree of loyalty.

However, there was much 'translation' in this replicative use of cosmopolitanism's participation and influence measures.

Gouldner argues that the dimensions are those of latent social identities. 'Social identities have to do with the way in which an individual is in fact perceived and classified by others in terms of a system of culturally standardized categories' (ibid., 1, p. 294). Such an identity is acquired by being located, categorized, typed by others, and realizing this the focal individuals 'mobilize their beliefs concerning it' (ibid., p. 293). This theory of identity involves, then, a very simple critical path of socialization by interaction and the existence of clear categories for the socialized. Basically, the Civic findings imply that such simplicity marginally scratches the surface of its identities. What lies beneath is probably more complex and realistic.

The essence of Civic's pattern is realism; that is, the younger, more qualified are 'academics' but the rest are much more peculiar to their case – their own admixture of age, industry, qualification and home situation. One respondent volunteered both ideas on completion of the questionnaire 'I found these questions difficult to answer. The comment which sprang to mind was, "It all depends . . .". If you are looking for people who are ambitious or mobile, would it not be useful to discover something about the factors which would modify their decisions? For example, the movers might be held back by house purchase, smooth relationships with colleagues, job of spouse, whereas non-movers might allow such factors to play an important part in their decisions. But perhaps you are looking for something else?' Theoretically, this is important as it questions whether cosmopolitanism is a latent identity projected by others or a role conception composed of a gamut of competing factors. Looked at 'realistically', looked at in terms similar to those of the lecturer's quoted above, the socialization process would entail individuals comparing themselves with similarly placed people; summing up their formal role expectations; relating these perceptions to their own attainments and aspirations and, then, assuming a

31

'latent' identity that is possibly reinforced by mutual association along significant axes. This allows for uncommitted as well as locals.

Such a process is complex in terms of its procedure and components. This would mean that the intervening variable of identity could be tackled either as its key dimension (commitment to professional skill) or as an involved factor. For it would mean incorporating novel, more sociological independent and intervening variables. It also begs a study of the process of acquiring a latent identity as well as a study of its product. These developments depend on an evaluation of the model's applicability.

Perhaps the locations were deviant or even exceptional. The comparison of characteristics (Table 2.3) showed that the only major similarity between Coop and Civic colleges is that they are universities. They differ in ethic, site, size and nationality. Civic's lectures are not 'pure academics' as faculty seemed to be at Coop. (See Table 2.12). Civic's lecturers could be 'neo-academics', 'managerial

TABLE 2.12 *Some background data from Civic College's lecturers sample*

Characteristic	Mean (x)	S.D. (x)	Observations
1 Length of service at Civic College	5·41	3·76	'New boys' predominate in a new university.
2 Length of industrial service	8·61	6·60	A 'norm' of industrial service less than 10% are 'pure' academics.
3 Age	39·89	6·7	Young lecturers; less than 10% over 50, and less than 20% over 45.

academics' or 'non-academics'. The cosmos thesis, theory or concept need not be applicable to Civic. But if it is not, is there a flaw in the measure; a qualitative difference between Coop and Civic Colleges; or a slap-happy, homogenizing use of the concept of 'college'?

Interestingly, the influence items divided into the educative and administrative functions of lecturers, with the latter being predictably less frequently recorded. A comparison might be empirically possible here on structural factors peculiar to Coop and Civic colleges. The Coop researchers observed (ibid., p. 297):

It was our impression that competents from within the college who might rank order the influence implied by different decisions would disagree considerably among themselves. In part, this was so because they were loath to make such distinction, since Coop College is strongly committed to a belief system which stresses the equality of different people and positions.

From my observations no such ethic exists at Civic College. This provides a further justification for standardizing at the lecturer level as different levels may well have significantly different degrees of influence. Gouldner, however, seems to have accepted Civic's ethic as fact, in that latent identity is much more significant than occupational level as a determinant of influence.

3   The quantitative method in theory

It may be too late for another essay on the quantitative method. So much has been said already and so many have turned away from its use. In fact, I would guess that if this chapter were to criticize the mechanical conceptions of man and society, the dubious possibilities of explaining social change and the predominantly trivial findings inherent, it seems, in the quantitative method, most of its potential readers would 'switch off'. So I wish to say something serious, sympathetic and fresh about the method. For despite my disengagement from its practice I have found the quantitative method exciting. There is a creative aspect to quantifying social phenomena. Admittedly the operations themselves cast still further doubt on the scientificity of the method but perhaps these operations are themselves subject to rules as yet unwritten.

And I have a further reason for writing upon the actual process of getting to quantifiable 'data'. It appears that the reductions from concept, to variable, to data are the least understood steps for novices. Most courses on the scientific method leap from 'This is a theory' to 'These are statistics.' The art is omitted. Students are then less attracted and more daunted than ever. Thus I write to give students the clearest understanding that I possess of the mysterious threads between theory and data.

Having accounted for concept construction, for that could be a name for the exercises involved, I move to theory framing. But in this second part I lay less emphasis on how to do it. Instead, I offer some reflections on the necessity of analogy in theories amenable to the quantitative method. I suggest that 'reality' must be approached indirectly from this perspective.

And how shall we account for this perspective overall? It has been called positivism, the scientific method, and yet I refer to it as quantitative. I shall stick, as an essentialist must, to the special quality that the method involves. Whatever else happens, numbers are made to speak more powerfully than words. The plan of the most extensive and articulate scheme in current sociology is to have the facts as figures. I have already implied that the teaching of this plan verges upon an obsession with the manipulation of its numbers. I wish to go into the exactitude of the plan; into how a researcher decides what to ask and what to watch. I begin, therefore, with concept construction: with the untold logic of approaching an idea through sub-categories of observation. And, I have again already said, it is a surprisingly imaginative operation.

Concept construction and operationalization

'Well,' he said, 'you get an idea and test it. I suppose that sounds difficult but you only need a couple of concepts to get going – and then you're away!'

'What idea?' she replied.

'Any old concept. You know, alienation, authoritarianism – that sort of thing.'

'What do I do?' she continued.

'Let Weber instruct you. It's in the first paragraph of 'Science as a Vocation'. And I quote (1948, p. 129):

> You wish me to speak about 'science as a vocation'. Now we political economists have a pedantic custom, which I should like to follow, of always beginning with the external conditions. In this case we begin with the question: What are the conditions of science as a vocation in the material sense of the term? Today this question means, practically and essentially: What are the prospects of a graduate student who is resolved to dedicate himself professionally to science in university life?

'There you are, Weber the practical scientist. He goes from science as a vocation to postgraduate job prospects. If he had asked what proportion of upper class degrees get grants to stay on he'd have had an MA thesis.'

Let us begin to construct a concept with Weber's aid. We need, first of all, the idea. The would-be researcher needs a magic mind. Well, not precisely magic; more of a complete involvement with a problem upon which he has temporarily turned his back. 'Both enthusiasm and work, and above all both of them *jointly* can entice the idea' (ibid., p. 136).

Here we might say that Weber's theory of the idea is that of an 'elective affinity' between work and enthusiasm which draws out, as if by sexual attraction, the 'inspiration'. Weber continues (ibid.):

D

Ideas occur to us when they please, not when it pleases us. The best ideas do indeed occur to one's mind in the way in which Ihering describes it: when smoking a cigar on the sofa; or as Helmholtz states himself with scientific exactitude: when taking a walk on a slowly ascending street; or in a similar way. In any case, ideas come when we do not expect them, and not when we are brooding and searching at our desks. Yet ideas would certainly not come to mind had we not brooded at our desks and searched for answers with passionate devotion.

I have no idea whether this attitude is true or false. It is simply important in the ideology of the quantitative method. Facts may stare you in the face, as it were, but theories, the ideas of a concealed rationality, must present themselves to their devoted pursuers.

'An inner devotion to the task, and that alone, should lift the scientist to the height and dignity of the subject he pretends to serve' (ibid., p. 137). Fortunately Weber rescues science from the immediacy of art, for he then writes, 'Scientific work is chained to the course of progress.' He notes that 'every scientific "fulfillment" raises new "questions": it asks to be "surpassed" and outdated. Whoever wishes to serve science has to resign himself to this fact' (p. 138).

And so, at least implicitly, Weber locates the researcher's idea in the imminent redundancy of ideas enshrined in earlier research. To cut a long story short, as it were, the new 'pure' idea comes from puzzling over old ones recently challenged by exceptions or other forms of inadequacy.

One day, while wondering why managers seem to encourage their jobs to dull their senses, I leafed through William H. Whyte's *The Organization Man*. In this grave and funny book Whyte explains how a manager is made grey by his experience and makes himself mediocre for his own good. Being a good author, Whyte makes his argument repeatedly plain. In the introduction he phrases himself thus (pp. 10–11):

The organization man seeks a redefinition of his place on earth – a faith that will satisfy him: that what he must endure has a deeper meaning than appears on the surface. He needs in short, something that will do for him what the Protestant Ethic did once. And slowly, almost imperceptibly, a body of thought has been coalescing that does that. I am going to call it a Social Ethic. . . . By Social Ethic I mean that contemporary body of thought which makes morally legitimate the pressures of society against the individual.

Here, before me, was the idea. Managers, in becoming organization men, had dumped the granite values of Protestantism and taken upon themselves the comparatively effeminate social ethic. However, even in 1968 I was not convinced that the transformation had already occurred in England. Even though I had but a hazy understanding of the ethic's substances I had already met managers who spoke of the joys of hard work *and* of working together as a team. These men are either in a mess, I thought, or they are making good, British sense. If it's good British stuff, I continued, the Protestant ethic gets you to work and the social ethic gets you to work for the firm. The 'ethics' collude with each other to have the manager identify work with working hard for the good of the company. To be on the safe side I called them the two parts of 'work integrative values'.

So far I possessed the idea and the wish to measure it. I turned to Galtung (1967), the most honest methodologist I had read. He said social scientists 'sample the space-time continuum' and that 'one problem of this methodology is its way of atomizing entities – "the ocean-ness of an ocean" and the "mountain-ness of a mountain" may disappear in the process' (p. 26).

Exactly. That was what even I had complained about. I could remember a visiting American professor telling me that you measure the amount of education in each country by counting the number of children at school! Moreover, there seemed to be a difference in style between a social survey and a sociological study. In a survey you asked a lot of people what they had done since they were born. In a study you asked a few people what they thought of things. I was going to ask about 'work integrative values', about the extent of managers' belief in the Protestant and social ethics. What questions should I ask?

The very term 'extent' makes the concept a variable. The phrase 'the degree to which' bulldozes the phenomenon into linearity. It makes the concept rather unimportant for the moment. The logic, that is, which one accords to a variable makes its preceding idea look something of a dilettante. Upshaw (1968, p. 60) says:

A variable is an invention, involving the abstraction of certain observable characteristics and the disregard of others. That which varies in a variable is some property which all members of a set of observations have in some kind or in some degree. In defining a variable, an investigator decides the exact property in which he is interested and, as well as he can, provides a set of standard procedures by which the presence or absence or degree of the variable property can be determined reliably in the individual case.

That's it then; I was to make up the variable in much the same way as I 'made up' the idea. The big step so far was to flatten reality in order to get a tape measure on it. I hoped that the next step was to get to grips with a tape measure. And I consulted the 'Scale of Atrociousness' (Lazarsfeld and Rosenberg, 1955, p. 54):

> Between November 1939 and June 1941 the Princeton Listening Center recorded short-wave broadcasts of news reports and topical talks disseminated chiefly from Berlin, London, Rome and Paris. Philip E. Jacob analysed the strategy of atrocity propaganda utilized in these broadcasts.

Jacob (1955) had defined his concept:

> An 'atrocity' is an abnormal occurrence; i.e. behaviour which departs from the accustomed patterns of human activity. It is, however, behaviour which so violates the deep-seated standards of social conduct, the ethic of those witnessing or hearing about the incident, as to shock them, cause acute nervous discomfort, and arouse the emotion of horror.

Jacob (p. 56) had his spine-chilling scale. 'The scale rates the victim of the atrocity, the effect of the act, the weapons or procedure used and the intent of the perpetrator.'

Each aspect was rated. Effect, for example, was rated as follows (p. 57):

Scale for Effect of Atrocity

A. Number of victims
   1 One object
   2 Several objects
   3 Many objects
   4 The whole of a class of objects

B. Extent of damage (property)
   1 Partial destruction
   2 Total destruction

C. Character of the injury (persons)
   1 Civic disability, robbery, etc., causing social and mental discomfort
   2 Physical discomfort, indirect injury to life and limb
   3 Death or normal wounding
   4 Mutilation
   5 Sexual mutilation.

The editors of *The Language of Social Research* had included Jacob's 'Scale of Atrociousness' because 'for the present purpose the most interesting aspect is *abnormality*, because for it the author develops specific criteria along a number of dimensions' (ibid., p. 56).

To get at the concept, they argue, you first say it is a variable, then give it dimensions and finally make up a scale. So the next move was to the dimensions of 'work integrative values'. Having taken Whyte's ideas, it seemed obvious to take his dimensions – whatever they might be. In his chapter on 'The Decline of the Protestant Ethic' (1956, pp. 18–26) Whyte emphasized four themes of the Protestant ethic:

1 A belief in competition
2 A belief in salvation through hard work
3 A belief in thrift
4 A respect for property which holds the property to be sacred.

And giving the themes of the social ethic a chapter each, he defined them as:

1 Scientism: 'the promise that with the same techniques that have worked in the physical sciences we can eventually create an exact science of man' (p. 27), that science can be used to bring about individual belongingness in a group
2 A belief in belongingness as a basic human need (pp. 35–48)
3 A belief in the group as the prime source of creativity (pp. 48–60).

Whyte had even gone so far as to call the social-ethic characteristics 'three principal denominators'; it seemed but another small change to call them dimensions. When we do so, the concept comes to occupy a space. For Lazarsfeld and Rosenberg (1955, p. 16) write:

The notion of property space is quite basic in the theory of index formation. The basic idea is quite simple and is an extension of the Cartesian Co-ordinate System known to all high school students from plane analytic geometry.

In their reader Allen H. Barton introduces the technique with other comparisons to show how 'quite simple' the idea is: 'The location of any point on the earth's surface can be indicated by giving its latitude and longitude, using as base lines the equator and the Greenwich meridian' (ibid., p. 40).

So if Whyte's 'denominators' were to be the latitudes of 'work integrative values', what were to be its longitudes? The answer being, of course, that I was making a 'data matrix' and to do so is to rely on 'levels of analysis' (Galtung, 1967, pp. 37–9); different spheres of life in which the work integrative values → Protestant +social ethics → dimensions of beliefs are to be found. As I had got to the stage of another decision I took as longitudes for a 'belief in competition':

1 Competition as a general value
2 Competition in national affairs
3 Competition in industrial affairs

After all, I was studying managers so it seemed appropriate to work outwards from industry, through government to culture. By this time it also seemed necessary to check on what I had done. I looked for some rules because I sensed I had made up my own. My three longitudes did correspond to Galtung's 'three kinds of superunits' (ibid., p. 39), being the 'category', 'the system' and 'the group' respectively. Anyway, before making up my questions I determined upon two related rules for the latitudes and longitudes of a concept's property space. If one refers to form then the other refers to content. So:

1 Make the latitude one of content, of culture or meaning and aim to have each dimension exclusive.
2 Make the longitude one of form, of structure or collectivity and aim to have exhaustive coverage.

These two terms 'exclusive' and 'exhaustive' I had once learned in a statistics course and suspected that they were part of some distant mathematical logic. 'Exclusive' meant that the feature of a dimension was not also part of the feature of another dimension. 'Exhaustive' meant that you had included as much as you could think of: starting with the individual and just stopping short of the universe. Thus emboldened, I considered myself ready to think up some questions. There are, however, a lot of rules abroad for the questions themselves. First, they are called by two different names according to different criteria: 'An *item* is a variable that is included by *intensive* criteria; an *indicator* is a variable that is included in a cluster by *extensive* criteria' (ibid., p. 78). In 'intension' the researcher decides 'on the basis of the *meaning* of the variable whether it belongs or not. This is usually done by some kind of thought experiment' (p. 77). And for 'extension', 'somehow there must be an homogeneity of meaning' (p. 78). In other words each question must fit and all the questions must fit together. Upshaw (1968, p. 65) calls fitting together 'functional unity'.

> The concept of functional unity implies some kind of statistical dependency among mapping operations, although the precise nature of the dependency varies according to the theoretical properties of the measured variable and practical considerations involving such matters as whether the instrument is intended as an assessment or predictive device.

He also says (p. 66) that items or indicators should fit together in a reliable and valid way:

In assessing the reliability of an instrument of known functional unity, an investigator faces the task of estimating how much fluctuation in numerical assignments can be attributed to momentary factors associated with the observed statuses of the observations in terms of the variable property.

In other words, will the questions get anything like the same answers on different occasions? Or will they be perverse enough to make each outing a 'special occasion'? And 'To question the validity of a measurement instrument is to ask whether (or to what extent) the numbers assigned to events correspond to the variable quantity that was intended' (ibid.).

Or more directly, do the resultant scores (p. 67) look at all credible? Do they look anything like measures of nearly the same thing, or anything different from quite distinct things?

These rules of Galtung and Upshaw are the big rules. There are a host of little ones. So at this point it seemed better to make up the questions and check them against the rules later. For rarely does a rule tell you how to go about something. So it was back to the bones of work integrative values made up so far. The property space is given in Figure 3.1.

FIGURE 3.1   *Work integrative values as a property space*

	(*as a*) general value	(*in*) national affairs	(*in*) industrial affairs
Protestant ethic: belief in	Scale	Scale	Scale
1 Competition	1.1.1	1.1.2	1.1.3
2 Salvation through hard work	1.2.1	1.2.2	1.2.3
3 Thrift	1.3.1	1.3.2	1.3.3
4 Property being sacred	1.4.1	1.4.2	1.4.3
Social ethic: belief in			
1 Scientism	2.1.1	2.1.2	2.1.3
2 Belongingness	2.2.1	2.2.2	2.2.3
3 Group as prime source of creativity	2.3.1	2.3.2	2.3.3

Every box was to have questions put in. The juxtaposition of the ethic's dimensions and its contexts made each box the space of a scale. Now I really was close to making up the questions. And now they were to fit inside these scales. I could either ask, for example:

Do you believe there should be competition?

or Would you like to see more competition?

or Do you think people should compete with each other?

or Do you think the nation is being weakened by lack of competition?

or How would you inject the spirit of competition back into our national life?

And so on. There is no end to the variations upon the theme. Some questions fix the answers, though – as if doing market research for the competition industry. The last two above depend upon a simple-minded nationalism that turns bloody-minded when forced into a corner. The rule of measurement says that in addition to settling the questions the researcher fixes the possible answers. After all, it's the variations in answers that he seeks. So a 3-point 'agree-disagree' and 'Don't know' or a 5-point Thurstone Scale (Upshaw, op. cit., pp. 90–4) of

Strongly agree	Agree		Disagree	Strongly Disagree
1	1	3	4	5

or

Always	Often	Sometimes	Infrequently	Never
1	2	3	4	5

is the choice of answers and the questions are phrased accordingly; a statement to agree with or a habit to be confessed. The easier option is an 'affective-subject' scale. You invent some statements and force all responses. The competition statements are in Table 3.1.

A scale, then, is much like a variable. It is a piece of invention and has no meaning without its variable and dimensions and no substance without its items. Once we have separated out dimensions the whole 'thing' is reconstituted on a smaller scale. The false antithesis is followed by an additive synthesis. The operation does not upset its operator as miniaturization always tends to make things look clock-work – it is a function of wanting to see things in the scale in which they occur and yet have an overview by categories for these events. The specification of items is necessarily the most vulnerable part of this process. No item or group of items need be the 'whole meaning'. The researcher carries only the lamp of an 'image'; the scale becomes a label that he reaches towards and also uses to consider the quality of his own reach. If the idea is brought on by 'inspiration' it is hauled down to earth by 'intuition'. And obviously we mean by intuition something that the researcher knew already 'from his stock of knowledge of everyday life'. It is not so much that the researcher makes his items up. He remembers

TABLE 3.1   *Questions on belief in competition*

Concept:	Work integrative values
Variable:	Profession of the Protestant ethic
Dimension:	Belief in competition

Scale 1:	*Competition as a general value*
1	Competition is the spice of life.
2	The survival of the fittest is a sound philosophy.
3	The experience of a competitive struggle is a basic human need.

Scale 2:	*Competition in national affairs*
1	Governments should be discouraged from interfering with the free play of market factors.
2	Too many weak firms are sheltered in the British economy today.
3	The state's main job is to inject the spirit of competition into the country.

Scale 3:	*Competition in industrial affairs*
1	Competition between firms always benefits the consumer.
2	There should be no such thing as the safe job.
3	Every effort should be made when recruiting personnel to pick them for their keenness to compete with their equals.

them and in so remembering crystallizes his social awareness and his need for items to fit in his scale.

It would burden both the reader and the theme of this part to discuss every item I remembered for work integrative values. And yet it would also be incomplete to omit them entirely. So the rest of the scales are given in Appendix 1 whilst we continue with what some authorities have laid down about items. The general problem has come to be described as correspondence. The items in fitting the scale should correspond to the spirit of the concept. The researcher is to take imaginative leaps up and down the 'ladder of abstraction' (Phillips, 1966, pp. 27–30) – and perhaps rest on a rung if he feels his balance going.

Thurstone (Upshaw, 1968, pp. 90–1)

> proposed a two-step procedure for the construction of affective-subject scales. . . . The first step in the procedure consists in asking a group of judges to sort a set of statements concerning the attitude object into categories according to the degree of favourableness towards the object which each statement implies. . . . The second step of the procedure consists in administering a sample of the scaled statements to the respondents whose degree of affect is to be measured.

This might be described as a psychologist's approach – he thinks up the statements and has a group of friends, associates or students sort them out. So I asked two friends to agree that my statements were opposite and generally they did so. 'On the face of it,' they said, 'the statements are valid' (Phillips, op. cit., pp. 159–60).

From this point it is necessary either to quote extensively or to refer the reader to two accounts of 'criteria for the selection of statements for the final instrument' (Upshaw, op. cit., pp. 91–2; Galtung, op. cit., pp. 241–2). In truth, all the rules are straightforward and, one is tempted to write, matters of common sense. Keep it simple, direct and meaningful; above all, cover the field and the possible range of feelings involved. In brief, the remembering process is partly modelling and partly faceting. Think of making the sentiment in clay, the shaping, thicknesses and lines. Think of holding up a diamond between your fingers – the light flickers, flashes, refracts and reveals it structure. When your pottery and pilfery are done, how many items have you got? For there are no rules as to how many you should have but convention says that eight or ten would be quite respectable. Such numbers would allow you to test mathematically the fitting together of the items. And really in the quantitative method the mathematical tightness of a scale is at least as important as its 'meaningful appeal'. In remembering many statements, choosing some and trying them out the researcher is prepared to 'lose' any that do not 'work'. If a few items do not fit in they are more trouble than they are worth. No matter how good they look the answers to them can encompass so much variance that they do not correlate with anything. You are half-way home with an intact scale but with a scale that has no correlates you are half-way abroad. The researcher can take out an insurance in case his scale collapses. He can make some items mean all of the scale's abstract meaning. They might be called starred items or key items. If the scale fails these items can be salvaged and stand on their own. Admittedly they will look a bit thin but they may still work to produce correlations. Thus the statement 'Competition is the spice of life' is a popular cliché put to work as a starred item for 'belief in competition'.

Now we turn back on ourselves. After the noise of the 'field', the tedium of collecting and collating the answers, we are ready to climb back up the ladder. A prime interest of the quantitative method is in the welfare of its 'measures'. The first question the researcher asks after fieldwork is 'Is my concept intact? Has it stood up to my subjects?' And so he carefully works his way back through the internal validity of scales, to dimensions and variables and onwards to the clouds of the associative validity of correlation. The first step is, 'Does the scale scale?'

Unfortunately, scaling is a complicated business. The easiest method is Guttman's scalogram but this involves recasting the answers into 'yes'es and 'no's. It also seems a particularly lenient test. Upshaw spends an unhappy nine pages on the pros and cons (op. cit., pp. 98–106). Levy and Pugh (1969) go through every known scaling technique and find faults in each. And McKennel (1970) offers the non-mathematical considerable succour in writing that the most straightforward approach is to assemble a correlation matrix, reject the items that do not correlate and work to an acceptance limit which he calls an alpha coefficient. Table 3.2 gives the coefficients and will have to be read in conjunction with Table 3.1.

TABLE 3.2   *A correlation matrix of the belief in competition scale*

	11	12	13	21	22	23	31	32
11								
12	0·300							
13	0·280	0·313						
21	0·128	0·351	0·042					
22	0·009	0·135	0·129	−0·023				
23	0·132	0·308	0·216	0·403	0·026			
31	0·256	0·322	0·188	0·198	0·297	0·305		
32	0·213	0·328	0·280	0·168	0·196	−0·006	0·275	
33	0·276	0·304	0·400	−0·010	0·077	0·134	0·374	0·320

Scanning this matrix, it seems that statements on competition and the government did not fare too well. The first two statements in this scale did particularly badly. The third is still touch and go. The researcher can decide to play safe and 'lose' items with the slightest weakness or decide by comparing the alpha coefficients of the scale both with and without its weak members.

McKennel (op. cit., p. 230) gives an approximate formula:

$$\frac{nrij}{1 \,.. \, (n-1)\,rij}$$

Where rij is the average inter-item correlation and n is the number of items in test. He also gives a table from which the alpha coefficient can be read.

Without items 2.1, 2.2 and 2.3 $n = 6$, $rij = 0·296$ and the alpha coefficient is approximately $0·7$.
Without items 2.1 and 2.2 $n = 7$, $rij = 0·264$ and the alpha coefficient is again approximately $0·7$.

The researcher must resort to face validity. If item 2.3 is included the scale's meaning barely enters competition in national affairs. Without item 2.3 he has combined two longitudes of competition; as a general value and in industrial life. If he decides to drop item 2.3 he may also decide to analyse all of this longitude separately. He may reflect that this is the political aspect of the Protestant ethic which should, on second thought, be treated as distinct. He may also be troubled by the implications of this decision. It seems that he is suggesting that religious ideas precede political ideas and make the latter a matter of 'unthinking principle'. The scale 'testing' has, however, just begun. The researcher is constrained to analyse each scale the same way. And then to analyse the sets of scales into dimensions. And finally to test for the 'whole' variable. At each stage the more he decides to include items because of their inter-correlation values the more he must puzzle the meaning of the answers he has combined. As McKennel says (ibid., p. 235):

> Reliability and homogeneity are essential preconditions for establishing the construct validity of a scale: without reliability there would be no correlation with any external variable; without homogeneity, measurement of one thing at a time, the meaning of any obtained correlations would be uninterpretable.

The ultimate test, therefore, of the validity of scales, dimensions, variables and the itemized concept is also its original purpose. The very fact that the researcher needs one concept to correlate with another concept necessitates all the stages of 'operationalization' and all the decisions to jettison wayward items. For at the end of this process I gave each manager a raw score from adding the answers to all the items that were left; from adding all the values that had a clear, single circle and where the manager had not modified the statement to answer it.

To date there are a lot of rules for each stage and a statistical etiquette for giving each respondent a mark. The rules are clearly 'guidelines'. They ask the researcher to chase up and down his ladder of abstraction and avoid oversimplifying or overcomplicating levels of context and spheres of meaning. It is still up to the researcher to decide upon how many rungs of abstraction suit his idea and how he will make one 'level' roughly correspond with another. The peculiarity of these freedoms is that they encourage the socio-logist to devise a psychometric test: a test used for sorting out people into potentials and types. It must be a classic instance of the end justifying the means. And the sociologist needs all the 'verstehende' he can muster to get through the process. For other sociologists will judge his skill in thinking up 'good items'. And institutional authorities may wonder if they can use it for 'sorting some of their own people out'. So the quantitative researcher may actually benefit imaginatively, occupationally and financially from the artistry with which he constructed 'his' concept.

Theory as analogy

'What's your theory?' he asked.

'Well, I don't really know', she replied. 'I suppose background counts for a lot. You know, father's job, schooling; things like that.'

'Are they supposed to explain something?' he continued.

'Not really. They might correlate with these identity measures', she suggested.

'Well, I'm sorry to pursue you on this but I don't really see how. I mean, how does what his father did cause what he thinks of himself now?'

'Oh! I didn't say "cause", did I? They're simply related. Look at it this way. The father is a bus driver. He's out on shifts very late and very early. He wears a uniform and carries his lunch. He doesn't get much money but it's regular. His son rarely sees him – unless he drives the school bus! His father just lives from bed to work. Obviously the son can be the same or different. If he's the same then he probably thinks of his father with affection. If he's changed from all that then he could reject his father completely. You see, his father's horizons would have to be limited to keep on bus-driving every day. He's bottled his frustrations and just got on with working for money. He was a clear example that the son could copy or ignore. Either way the son would have to see his father as an identity. He would have to think on all this and come to some working conclusions. You know: he would have to make up his mind about his father and in so doing have a clearer picture of himself.' And she paused.

'The subtlety of your sociology has charm', he said quickly, 'but is that a story or an explanation?'

'It's neither! Can't you see it's a model? It's a working description of what might actually happen!'

'All right, all right', he countered, 'I give in. The story may be true . . . but how the hell are you going to prove it?'

'For the last time', she growled, 'I'm interested in how it works. I don't make a theory, I make a model.'

'I'm sorry', he said gently, 'I didn't mean to chase you about. I just can't understand why you want to call it a science.'

The quantitative method rarely has direct dealings with 'sociological theory'. Occasionally so and so's proposition might be 'tested', and then both the contexts and the concepts are drastically reduced. The quantitative method, that is, tends to produce its own approximation to theory. In the convention of the day there are different sorts of variables. They are respectively independent, intervening and dependent types or, roughly, causes, influences and effects. But it must be remembered from the outset that terms like cause, explanation and prediction are almost never used. An imprecise vocabulary has been developed which conveys an exactitude between its users. Always the emphasis is upon the 'analysis', the 'pattern', the 'path' and the 'probability'. There is, in truth, no need to bother with the outmoded imprecision of sociological theory. It has become more interesting to consider a few things 'well' than the whole issue 'woollily'.

It appears that the testing of just a few propositions is a lengthy and even risky business. A formula is needed for each with its 'error term' and its 'partialling out' for each factor. The hint dropped by methodologists passing to and from the frontier is: keep it simple and it may work; if you must, call it a model.

And it is truly amazing: the sacred marriage of positivism and organicism is bringing forth yet another generation of progeny. A model depends upon the concept of a 'system'. Whatever it is is a thing; a working thing, a living, breathing thing with parts all pulling together. Whatever the system it is unlikely to be more complicated than Spenser's 'head, heart and hands'. And they could well be called the regulatory, distributory and sustaining sub-systems. Calling whatever 'it' is a system, however, means that the researcher is no longer limited to a biological analogy. This is very convenient. A biological analogy is detailed and extensive. A system can be analogous with anything more concrete or more familiar than is the 'it' under scrutiny. In fact it is well worth a researcher's time to draw up a list of analogies ready for use. The object is not to explore the analogy in full or in terms of fittedness but rather to explore the range from which analogies can be drawn. The researcher will then learn the mileage ingredient of each analogical subject; a light switch has clearly less potential than a hydro-electric dam. Thus a lower order of analogies may be designated. They have the potential for 'driving the point home' or giving 'a practical application'.

To further the development of this sub-science I list analogies that can be made with other 'science' subjects (thereby proving mutually entrancing).

'Scientific' system		Sociological system
1 Geology:	the formation of ex-bow lakes	the formation of sinecures
2 Astronomy:	the structure of galaxies	the role-relationships of leadership

	Scientific system		Sociological system
3	Physics:	the light refraction of a prism	man as the carrier and creator of culture
4	Mechanical engineering:	a spanner in the works	deviance as sabotage of the state machine

The light-heartedness of this list should detract from the potential of science as a field from which sociological analogies can be drawn. Geology offers rifts, ruptures, sedimentary deposits and fossils. Physics has lenses as well as prisms, levers as well as light. Astronomy probably offers the most picturesque form with quasars, pear-shaped earths and exploding stars.

In fact stating that the quantitative method in sociology needs metaphors for its theory is falling into the trap of analogical thinking itself. The point being that to give the workings of something is to see it as an object – like any other object with working principles common to a whole class of objects. The analogy conveniently 'proves' that the subject under consideration is 'just like' a whole class of objects. It is not that 'reality' must be stalked as if a wild beast; it must be sliced as carefully as warm bread. Anyway, analogies are usually used either as a 'coathanger' for the model or as an impression of one of its relationships. There are no rules of correspondence between systemic reality and reality systemically seen. No quantitative researcher is going to pursue a machine analogy with a pump down to the last c.c. of displacement or the frequency with which it needs greasing. The unwritten rules of correspondence are roughly:

1 Use a choice analogy to add a poetry of expression.
2 Limit the usage to what is immediately needed.
3 Test for correlations and not for parts of an analogy.

For even though the simple-minded may come to read 'it is' from 'it is just like', their mistake is unimportant. The researcher himself has never held anything other than an heuristic opinion of an heuristic attitude – he has a workmanlike criterion for a child's drawing. This drawing; this model; this pathway is what matters. To put it another way, an analogy is advanced by analytical rhetoric and is not subject to methodological rhetoric. The statistical tests between the variables are the 'master rhetoric'. This latter rhetoric is, at the time of writing, generally called path analysis.

Path analysis is a method of 'linear causal analysis'. I am unable to see why it should warrant a name other than that of regression correlation. But its proponents have been very busy in naming it, applying it and working out its 'own' rules of correspondence. Invariably the analyses have something to do with 'socio-economic background' and generally the examples contain amply significant correlations.

It is generally agreed that Blalock started it, or rather Blalock made the work of Wright, Simon and Wold readily accessible to sociologists (Blalock, 1964; 1968). Otis Dudley Duncan, with customary clarity, has summarized the success story (1966, pp. 1–2). Costner and Leik have worked hard at the same problems (see, e.g. Costner 1969a) and only Boudon (1965) has so far rocked the boat by 'proving' that both regression analysis and the Simon-Blalock model are special cases of dependence analysis. At least one 'proselyte' has so far written to say: 'The technique of path analysis, recently introduced into the sociological literature by Duncan, can be a powerful aid in clarifying complex causal arguments' (Werts, 1968, abstract).

We may expect a virtual avalanche of studies using four or five variables and proving their mutual dependence by path analysis. Blalock, Duncan and Boudon have all given the appropriate formulae and no doubt computer package problems are already available. And Hilton (1971) has performed the even greater service of testing the method with data.

It is worth paying close attention to Hilton's paper for it contains both an account that is faithful to the method and a devastating criticism of its use and value.

First, Hilton enters the problem of assumptions. Every statistical test makes assumptions. The best known require that the data be 'randomly collected' and 'normally distributed'. And, of course, data rarely satisfy these requirements. Hilton says that a researcher must make 'valiant assumptions' to use path analysis and that these are rarely realistic.

Second, Hilton spells out the Achilles heel:

> This is to do with the inability of the technique to discriminate
> between various causal networks. . . . Causal inference
> techniques are rarely capable of discriminating between several
> intuitively plausible causal networks. They may be able to
> reject unrealistic networks but most of these will have been
> rejected *a priori* anyway.

He then processes 'three perfectly acceptable and vastly different theoretical frameworks for organisations'. . . . 'The data do not reject any of them.'

Next, Hilton gives 'a full parade of all the difficulties associated with the use of the technique'. This discussion is the most thorough account of the 'nuts and bolts' that I have read. Time and again the difficulties are insurmountable. He finishes the paper, justly, without hope.

But despite Hilton's honest labours the 'modelling' and 'analysis' will probably continue. For obviously where there is more interest in results than in reasoning, analogies and path analysis can easily pass for theory and method. The problem seems to rest in the excuse-term model. It is no longer necessary to know Bridgman's definition and strictures, or to recall Nagel's nightmare of a chapter on the subject. Perhaps, however we may still hear the faint voice of an eminent anthropologist (Leach, 1964):

> The concepts of social theory are so lacking in concreteness
> that every social scientist must construct his argument around a
> model of some kind. . . . If the aim is only communication then
> analogy is justified, but in that case simple models achieve their
> purpose much better than complicated ones. . . . But what
> we must never do is confuse our objectives; we must not
> imagine that we can solve problems by means of over-simplified
> analogies or expound a simple metaphor with the aid of
> complex algebra. The model in a matchbox won't fly.

The goals of quantitative sociology: by way of the goal-scorers

> Real advancement in sociology, and not mere discussion of
> legitimations, is now needed. Indeed the only answer to the
> challenge of the 'new sociology' is in significant scientific
> development – not in another critique of existing methods, nor
> even in their refinement. Refinement may be necessary, but it
> would not be sufficient. Nor would yet another call for a new
> direction be of value now. Instead immediate progress must be
> made. Until those who believe sociology should be a science
> can demonstrate effective scientific advancement, the challenge
> of the new sociology will remain unanswered. The problem is
> now the direction of that progress (Willer, 1967, pp. xix).

In this quotation Willer puts the problem of quantitative sociology in a nutshell – many sociologists have simply walked away from it. And as Willer also says, albeit somewhat dramatically, it is for quantitative sociology to blaze along its own trail and be the brightest star of all. Like many adherents, that is, he would like to think that quantitative sociology is the surefire winner. Unlike its main proponents, Willer is dumb enough to admit serious rivalry. For the characteristic manner of the top quantitative sociologists is a measured calm; a surefootedness along their pretty path. Willer's distress is most unbecoming. The best men in the field simply pursue their own excellence.

Quantitative sociology is a world for its practitioners; a world of assumptions and satisfying them; a world of dilemmas and a world of practical promises. As Hindess wrote in a book review of Blalock's most recent collection, it would doubtless be rewarding for someone to analyse the rhetoric of this style in terms of a myth. But I cannot undertake this for I fear that the form of the myth would become more important than its content. Instead I shall settle for a sub-mythological presentation of the goals of quantitative sociology. In its own clichés one can sense the defensive walls of a garbled reasoning. This is not to say that its clichés do not contain the customary trace element of truth but rather that the current state of philosophizing has degenerated to oblique referencing of a little cluster of terms. The style of quantitative sociology is true unto itself. There are basic premises held by a community of scientists that they may make certain practical judgments about the shape of the next developments. But despite engaging in the exercise of charting the cluster of home truths I should make it clear from the outset that the 'goals' are much less important than the individual and institutional investment going into the style. It is this latter 'practical fact' to which we always return in the end. And, *en route* so to speak, we can but marvel at the sheer volume of work being produced by the style's adherents. On our way to judgment, that is, it becomes clear that the quantitative style is held to be both a 'whole sociology' in itself and the nexus of integration for all of the 'social sciences'.

There are obviously grave analytical problems in presenting a style in brief form. I could make the truth cluster linear and then taunt its naïveté. I can pick on each star and have it explode with contradictions. I can itemize the best expressions in the works I have used and challenge their truthfulness. However, I shall try to make a composite picture, an ideal type, that gives the sense of so many good minds pursuing a sterile exactitude – that is, of many men who find it too painful to look the world in the eye. Nevertheless quantitative sociologists are honest men, at times apparently obsessed with the procurement of the way to know their truths, and at other times seeming barely aware of the 'world outside'. For it could be said that a scientist must live in an ivory tower. But there are neither ivory towers nor pure scientists to inhabit them. To begin, then, quantitative method is a definite form of scholarship; definite in its determination to make this scholarship acceptable to all and accessible to some.

We begin with a roll-call of paradigm-pushers. Disrespectfully, that is, it is important to realize that two generations of American sociologists have been small in number and yet dealt in illicit drugs well enough to have their trade legalized.

In the beginning there were modest men. In fact there were Lundberg and Hempel. Both thinkers engaged the problem 'How is social science possible?' Hempel made striking advances in the logics of concept formation and 'explication'. His answer was that social science is just possible: providing it is painstakingly simple and as Lundberg said (1939) keeps its claims to those within its own emergent field. Hempel continued his life's work (1949, 1952, 1963). His contribution was that of making useful distinctions in a cogent, unhurried manner. Both Hempel and Lundberg went to great trouble to be specific.

Lundberg has largely been forgotten, his weakness being that he so limited sociology as a science. Further, Lundberg was of the opinion that sociology would barely constitute a science for a long time to come. Finally, Lundberg's strictures on disengaging from all social-policy activity were simply unacceptable.

Meanwhile Hempel became incorporated by a group whose specific policy was to sell sociological research. I refer to the Columbia school, the Lazarsfeld school or initially to the young turks who studied the 'American soldier' (Stouffer et al., 1949). These three volumes contained a mass of closely reasoned and researched accounts of the second world war that was fought between the ranks and within each soldier. The studies developed method sufficiently to produce a further volume (Stouffer et al., 1949–50) and a volume of restricted criticism (Merton and Lazarsfeld, 1950). There is no doubt that a style came from this work that is now, twenty years later, both the easiest and most extensive method of social research. It produced the 'variables and variance' approach and so with it came scaling, trend studies and panel studies. More to the point, this mass of research blurred the distinction between data collection and data analysis, or the distinction between technique and methodology. The researches proved clever – to see how a GI felt about the Army he was asked whether the uniform was respected by people in Civvy Street (Kendall, 1950). The distinction between what you study and how you study it was blurred because this 'team' could study virtually everything and did so. In the process they produced proofs about their indicators. They were 'getting at' what people did and felt in a way which no sociologist seems to have dreamed of before. All their questions were personal and they all pointed to a new social psychology of normality.

It would be foolish to say that the Columbia school consciously spread its influence by propaganda – unless, that is, they say they did. For half a decade funds flowed in and studies flowed out. The technique was quickly taken up (Lipset, 1953, p. 571, n. 3):

The six questions were agree-disagree statements concerning the Taft-Hartley Law, socialized medicine, government breakup of large corporations, government ownership of public

utilities, belief that most strikes are unnecessary and belief
that the British Labour Government deserved to be re-elected.
A conservative answer was given a score of 2, a liberal answer 0
and a don't know a score of 1. A perfect conservative score,
therefore would be 12, while an extreme liberal score would be 0.

And a textbook was produced specifically intended as a manual
from which a student could be instructed, as 'during the period of his
training, during the time when he tries to acquire the knowledge
and the modes of thinking which he might use later – during this
formative period a thorough grounding in methodology will be
valuable' (Lazarsfeld and Rosenberg, 1955, p. 12).

That is to say, the Columbia school was, and is, self-consciously
concerned with the hearts, minds and flexibility of future researchers.
The text is a magnificent blend of interest, practical guidance and
philosophical anecdotes. There is no base reference to Braithwaite,
let alone Bacon. There is no need to go any further back than the
triumph of four living volumes that arose from six years of death
and destruction. The Columbia school capitalized upon its success
quickly enough to be the major shareholder in post-war methodology.
And what to study never seems to have been much of a problem.

Hempel and Lundberg did have more direct heirs, however.
At the philosophical end of things were Carnap (1958) and Kaplan
(1964). And doing their best with 'being a science' were Coleman,
O. D. Duncan and Blalock. These three men do not constitute a
school. They are methodologists who have made extensive reference
to each other and to two scientists who surfaced to communicate
their method. Herman O. Wold (1953) seems to have been the man
who organized the principles and Sewall Wright the man who set
the practice down (1960). And it is truly remarkable to observe
the devotion which these two little papers are given. They have
apparently provided the impetus for the last ten years' developments
in 'path analysis'. Those who adhere to the arguments of Blalock –
path analysis's main advocate in sociology – make reference to all of
Wold's and Wright's rare offerings (see index). For the Blalock
school, as it may come to be known, still takes scientific examples for
matters of probability and frequently compares the operation with
one similar in contemporary physics. To put it too crudely,
Lazarsfeld's school is preoccupied with variables and Blalock's
school is fascinated with variance. In either event, both schools
claim to have turned a corner; to have broken from early days into
adolescence or to have moved from creation to application; or to
being as scientific as it is possible to be at the moment.

There have been similar generations in European quantitative
sociology. Or more categorically, the fringe Teutonic countries of

Scandinavia, Holland and England have somehow kept abreast of American developments. The earlier generation was devoted to surveys in England. These men were Caradog-Jones, C. A. Moser and D. V. Glass. The new men are A. P. M. Coxon, P. Abell and K. Hope. But in the case of the first two there is more than the American passing reference to the shape of sociological inquiry. Reviewing the books of Galtung and Blalock that have been extensively used in this chapter, Coxon (1969, p. 250) wrote:

> Sociologists have the right to expect that methodology will help to provide the models and procedures for the analysis of social phenomena and behaviour which is substantively important to them, just as methodologists have the right to demand coherent and rigorous statements of the problem from sociologists. The new methodology shows some signs of providing the basis for much closer interaction, and this may well involve a radical restatement of what sociologists consider to be substantively important, but it would be sad if greater methodological competence led sociologists to suffer from goal displacement. Both texts leave one with the feeling that however these advances are, the tail is sometimes wagging the dog.

In this paragraph Coxon recognizes the separation of sociologist from methodologist and the part played by 'the language of social research' in this process. His final comment that methodology may usurp sociology in the making of theory is untypical of the writings of American methodologists. Coxon thereby registers a primacy of sociology in the making of sociological theory.

So, too, does Abell – even in his most cryptic writings. Abell is continuing a characteristic English concern for the structure of things. He is also 'working out the maths' of situations of social interaction and as such blending two major styles as best he can. He writes (1969, p. 500):

> If a systematic social theory is a logical possibility then it will emerge from a close inspection of the structures that actors generate in the complex process of social interaction. Our focal point at the present stage of development should be far closer to the empirical plane than theoreticians would lead us to believe. Most of the theoretical concepts at our disposal should play the role of *naming* different types of structures, not the role of propositional terms within the theoretical system itself. If this is accepted we can appreciate more easily the importance of the various structural levels of measurement.

And in footnote 3 of the same paper Abell charts the future of sociology and its mathematics in one contention: 'In fact I would contend that the laws of sociology are unlikely to be probabilistic in nature, much rather they will be structural regularities where the appropriate formalism will be abstract algebra of one sort or another' (p. 410).

Sociology has, however, been going long enough to resist the call for all to travel in a unified, purposeful direction. The significance of Abell's prognostications is that he is making his own quantitative sociology and using mathematics rather than the natural sciences as both model and source. Thus he writes upon topology and from the little I know of this field I would guess that he has found a subject for his mathematics, and a mathematics for his subject. But to revert to Coxon's observation, it is doubtful if this subject is 'really' sociology.

The relevance of these two generations in the two countries is that there are very few men with enormous influence. These men are untouchable in their own field. They have very little reading to do. They can illustrate a paper with a soupçon of data. And they are all moral pragmatists. By this I mean that all methodological discussion has gradually shifted from:

a. What is science?

to b. What should 'our science' properly be?

The very quality of these leading methodologists is in their unending capacity to make up and discuss their own rules. The quality of a methodologist is, therefore, a sense of discipline and a nose for the lawlessness of the current research process. In this way all the methodologists mentioned are careful to develop their rules without punishing the many violators of these rules to date. In effect, methodologists are characteristically careful not to condemn those who may mend their ways when given a good example.

There is one outsider to these schools and generations, who is nevertheless influential. The final chapter of Galtung's text (1967) shows how he answers what our science should do by saying what a science does. Galtung does not compromise or make special claims. Instead, he has the head and tail wagging furiously. By this I mean that Galtung, like Abell, has his own 'social research'. Data collection and data analysis are in equal halves. They are joined by his itemizing of the units of analysis. But this point will concern us quite soon. The point here is that a consideration of the community influentials in methodology shows a shift from the philosophical to the practical issues and yet in actually doing it methodologists have become a breed apart with just part of one foot in sociology. This state of affairs is neither peculiar nor precarious because of the success that quantitative sociology is having in the open market. To repeat a theme with slight variation, these few methodologists are largely unchallenged because so many are trying to practise their most recent teachings.

Nevertheless it is often privately suggested that the men named here are dull or even stupid. Perhaps this impression is gained from the writing style adopted by so many. For this style is admittedly embarrassingly simple and jargon-bound. A few sentences can contain bald, weak everyday English and a string of terms. Worse still, the poor English is usually devoted to a terminological discussion. The methodologist breaks into an example and, as quickly as possible it seems, into algebra. In truth methodologists are generally quite uneasy when discussing why they have bothered to make yet another distinction and coin yet another neologism. And yet it should be understood that the 'ideologists of quantification' are hard-working, sincere men whose style is dictated by a bewildering range of forces. Or rather, methodologists themselves feel forces from all directions and so rather than appease one force they try to keep their cool and be above the meeting-place of these forces. Let us list these forces somewhat arbitrarily:

1 A need to speak with other methodologists in the most congenial terms.
2 A fluency in mathematics to the point of appreciating implication and nuance.
3 The problem of having isolated researchers keep abreast of methodological developments.
4 A very slight grasp of sociological reasoning to the extent of a studied ignorance of classical European writers and contemporary writers in other schools. For example, Durkheim is in no sense recognized as the founding father; H. Stuart Hughes is as unlikely to be referenced as Everett Cherrington Hughes.
5 A facility with computers and an admiration of their speed with the drudgery.
6 A feeling that sociology as a science is at the watershed of classification with explanation and is in need of very detailed focused guidance.

Now just as methodologists' writings can be barely articulate so are these forces kept unarticulated. In fact the real 'feelings' have been so suppressed that the few men actively engaged in developing quantitative sociology have become both breathless and conservative of late. They are breathless because the 'watershed' has actually been sighted in the last twenty years. They have become conservative because of the awesome assumptions necessary in scientific practice.

In effect, the Columbia school of applied classification was getting much further with sociology than the models men now find themselves. For the Columbia school really worked at a phenomenon, they made extensive forays into previously closed territories. The mass of studies on communication, voting and general market research did produce 'sociological concepts' (see, for example, Lazarsfeld *et al.*, 1948). More especially the teaming of Merton with Lazarsfeld was particularly productive. For a while it looked as though there was nothing that they could not research. And finally, the method was still part of the meaning. By that I mean that the Columbia school found out about things and in the teaching of these facts expressed their method.

The mathematical-models methodologists have changed the subject yet again. They have shifted 'back' to survey style: to finding out a lot less about many more people. In the process they have tried to contain one of quantification's thorniest problems, namely that of spuriousness. To put it simply, it might look right but it's wrong. If you have a lot of 'respondents' your correlations can be very small and yet 'significant'. For example, in the paper on class in this book there are over 500 respondents. Well, roughly, 'a correlation of $0 \cdot 12$ is significant at the $0 \cdot 05$ level'. That is, there is $0 \cdot 88$ of the relationship's movement still 'unexplained'. Consequently, the honesty of those engaged in path analysis has driven them to consider spuriousness more of a problem than that of getting a significant relationship. This in turn has turned them in search of an error term and made the algebra of the theory very complicated.

To round this account off with an impudent analogy, then, the Columbia school scored goals from the penalty spot against a midget goal-keeper. And now the Blalock school (though it is still not fully formed) is trying to score from the centre and asking its own team to stand in the way of all bar the finest shots.

Quantitative sociology as a science

We must now face the key problem directly. Why is it so important for quantitative sociology to be a science? For the claims of its practitioners all point in this direction. Let us concentrate upon Phillips's text (1966, p. vii) for a few moments and draw upon his major articles of faith.

> Theory constitutes the most important research tool available to the scientist, and . . . research methods may be fruitfully conceived of as strategies and tactics adopted by a community of scientists. . . .
>
> From this perspective the choices that each investigator makes may be evaluated in terms of how effective they and this community are in reaching the goals of science.

These two excerpts contain Phillips's cluster of importances. They go roughly:

Science is good. Scientists are good.
Research is science. Theory is scientific.
It's a matter of getting a good strategy.

In the following chapter (pp. 3–4) these absolutes are related to the reader once more:

In the universities social research has attained a degree of respectability not far removed from that achieved by physical science research. . . .
The fundamental goal of social science is to achieve accurate explanations and predictions of human behaviour. . . .
Few would deny that a great deal of progress has already been made in the scientific study of human behaviour. . . .
Such knowledge of human behaviour has provided the basis for a wide variety of social technologies. . . .
For the person with intellectual curiosity social research offers hope of fulfilling man's ancient quest for self knowledge. For those caught up in the misery of urban slums, social research can lead to hope for a better life. For mankind as a whole, social research may help to provide the means of avoiding nuclear destruction. There is, of course, no guarantee that social research can lead to these results, but there is also no evidence that such achievements are beyond its scope.
In view of the importance of social research for extending the boundaries of our knowledge and for the development of effective social technologies, a grave responsibility rests on the shoulders of students of human behaviour. It is their achievements or lack of them that will determine the degree to which the promise of social science will be fulfilled.

So social science is respectable, useful, interesting and promising. The last adjective is a little troublesome in that Phillips is sure that social science is full of promise but not sure of what these promises might be. He is saying, 'Social science might work, you will enjoy it and its findings may help the world.' Repeatedly, that is, for Phillips the biggest problem of all is nuclear destruction. Social science he suggests may somehow prevent its subject matter from annihilating itself. And in the next chapter the somehow is turned into a maybe, for in further specification of the goals of science Phillips identifies them all as aspects of control. Social science is the answer because the science will determine the controls of the 'social' (p. 49):

The goals of science seem to involve the nature of reality, prediction and explanation. . . .

The conclusions of science as to the nature of reality are viewed as being fundamentally uncertain. Scientists have learned to live with this uncertainty. The scientific process seems useful in coping with this uncertainty, because it at least substitutes a collective estimate of the nature of reality for an individual one.

The broad emphasis is on that kind of behaviour which can be shaped in different ways by the environment and is not predetermined by heredity.

Scientists are interested in prediction in order to be able to cope effectively with their environment.

So far, that is, science reassures scientists. The clues are there for the use of science too; the use is to control the environment. The problem for the scientist is really the rationality of his subject. Science is tireless in its pursuit of 'internal logics'. A rational explanation can always be found for the irrational. To put this directly, scientists can have a different rational explanation from the irrational one of their subjects (Kaplan, 1964, p. 359, quoted in Phillips, 1966, p. 54). But this is sliding from prediction into explanation. In science a prediction is what will happen and an explanation is why it will happen. It is truly unfortunate that they are practically synonymous and tend to amount to the same thing. As Phillips writes, 'Just as predictions may vary in their accuracy, so it is true that explanations may vary in their completeness' (p. 54).

In fact the more 'pure' the theory the better, but more 'partial', it is. And it is not worth anyone's time to pursue these distinctions. They are made to find a way through the problems that seeing reality as one and science as another have created. And the mess is largely attributable to followers like Phillips looking for certainties, for linearity and obvious utility. Such followers are forced to list the characteristics of science, make comparisons with physics when they can and create polarities to bypass imponderables. There is always the danger of following this meandering path wherever it goes in the hope that it covers the field. The fact is that just as the frequent opposites are obfuscating, the equally frequent assertions are tautological.

In addition to the regularities that are obvious to most individuals, social scientists have unearthed many regularities that are or once were not so obvious. (ibid., p. 51)

The path to more accurate predictions seems to lie in the further development of theories out of which more accurate predictors may be put together. (pp. 52–3)

Explanation is also pursued by the scientific community for its own sake, and this seems to be one of the most important factors motivating scientists generally. (p. 56)

Men like Phillips turn up their science full blast to cope with some apparent uncertainty. They take Reichenbach's (1964) distinction between the 'context of discovery' (theory and idea) and the 'context of justification' (data collection and analysis) seriously so that they may relate them or argue that sociology has matured to some second stage. There is no hope of having an answer to this section's question in this way because the strength of science is shielding and spurring an undisclosed weakness. It is the weaknesses that can be listed. For then the piety of science does appear as a protection. And the listing of weaknesses can begin with those that quantitative sociologists see for themselves. These are really issues in the method itself.

The first weakness is the one with which this chapter's second section began. Where does the idea come from? Clearly this is a big headache for the student. There are three devices used to cover this problem. First, students can replicate their teachers' work and not face the problem at all. Second, a student can be told to find out about something and make an operational model for himself. Third, the student can try to make an operational model of something that genuinely interests him. In effect, the making of an operational model becomes the problem and then all the issues of causality, contingency, explanation and prediction are secondary. Willer (1967 ch. 5) claims that most sciences have two 'levels': theoretical and empirical. His chapter provides an example of the way in which an operational system unifies these two as closely as possible. Blalock also guides towards modelling but, being more concerned with the mathematics, prefers to call his diagrams linear, additative, recursive systems (1968, pp. 165, 171, 178). But the 'idea' is not provided by a model or by operationalizing concepts (see Adler's criticisms in Blalock, 1968, p. 12). In fact it is something of a regression to advance to modelling. It is a regression to overlook the criterion that concepts should refer to 'observables'. As Dumont and Wilson (1967) cogently argue, an idea may be contained in a model but its theoretical status can be that of an implicit theory, a theory sketch or an explicit theory. And much of this depends upon how rigorously the concepts have been explicated. For models often juxtapose all sorts of concepts in the rush to get the picture.

Dumont and Wilson (p. 994) are in fact particularly generous towards the cavalier approach to concepts adopted by most model-builders. For if they are read in conjunction with Shanin (1972) a very different opinion can be gained. Steadfastly Shanin pursues the problem of 'units of analysis' in sociology. If sociology is a science what are its elements (*pace* chemistry), its forces and energy principles (*pace* physics) and its organisms (*pace* biology)? He offers six basic units of sociological analysis (see his typology on p. 354) and discusses their development. As far as I am concerned this is a truly scientific approach, or rather would constitute the beginnings of such a science. But quantitative sociologists have gone round, rather than through, this stage.

All in all, the weaknesses intrinsic in the method are those of being in a hurry to get through birth pangs and teething as quickly as possible. And now the infant science is tottering rather than toddling; the point being that for all the progress there is little solid achievement. It may be that these weaknesses derive from copying and modifying a style that was only stereotypically understood. Yet I suspect that the weaknesses are inherent because of the desire of quantitative sociologists to 'accommodate to changing conditions'. To put it more directly, quantitative sociologists have weakened their own discipline by offering to apply it as quickly as possible.

Throughout their writings there are phrases about 'given the present state of practice', 'in order that we might make some headway' and 'accepting the practical issues that surround us, then we should do this next'! In this way quantitative sociology has had an *ad hoc* career, not the measured evolution suggested by its apologists. And nowhere is this more evident than in their attitude towards being methodologists. There is the desire to be of service, a studied neutrality and an insistence that methodologists make good employees. In fact the suggestion that 'tame statisticians are being produced' is hardly unfair. For the demeanour of methodologists does mix attributes of mastery with the attitudes of servility. The 'natural comparison' would be between the methodologist in the team (see Appendix 2) and the accountant in the firm. The accountant does not 'make the decisions' or 'bear the responsibility' and yet he meticulously checks the figures of other employees and his 'advice' can have the force of law.

Beyond the weaknesses of the method and the weakening posture adopted by methodologists there is the final thread to this section's question. For it may be 'scientific' but is it really 'sociological'? The books and articles cited generally speak of 'social research', or 'social science', or 'behavioural science'. There is little direct mention of sociology as such. In some instance even the facts dealt with are barely social. Phillips and Lazarsfeld and Rosenberg think this is all to the good. Lazarsfeld and Rosenberg eulogize the qualities of methodology in the following themes (1955, pp. 9–10):

One function of methodology is to provide formal training for young social scientists which will enable them to do better research.

Methodology also increases the social scientist's ability *to cope with new and unfamiliar developments in his field.*

A third way in which methodology can aid in the advancement of the social sciences is through its *contributions to inter-disciplinary work.*

The quantitative method, that is, blurs the human sciences and co-ordinates mass studies. As such the quantitative method is in no sense the future form of sociology. Its advocates care for science, not for sociology. To them sociology is doubtless something in the past. They think that science is 'a risk worth taking' (Blalock, 1968, p. 11) and that really the endeavour should be science at all costs (Blalock, 1968, p. 157). The remaining sociologists may, however, be puzzled over any reconciliation between science as quantitative sociology and sociology. And so it should be of help for them to realize that those advocating quantitative methods are rarely interested in sociology as such.

This is no fresh conclusion. Recently Sklair (1972) reviewed a volume entitled *Explanation in the Behavioural Sciences: Confrontations* (Borger and Cioffi, 1970). For his part he concluded:

This is a book for philosophers and psychologists. Sociologists will find almost nothing new in it, and what they do find in it seriously neglects many pressing issues in sociology. But perhaps these do not merit inclusion in a work devoted to the *behavioural sciences* and this might cause us not dismay, but relief.

We might put it as simply as this: there has always been a caring for people in sociology and quantitative sociology is a rash of 'social ethic' in comparison.

4   The practice of quantitative research

The most obvious criticism of quantitative research is that it 'cooks its books'. Not that the theory is made to fit the data but that the actual mode of presentation presents the good side of the research in a revelationary manner. Step by step reality is stripped to its bare essentials – the show gives you all in the end.

Quantitative research offers the chance of flair – of the exposition of the researcher's skill. The chance is to make it all look easy: theoretical grounding, aptness of measures, telling tests and inspired secondary analysis. Yet this chance characterizes a successful 'piece of research'. Really the obverse is true. Every stage of the research process is fraught with the hazards of following an etiquette. The results of quantitative research may come to nothing. Loads of collected data may be dumped. The slim monograph may never appear. So a less obvious criticism of quantitative research is that it 'burns its boats'.

Quantitative research begins with a problem. Characteristically this problem is phrased in a 'middle-range theory'. The theory says that a feature of a type of collectivities is that generally people behave the same way by virtue of the same forces and that the variations in types of reaction vary with the strength of forces filtered as types of people. The problem is to prove that the particular features do vary, form types and go up and down with each other. The problem is to pick features that are accessible and sociologically organized. Concepts do the organizing. These concepts form part of a theory. Quantitative research is a matter of accounting the system.

The system can also be accounted as a system in itself. The form of the collectivity is as amenable as its people-content, to being looked at as a whole. The problems of relationships and types are just the same but the people therein are informants rather than subjects. In any case, the middle-range theory used invokes both 'macro' and 'micro' in its explanation. For empirical purposes, that is, the researcher is treating the collectivity as a world and the incumbents as wholly occupying their respective roles. It is the variables that matter, those concepts made to measure, and just how they vary – all things being equal.

The researcher is quite entitled to pick his theory; it is his stand as a researcher. He is less entitled to pick the system he studies, as sponsorship usually states where he is to work. His theory is that this world fits together in a particular way and has particular effects. People are patterned and behave alike. The theory does not really have any problems. The researcher is to fit the theory; to make use of it to find out what people think, feel and do. The problems are practical. Yet a doubt enters – there is the hope that the theory will work and will not produce insignificant results. For the researcher is not employed to produce changes in theory. He is not asked to relate insignificant results with expansive criticism. The researcher is to get on with the job, get the data, analyse the results and get a paper out of it.

Having been given a field, area or topic the researcher sets to work out theory. This proves to take a long time. There are a lot of variables which might have an effect but if he takes too many there may not be enough variance for each to explain. He has to consider all the likely factors and produce diagrams, or equations or a list of hypotheses. He has to work this all out before he can make his measures. He has to produce a way of getting at the data.

Getting the measures is surprisingly simple once the variables have been finalized. Many have been there before. They have left some tools with good correlations; lists of things that save a lot of time. There is always data available so the researcher might as well use it. What to actually explain may still be a worry but calling something a dependent variable settles the matter. The dependent variable has to be interesting in itself. The measures should get at the dependent variable particularly well. The measures should get some good independent variables too, like background, socio-economic group and the size and structure of the system. Everything must be got ready for the field beforehand. Interview schedules precoded wherever possible. Questionnaires with columns; circles; squares and ticks. An introductory letter asking for co-operation, hoping the respondent finds it interesting and promising anonymity and confidentiality.

The field has still to be entered and actually getting into it is a worry. Respondents may not co-operate, someone might object to the questions (not a respondent, but someone important enough to effect a veto). The response rate might fall too low (although there is always the possibility of 'extending the sample to include . . .'). For the system has been overviewed by the researcher. He has worked out how many people he should take; what proportion or number of the parts of the system should be representative or even just respectable.

Getting the theory right for the system is partly a matter of aesthetics. Getting the numbers is largely a matter of adequate coverage. The researcher has to cover himself. He has to have taken enough cases to write a result as a generalization – thirty for an experiment; fifty for correlation; a hundred for analysis of variance, one thousand or so for an area study. But initially when the first replies come back, when the first few people have been friendly and spoken their mind there is a euphoria to replace the depression of design.

The analysis of results is simply tedious. It all has to be coded. Some replies are incomplete, some pages have been omitted, some people give two answers and some people redefine the question to give a standard answer to it. There are a lot of little decisions to be made and noted. The design is beginning to suffer at the hands of the respondents.

The design really suffers, though, across the hurdles of analysis. A lot of answers might be virtually the same. The distribution is rarely normal and the testing for it can reject the bulk of the data. χ^2s and correlations are the easiest of analyses because they let slight trends be significant if the numbers are big enough. F-tests and regression analyses are more stringent but they look better. Factorial analyses are bound to produce something but they bring the problem of identifying what has been found. Factorial analyses, however, promise to salvage something out of the data. Data analysis is a clerical matter and there are clerks to be had to do it.

By now the theoretical problem is coming back into sight. Many respondents have given enough 'soft data' for the researcher to get new ideas on organizing the results. Some correlations are truly significant. Others, sadly, are not. Some linkages have simply not worked. They should have, even an 'eye-ball scan' said they might. But they did not. So the whole framework cannot really be presented. The report will have to be restructured around the interesting findings. Anyway, also by now, there are problems of audience. There are 'external theoretical problems'. A factual report should be written for the interested parties. A discussion paper could be mounted on a concept and its correlations. And there are a few methodological insights that could be worked up into a research note. The sponsor's demand is naturally the strongest but can be met in cold fashion by teaching him the method and discussing a few hypotheses light-heartedly. The paper being written is for the 'practitioners in the field'. The academic paper has to wait. The external theoretical problem is that considerable change is planned which would affect the results. However, the sponsors want to know what to watch – which results would go more against them. The old theoretical imagery of the system comes to the rescue. The system will change, there'll be some resistance, but the system is bound to survive. The system is probably better off bringing resistance to the surface and dealing with it man after man.

And having worked all this out of the data, the researcher finds the academic paper is much easier to write. There are concepts to be coined and put into currency. There are all the tests, detailed results and some sample measures. Best of all there is the literature to be evaluated and brought up to date. In an obvious way it's all a plea for more research using a particular 'orientation'.

The methodology paper is rarely written, for methodologists are 'great men'. They are on speaking terms with scientists. They can always do something with data. They are mathematicians. They are bringing the tests in from astrophysics, biology and econometrics. The researcher is unlikely to claim to be a methodologist.

Resting back a little, the researcher may realize that he has produced tendencies, types and difficult cases. The system does have some systematic properties and some sources of tension. The research has identified the flow, the massed majority, and brought a few instances bobbing to its surface. The researcher has the tabs on these places and people. He can, in fact, divulge a little of what he has found discreetly to an appreciative audience. In fact the rare, nagging doubt may be that the only audience he has not considered is that of the respondents themselves. This is nevertheless convenient. For frankly, it would be embarrassing to tell them what happened to their laboured answers. Nearly all of what they said has disappeared. What words are actually reported have come from a few especially talkative people.

Some sort of report has to be written. The researcher has to 'deliver the goods' and into the right hands. He may then realize that his categories are to be used; people are to be their types; systems are to change into shapes which give the least trouble. The researcher sees his efforts being put to work as a tool for greater administrative control.

The quantitative method is rigorous, aesthetic and almost humble before its facts. It gets its facts right time after time. It has a proven capacity to make facts. For its findings are usable. They are practical. They serve to enable an ordering worthy of more penetrating quantification. Some situations *suit* quantitative sociology. Studies of so-called organizations and their inmates do. Studies which involve extrapolations of having been 'in' organizations do. Wherever there is a pressure for conformity, for uniformity, for mediocrity,

F

for concealment in the grey mass, there is an opportunity for good quantitative sociology. And then it works. The inmates are sufficiently similar to be treated the same and their slight differences are exaggerated to the convenience of qualitatively distinct types. And, if there are a few hands guiding the future course, prediction is rather unimportant.

The realization that comes to a quantitative sociologist is that very few professionals are interested in his work. Some 'practical men', however, do show some interest. From across the continents come cryptic greetings. They have their source in strange-sounding institutes where everyone is a doctor. These 'colleagues' poke hard into the findings; identify types and adopt the 'ways of getting at things'. These distant friends are behaving the same way as the practical men 'in the field'.

Only as time goes on is the practical aspect properly revealed. The quantitative method produces a process for reducing variance – for lessening the unexplained and the error. Later, then, the quantitative researcher can discern his true audience. And by then this audience, this willing sponsor, solves at a stroke the problems of finding a problem and somewhere to do a bit of research. Quantitative sociology is thus whipped into its proper place by its own practical backlash. When the researcher fumbles and falls he is helped to his feet by friendly funds.

The criticism of the quantitative method in sociology is not that it measures people as if taking the yardage of their consciousness. Nor is it that the data is useless to its subjects, turns them into objects and furthers their manipulation by controlling élites. Nor is it that measurement stultifies the chaos and mystery of life to a few feeble mocking mechanisms. Nor is it that quantification fails to find the circumstances of prediction. The core criticism is that the quantitative method in sociology replaces scepticism with ignorance. The researcher is not sure what he has got or what to make of his results. Or, more simply, how his method works. Sponsorship aside, the quantitative method in sociology is *personally* inoperable.

part two

The qualitative method

My introduction to qualitative sociology

In leaving quantitative methods for qualitative methods I felt I was leaving statistics for real people in real situations. I was seeking the significance of the little bits and pieces, of conversation that had revealed so much to me. I was also looking for an easier method. One with which I could start right away, make it up as I went along and write it up quickly. It was not so much that I felt inspired by qualitative sociology but more that I was frustrated to the point of paralysis by the business of having a computer produce my facts. I did not want to look at another print-out and read that there had been an incorrect major control block. I wanted to see the real thing.

The opportunity came in a research job 'to research the concepts of health and illness'. I thought to compare these notions and their usage in spiritualism, herbalism and orthodox medicine. I dreamt of being a caretaker in a local Christian Science church, an apprentice to a nearby herbalist and a receptionist in a surgery. But, by the time I had pottered through some literature, I was cursorily told I was a 'general practice person'. Apparently I should have been studying doctors all the time. In a panic I realized that I was half a year in and with no fieldwork under my belt. So I 'tapped up' a friendly doctor and sat, safe for a while, in his surgery.

An introduction to part two

This part is altogether more readable than is part one. Qualitative sociology lifts the lids from hygienic dustbins. One example is probably enough. More professional papers are Egon Bittner's 'The Police on Skid Row' and David Sudnow's 'Dead on arrival' (1968). These papers exhibit more clearly than mine the art of grounded classification that gives the researcher so much childlike pleasure.

5 Observations in a surgery

Ordinances of observation

I was lucky, for having been told to study GPs, I came to know a doctor well enough to observe him at work. I wanted to enter the sanctuary. I asked to sit in his surgery. And so two series of observations were made; the first during a fortnight in February 1971 and the second during a week in the October of that year. As it happened, during the first series I found myself observing the doctor and was then more able to observe his patients the second time around.

Consultation seems to be a multiple situation. Each consultation is an event. Patients come and go and their different faces catch different reflections from the same doctor. Each is an entity in the doctor's total morning or evening surgery, and these surgeries are but one set-piece in his practice. In the beginning there is variety.

More than two reference points, or ordinances, are required to take a bearing on a moving point or process (Rancière, 1971, pp. 45–6):

> For an understanding of this concept 'process' let us first recall Marx's definition: 'The word *process* . . . expresses a development considered in the totality of its real conditions'. Let us complete this definition by mentioning the two essential characteristics of a process i.e.
>
> 1 Its development leads to a constant reproduction of its starting point.
> 2 The elements in it are defined not by their *nature* but by the place they occupy, the *function* they fulfil.

I have chosen to develop two parts and their functions. The doctor has a diagnostic routine. He asks questions, pronounces the disorder, projects a therapy, gives treatment and dispatches any related paperwork. This is the core of his consultation. Around this core he can wrap many 'human touches', developing the patient as a patient, informing himself and patient. The patient, meanwhile, has made a rehearsal. He has worked out what he feels he has to say. These matters confirm and confound the doctor's routine. They confirm it by 'sticking to the formula' and confound it by stretching out the time a normal routine is scheduled to take. The patient's rehearsal is subordinate to the doctor's routine. The theme is that of the doctor's dominance throughout the event. This dominance is appropriate to both the patient's condition and the doctor's and patient's respective class situations. And further, dominance maintains the integrity of two opposing worlds.

Let me polish this pedantry. The doctor did not have a precise routine any more than the patient had made an incisive rehearsal. Nor, crucially, did the doctor 'try to dominate' the patient. To be utterly naïve, it just happened that way. To be more abstract, routine and rehearsal enable the consultation to reach round to its identical beginning and their function is to reconstitute the dominance of the event.

To use these ideas, and to permit the stating of several lesser ideas, I have made three assumptions. First, the patient is, in each consultation, in some sense ill. This means that when a person comes to this surgery there is something wrong with him. Second, at the time of consultation, both doctor and patient take the world as it is. There is nothing sinister, no intentional indirectness or inappropriateness on the part of either doctor or patient.

The third assumption seeks the reader's charity. I hold that my observation did not qualitatively affect the process. My presence may have made some patients keep their part to a minimum but, as Dr Rogers observed, most patients were not discouraged. Dr Rogers also said he had felt himself slipping back into a routine. It became clear to both parties that I did nothing apart from sit behind him, bow my head and write. The patients had no choice; they were driven on by their own rehearsal and deterred from protest by the dominance of the process.

In part the relevance of my observations is still unclear. For my own problem was, 'What is wrong with the patient?' By the fact and actions of friendship I was incorporated by the doctor.* Being 'on

*During the first series of observations 'Dr Rogers' came to collect me from the waiting room; ushered me in whilst a patient was present; discussed a previous patient whilst the next was making an entrance; referred once to me as 'Dr Fletcher, here' and on another occasion encouraged a three-way discussion on a man's complaint.

During the second series he said that he became unaware of my presence. And then he became increasingly anxious for me to complete my observations. I held out as long as I could and then abruptly stopped before he felt it necessary to prohibit me.

his side', I discussed what I would do. The doctor's problem was my problem even though I was at liberty to dwell upon diagnosis. It may be that 'playing doctor' has concealed all but the technicality, sincerity and urgency of consultation. Yet having tried them on, I have felt a little of their force.

In a further part relevance is secondary in this essay because of the effort to establish neutral reference points for its subject matter; to develop generalizations about a surgery and not to say that the world at large is so or should be so. Its relevance is to reveal what I have seen, though darkly, that others may piece together change, in and for themselves.

Lines on a sketch of the surgery

On a main road, close to the centre of Midtown, a corner house serves as a surgery. Alongside the house a rough road rides up towards an expanse of more slums beyond. The slums are slats of Victorian terraces stretched around a hillside. They are not really slums: overall they need fresh paint, new window frames and roof repairs. Nevertheless their greyness speaks as sullenness. Landlords will profit by clearance and close traffic will serve as a cause. Occasionally, in early morning, after a shower, roads and roofs reflect their street lights and warmth joins the houses into a street. Usually mechanical thunder and emetic sulphur drive the inhabitants apart and indoors.

The surgery offers no contrast with its surroundings. A brass nameplate is its only mark; a mark that is scored by the steady pace of people to see one of the five partners. Entrance, waiting room, reception desk and file store are one room. Telephone rings and buzzes are nearly continuous. Two women answer these calls and weave their arms to record appointments. From 9.00 a.m. to 10.00 a.m. they are making appointments, moving the queue; finding things for the doctors and ensuring that each patient's card is on the doctor's desk. From 10.00 a.m. onwards they are also writing prescriptions for the doctors to sign and do so by looking at the bottles and pills people bring in their pockets.

'Who do you want to see?'
'Dr Rogers.'
'You can see him at half-past ten.'
'Oh no! I have come to watch him, to sit with him. I am a colleague of his.'
'Oh. What is your name?'*

---

*This request for privilege was not needed a second time when the older woman said, 'You're the one that goes in with him', and broke into a long smile.

73

In a room behind the counter are an office and treatment rooms, a secretary and 'Sister'. In front of the counter are three long, red benches.

Patients wait on these benches. A young woman in a brittle scarlet coat, her figure beginning to slacken. An old man deep within a green-grey overcoat. A youth with hard rims to his eyes. Two women with teenagers chatting as if they were in a coffee bar or on a bus. No one quizzing another's face. Few concentrating on anything. (Cf. Dennis, 1955, p. 44.)

Beside the benches runs a corridor with three consulting-room doors marked and numbered. The rooms vary little and then only in size. Between the glossy cream walls are a couch, desk and chair, sink, screens and three wooden chairs. Two of these chairs are at angles in front of the desk and one floats behind. Each time I made for the latter's cover I failed to acknowledge the patients sitting in front of the desk. Their eyes never left the doctor.

An account of Dr Rogers's surgery

I observed 214 consultations in Dr Rogers's surgery and noted what was said in just over half of them – for the rest I simply watched. Every usable recording is given fully in the following account. As I wish to argue that Dr Rogers's consistencies can be understood as his managing of his patients I feel that the reader is entitled to the fullest possible account. For I am arguing about the presence of a tone or taste to the event. Yet obviously each dialogue is placed to substantiate a particular part of the argument. So the exchange of interest is emphasized by being set in italics.

A further convention which has been adopted to present the data is that of a script. Dr Rogers's words begin well to the left of the page and are signified by a preceding dash.

—'Hello, how are you?'
   'I've got a pain in my side.'
—'Where?'
   'Here.'
—'Any headache?'
   'Bit.'
—'Did it hurt when you passed water this morning?'
   'It stung.'

Doctor walks round his desk briskly, and the man stands up, looking at the place of his pain.

—'You've settled down at work since that head injury? Point with one finger where you feel the pain.'
   'In the top of my head. I feel a bit dizzy.'

—'Did it hurt when you went this morning?'
    'Yes.'
—'I think you've got an infection on the bladder.'
    'It's just like a stitch when I stand.'
—'Any headaches since your injury?'
    'I've changed jobs. I was made redundant, I'm at Smith's.'
—'Doing what?'
    'Odd jobs, you know.'

Doctor returns, just as quickly, to his seat, takes a pad and completes it from the man's card.

—'It should be completely better in 48 hours, but take them all, even if you are completely well.'
The man stands and takes his prescription.
—'Take today off and go back tomorrow.'
The man moves sideways and takes his sick-note.
    'Thank you doctor.'
—'Bye-bye.'

This is the most straightforward record of a consultation that I possess and obviously every word, idea and *non-sequitur* counts. To show how this is so, and to discuss the functions of the parts the 'film' will be staggered down to its frames. And first we project the film:

From the doctor to the patient

We begin with the patient's entrance. Dr Rogers is starting from cold and yet preparing for a decision. The first frame of 'his movie' (cf. Wolfe, 1968, p. 117) is the familiarization of the patient to himself.

—*'Well, what's the problem?'*
    'I went to Jones's but I'd lost the note and I need one for
    the insurance from the last place.'
—*'You want another note?'*
    'Yes.'
—*'How's your mother?'*
    'All right, bronchitis, flu and that.'
—*'How's the girl friend?'*
    'She's like my mother, bronchitis, flu you know.'
—*'When's the wedding bells?'*
    'When we get a place and some money.'
—'If you're like me you've never got any money, so you'd better get a place and go from there.'

There is a pause while Dr Rogers rapidly writes a note and records the consultation.

—'Is that trouble cleared up now?'

'Yes, I drive past Ford's and I feel good not turning in. I like it you know.'

The following example of familiarization comes from a consultation with an attractive young woman.

'The pills make me drowsy and vicious. I've got this rash too. It's worse on the back than it is on the front.'

Dr Rogers signals to me and I leave whilst an examination is made.

—'*How is it at hone? . . . and the little boy? . . . and the dogs?* If I said how can we help you what would you say?'

As I return Mrs F. and Dr Rogers are talking of her husband.

'He's a terrific organizer but he never finishes anything.'

—'And you tidy up the loose ends.'

'He's still got the club but he's dropped the other business.'

—'I'm giving you some specifically anti-anxiety pills. Take them an hour before going to bed.'

Whilst handing over a prescription Dr Rogers helps Mrs F. on with her coat.

'What service! I think I'll be ill again.'

In familiarization Dr Rogers also familiarizes a patient with himself. Already he has conveyed a financial attitude in saying, 'If you're like me you've never got any money. . . .' He also uses himself and his family as medical examples.

A pregnant woman asks:

'Is my blood group all right?'

—'Oh yes, you're all right. You are positive. I'm rhesus negative and so's my wife.'

A mother says her daughter feels that 'she's walking into things'.

—'Oh yes, it's otitis media. An infection of the middle ear. *I'm an expert on it, my little girl used to get it a lot.*'

Familiarization both opens a consultation and sustains it with personal asides. Once acquainted with the patient Dr Rogers passes on to diagnosis proper.

'I'm shattered all the time and it's not work. Yesterday I had a terrible headache.'

—'How's your aggression?'

'I can control it now. I'm a changed person, everybody says so.'

—'You don't feel frustrated?'
　'I still want things.'
—'What's the mood?'
　'Fine.'
—'and breathing?'
　'All right.'
—'Drinking?'
　'Quite a lot.'
—'Pain in the chest?'
　'Yes.'
—'Tummy trouble?'
　'A bit.'
—'Bowels?'
　'O.K.'
—'Eyesight?'
　'I think so.'
—'Hearing?'
　'I miss sometimes.'
—'Thirsty?'
　'Yes. I drink a helluva lot.'
—'Right. We'll test for diabetes. Bring two specimens. Number
one before breakfast and number two afterwards. When you
eat it can lift the level of your blood sugar and this can affect
your mood.'
　'The bottles?'
—'Any little bottles will do . . . any chest symptoms?'
　'I'm not sure.'
—'Oh yes, bring a number three from after lunch. I'm not
saying you've got it but we'll see.'

Diagnosis locates suffering. Diagnosis often brings Dr Rogers into
physical contact with the patient.

　　'I have a pain in my shoulders, I've tried to beat it for
　　weeks.'
—'Right, let's have a look.'

Dr Rogers moves alongside the now standing patient.

—'Is there a pain when you take a deep breath?'
　'Ouuh!'
—'Pop your shirt off.'

Dr Rogers places his hands flat on the man's back.

—'Can you lift your arms?'

Mr W. tries and his eyes water.

—'Can you touch your head?'

Again no.

—'Can you kneel?'

Mr W. winces and staggers. There is not an ounce of fat on him, his arms and stomach are firm.

'It's probably my age, I'm 58 next birthday.'
—'Can you take a couple of days from work?'
'I'm a baker and confectioner. We've got a stall in the market. We can't make enough of it. It really goes well.'
—'It's sinovitis of the shoulder. I'm giving you some pale yellow capsules to relieve the pain and some stuff to rub in. Get your wife to massage it in for you.'
'We've got a stall in the market — Albert's. We've been making bread for years.'
—'Do you need a private note? I'll have to ask you for three bob for it.'*
'All right.'
—'Rest for two days at home and put a board under the bed. Come back next Friday and we'll see how it's going.'

Internal diagnosis of illness in women requires a witness as well as a couch.

—'What's the latest?'
'I haven't had any letter from any department.'
—'Can I see what's cooking?'
'It's the burning and the smell.'
—'Is there pain in the side?'
'The smell is exactly like an abscess I had last year.'
—'I'll get the Sister and we'll have a look at this. Will you just pop up here.'

Dr Rogers draws a screen round the couch, leaves and returns in less than a minute with Sister, who says, 'Ah, my friend, how are you?'

—'It's our Patricia. Just make sure there's nothing up there, Sister – it's miserable for you, isn't it?'
'I can't get up in the mornings.'
—'O.K. pet, get dressed now.'

As Dr Rogers is folding back the screen Sister is wiping the couch.

---

*In fact there is no fixed charge for a private note. It is a 'perk' of the surgery. The doctor can charge what he likes and pocket the proceeds. Dr Rogers regards this revenue as his 'petrol money'.

—'You've got a chronic inflammation in the neck of the womb. It's possibly a tear due to childbirth.'

Dr Rogers turns momentarily to Sister.

—'Will you get Mary to phone?'
—'Do you want any more nerve tablets? I'll give you tablets and some other pessaries.'
    'Will they help the burning?'
—'They've got to some time!'
    'Do you think I'm wasting my time for that?'
—'No! It's good to have you.'

Patricia stands and takes a prescription. As she is closing the door Dr Rogers turns to me.

—'There's some patients that come in and your heart sinks. You name it and they've got it. She's a widow with four children.'

At the point of diagnosis Dr Rogers may touch the patient. Touching is normal in diagnosis, the doctor's hand is guided by the patient's answers to his questions (Emerson, 1970, pp. 77–8).

Diagnosis proper is a distinct routine in itself, as if a special sub-routine in Dr Rogers's consultation. Aches, pains and discharges are all symptoms. And so, peculiarly, are the side effects of drugs; in this way drowsiness, diarrhoea and full anger are not sicknesses but coincidental with cure.

Diagnosis has a logic; questioning pursues discomfort to its source. As discomfort becomes more precisely located 'the picture builds up', a case is made for there being only one serious alternative. The questioning procedure has been learned the hard way, mastered by repetition, that is, before the awesome teachers at medical school. These mechanical pathways are evidence of deep-seated training. For coupled with cautionary tales came the operational rule that an adequate diagnosis may have to be made at half-past four in the morning with an overcoat over the pyjamas.

In the diagnostic routine there are full-dress outings and safe shortcuts. The procedures can be suspended for friendly asides, tips on self-treatment and tentative discussion of therapy. The method permits an apparently unmethodical approach. It ends with naming the disease (Berger, 1967, p. 74).

Once the disease is named it is known and can be assailed. Dr Rogers devises a therapy. Therapy is what to do next; it is what Dr Rogers expects to happen and intends to happen. Dr Rogers can have a time projection from 24 hours to 26 weeks in which irritation will be relieved and a condition ameliorated. Therapy may be simply instructions on chemical treatment or dosage. Therapy may also be words of encouragement, good faith and hope. In practical terms, therapy is giving specific instructions in near-telegraphic phrases.

> 'Dr Jones is my doctor. He said to see him about my blood pressure.'

—'I'll get the sphygmo. What a place! One piece of equipment between two doctors!'

Dr Rogers leaves and Mrs D. addresses me.

> 'He's a good doctor. He's kind. Not like some of them where you're just in and out. I'm the panicky type.'

Dr Rogers returns.

—'What happens when the pains come?'
> 'It's just like someone sticking a knife through my back.'

Dr Rogers binds the pressure sleeve, pumps and reads the result.

—*'Within forty-eight hours we should have got you better. A bit to eat every two hours and two teaspoonsful of mixture. Nothing fried or fatty. Come in Thursday morning.'*
> 'Can I have some ointment for the three-year-old's botty?'
—'What is it?'
> 'It's a sort of rash and pimples.'
—*'I'll give you some of this. It's a bit yellow so use an old pair of pants. It should be clear in twenty-four hours. Put plenty on.'*

All therapy is what to do next. Dr Rogers takes charge of the patient's next move. His instructions to Gaynor who had inflamed tonsils were:

—'Take one four times a day of the antibiotics and one four times a day of the others until they're all gone. Drink plenty. Don't go out today. We'll have you feeling 100 per cent better in twenty-four hours. Go to work on Wednesday or come back here.'

The patient's next move may be deeper into the medical world by way of a barium meal or a psychiatric examination.

—'Hello. Come and sit down. Now Mr . . .'
> 'Mr Adams. I've had these pains. I took some tablets but I'm in a daze all the time. I've stopped taking them.'
—'Well, that won't improve you, will it?'

There is a long pause.

—*'Have you ever seen a psychiatrist?'*

'I saw one once and he said I was to go into hospital.'
—*'Would you be prepared to see a psychiatrist, Terence?'*
'Yes, O.K.'

There is a further long pause.

'What's this electrical thing they've got?'
—'You can have it outside or inside.'

And there is another, shorter pause.

—'What's your occupation normally? Labourer?'
'Plasterer.'
—'What's your address?'

Mr Adams dictates his address.

—'How would you feel if I said don't have a drink?'
'I'd stop.'
—'How would you feel?'
'I'd be shaking and jumping all the time.'
—'How much beer do you drink?'
'A few pints.'
—*'How depressed are you?'*
'Terrible.'
—*'Suicidal?'*
'No, I've got over that stage.'

Dr Rogers laughs.

—'How do you mean?'
'I had a girl friend and when we finished I felt like it.'
—'I think I'll send you up there. Are you married?'
'I'm at home.'
—*'Right, we'll see about it.'*

Alternatively, the patient may appear to be looking for a move out of the medical world, a move out of the impasse of illness.

'I've spoken to people who've been to rehabilitation at Midtown Centre.'
—*'Do you want a light job?'*
'If it's outside. I feel I could go back and do my own job but it's up to you doctors. Dr Jones threatened me. He said, "Forget about it, don't upset the things I'm doing".'
—*'O.K., I'll get your manager and Dr Jones on the phone and see what we can do.* How long have you been off?'
'Seven and a half months.'
—*'What was your job?'*

'Asphalt roller.'
—'*O.K., leave it with me.*'

Therapy is not provided by the flick of a switch. Dr Rogers's design 'firms up', he becomes more resolute with the patient's support of or non-objection to his scheme. And as he firms up he becomes increasingly more reassuring. He says exactly how long the illness will last. He seems to have great confidence in the chemicals he prescribes.

—'What's she done?'
'She's got a festering coming up on her knee.'

Dr Rogers rounds the desk and looks closely at the sore as the little girl bends her knee upwards.

—'It looks as if she's got something. I'll get her to nurse and give her some ointment. Keep it in the cupboard and if ever she gets a spot or cut use it. It'll keep for a couple of years. Come on.'

The girl stands before the desk and, looking up, gives a cough.

—'Got a bad cold eh!'

Dr Rogers laughs and leaves with the girl behind.
Therapy may be a corrective; there are cases of patients making themselves ill with abusive treatment. Dr Rogers is quite prepared to criticize inappropriate therapy.

'I've already had blotchy skin but this last two days I've been itching all the time.'

Dr Rogers walks around the desk and holds her inflamed face and neck by the chin.

—'*It's Valderma. Never use it. It's for boys with galloping acne to give them a twinge! I've seen lots of cases like this. Use Nivea or something softer. It'll be cleared up in a day.*

When therapy has been pronounced the medical business is done. But usually Dr Rogers has not finished. If the patient is an employee he 'needs a sick-note for work'. The doctor provides him with a formal excuse for a finite period. Thus in establishing what is wrong, and how long it will take to get it right, Dr Rogers works out how long the patient is to have off. Having projected the course of illness (or, alternatively, predicted its trajectory), the doctor informs the patient when he can go back.

—'Is there any improvement?'
'It's a bit better but there's still pain.'

—'Would you say you are beginning to improve?'

She gives a bottle to Dr Rogers's outstretched hand. He takes it beyond the door. On returning:

—'*I would think it's beginning to respond to the black and red.*'
His telephone rings.
—'Hello, Millway Hospital paediatrician, please. . . . Dr Rogers, Midtown here. . . Yes. . . that's fine. I'll get the mother to post the letter today.'

Dr Rogers stands and leaves in the direction of the dispensary. He comes back within the minute.

—'*That's tons better. I think we can leave you until your next antenatal.* Finish with two in the morning, and two at night. When are you due for another note?'
  'Next Tuesday.'
—'If there's a queue just go to the desk and get one.'

Another patient is given to understand that his illness is over.

—'How are you feeling?'
  'Fine but I've still got the giddiness.'
—'Do you feel dizzy when you stand up?'
  'No it's more when I'm bending down.'
—'That's right.'

Dr Rogers moves to listen to his chest.

—'How's the mood now?'
  'I'm not as depressed. Doctor, will you look at my gumboil for me?'
—'How's the depression?'

Dr Rogers quickly looks round the sides of the man's mouth.

  'High in the morning and then it goes down.'
—'Get up slowly in the morning. And the wife?'
  'She had a big operation some years ago.'*
—'*We'll get you back to work.*'

Dr Rogers turns to me. Mr Thomas has been a bus conductor and then worked in a factory

—'What does your wife think about going back to work?'
  'She doesn't want it. She's got used to it. I know it's a business to manage but we do.'

*The phrase 'big operation' is usually used to imply a psycho-surgical trauma since when things have not been the same. A weakness has been made permanent.

G

83

—'*Well, you can go back if you want to.*'

Earlier you may remember a baker and confectioner was asked if he could 'take a day off' work as if easing him into acceptance.* The patient may have already eased himself back into the idea.

'I went to casualty.'
—'What happened?'
'They never X-rayed but they covered me in bandages.'
—'Are you ready for work?'
'I think I'll go back tomorrow.'

The issuing of a prescription and a sick-note complete the formalities. Dr Rogers should then be ready for the next patient.

His routine consists of familiarization, diagnosis, therapy and prescription with the possibility of giving a sick-note. Dr Rogers, however, fits a bit more in. His interests are social as well as clinical. He believes in 'holism' and this belief means that he fits an intimate consultation within his physical consultation. He asks about family and work in an easy manner. He appreciates that somehow sickness can be caused and affected by the person, his milieu and his culture. He knows cause and effect are too crude to be true. He seeks to untangle all that bears on the patient's disease. In particular he suspects that frequently a somatic disorder is a cover for a psychological condition. He thinks that the patient is then trying to get through as well as trying it on. In this way asking 'How are things at home?' can be part of an alternative diagnosis rather than simply being a breathing space in which the record of the consultation is made.

—'Did you get a message?'
'To come and see you today.'
—'How's she been?'
'Sleeping a lot during the day.'

Dr Rogers goes out and returns holding a letter.

—'A little bit brighter is she?'

There is a pause.

—'How are the threadworms?'

---

*Consultation is called a routine and diagnosis a routine within it. There may also be a routine to determine how to ask a man to disengage from work. The phrases Dr Rogers uses vary. For leaving work he asks, 'Can you take a couple of days from work?', 'Do you need a note?', 'How long do you want?' and 'When do you want to go back to work?' He assures me that he has developed these phrases in response to patients' objections. At the time of study he had spent ten years in general practice.

There is another pause.

—'We start by knocking out the threadworms. They can check
the urine and we can clear the bladder.'

And another pause.

—'How many in the family over six years?'
   'Four.'
—*'How are you in yourself?'*
   'I'm . . . you know . . . tired all the time.'
—*'We'll get this cleared up and see if we can help you.'*

When mother and daughter have left, Dr Rogers turns to me.

—'I'm not so sure it isn't the mum.'

If the patient is, or has been, drawn out by 'any other problems?'
the consultation moves to a new vocabulary. Dr Rogers has a language of feeling. He also has a way of relating feelings to his drug
therapy. He has psychotropic drugs to 'relieve the symptoms' of
mood and depression.

—'Is the depression lifting?'
   'It'd be all right if I could get a good night's sleep. There
   are times when I wonder if it's worth it. It's the wife I'm
   worried about. She's a cripple . . . the health visitor says
   she'll help us all she can.'
—*'The type of depression you've got doesn't lift easily. You'll get*
better. Sometimes it's weeks or months before it really lifts.'
   'I hope so. I don't want to go on like this. I want to be
   back at work within two weeks.'

And with another man whose mood had previously been established:

   'I did a lot of walking last week, but I didn't get a lot of
   sleep.'
—'What seems to be the trouble?'
   'I get this pain in my groin like someone stabbing me with
   a knife.'
—'Are you getting short-tempered again?'
   'A bit, yes.'
—'How depressed are you?'
   'Off and on.'
—'How anxious?'
   'Very. Especially with new things, things I've got to do.
—*'We'll give you something to relieve the tension.'*
   'I'd like to get this right. It's annoying me, it is. The pain
   is always there.'

Diagnostic holism and therapeutic narcotics are clearly a different category from the 'personal extras' of familiarization. And similarly the advice that Dr Rogers gives within an holistic consultation is definitely heavier than tips on self-medication. He encourages the patients to make them see sense; tells them to march out of their dilemmas.

—'How's it going?'
　'It's not so shakey.'
—'And things at home?'
　'The daughter's left home, she left a note. We want her to come back but she says she's all right. She's got a room somewhere in town and the boyfriend's close. She left a note but she won't come back. The wife and I want her back.'
—'How's she taken it?'
　'Same as me, she wants her back, if I'd have thought . . . I should have brought the letters down. I've spoken to her on the phone but she says the same thing.'
—'*She's probably better off. Only good can come out of this. I think it's for the best. The best way for you to help her would be to say that she had done the right thing. How old is she?*'
　'Eighteen.'
—'Oh well, she's old enough.'
　'That's what the police said. They said they can't do anything if that's what she wants, she'll only go away again.'
—'If you'd had this before you'd really have been on the tremble.'
　'Yes I would. I think I've got enough Valium now.'
—'How many?'
　'Sixty-one.'
—'What happened to your job?'
　'I've been gone so long, it's gone.'
—'Have you enough?'
　'We get £10 with £3·24 rent. They gave us another £2 and said it was for the rent. It must be automatic. I didn't claim it, it just came with the rest.'
—'How's the wife?'
　'Not too grand.'
—'*Well, look, if the daughter phones tell her she's done the right thing. Tell her you wish her luck and that you'll like to see her sometime. You can't do anything about it, can you? Well then. Tell her it's all right and don't nag her.*'

But holism is not always associated with the sedation of anxiety.

Dr Rogers can relax with some patients sufficiently to close the consultation with good advice.

A young woman enters carrying a small boy.
—'How's the ear now?'
　'All right I think.'
—'And eating?'
　'Still picking a bit.'

The telephone rings.

—'Right. She's ready for her injection.'

And turning to the young woman:

—'How's his ear now?'
　'All right.'

Dr Rogers wheels around the desk and holds the child's head. The boy resists, shaking and stepping backwards.

　'Who's going to get sweeties now?'
—'That's a good boy. Back to normal. So the question is why is he a bit fretful?'

Dr Rogers pops a kiss on the boy's head.

—'I won't be a minute. I'll just go and inject this woman, O.K.?'

He leaves and returns as the mother is telling her son about 'getting a bike for Christmas'.

　'Will you look at his bottom as well?'
—'Anything for you!'

Dr Rogers smiles and bends to look.

—'It's probably the antibiotic. Put your finger on there. You can get lumpy glands when you treat a cut. Is he fretful at night?'
　'Some nights I don't know what to do.'
—'He should be settled now. I can sympathize because my daughter was all colds and ear troubles.'
　'Can I have a letter?'
—'Oh yes, for his stretching and circumcision.'

Dr Rogers writes and looks up.

—'It doesn't get better, it gets worse. Can you put a stamp on that and post it?'

There is a pause.

—'He's probably too intelligent and likes less sleep than the average. I'll send the health visitor in this week. It's difficult because it's a problem of management. We'll give a little something to relax him.'

He writes a prescription.

'He's ruined, see . . .'
—'*What we've got to do is break the vicious circle. I don't think you can spoil them. I think you only try your best and sometimes they win.*'

The fullest possible record of each consultation has been given to make each particular point and to illustrate the argument. Each point has been a location, a pointer to the routine perspective upon consultation; gained as if through Dr Rogers's eyes. The whole thing, as it were, is a routine, its parts are tidy in themselves. Each consultation is an example of how Dr Rogers is a manager to the patient: managing the routine and its routine parts. As the events were orchestrated before me, I sensed music. I had expected each event to be special or even unique. Instead I recognized rhythm and melody time and time again. Dr Rogers handled his patients in every sense; by touch, guidance and control.

To Dr Rogers this part, this routine, is a whole. He does everything he has to do and wants to do effectively and efficiently. He takes responsibility and uses it. He spends money and watches this expenditure without worry. Dr Rogers's routine is how he wants a consultation to go and how it should be. Thus the function of this part, from him to his patients, is as a whole. He 'runs the surgery'. To repeat a previous analogy, the routine functions to manage his patients for him. And further routine welds together the parts of himself which Dr Rogers brings to his surgery. He too is made whole by clinical skill, therapeutic responsibility and the practice of everyday wisdom.

The function of the routine is to make people patients; to recruit a person to a sick career (Goffman, 1961, p. 119). Dr Rogers has the power to offer alternative employment.* Through him people become patients with diminished responsibility and with eligibility for sickness benefit. Dr Rogers offers a viable alternative to mainstream occupations. And as a career there are the appropriate stages of hiring, putting to work and firing. In hiring the person becomes a patient and changes to this legitimate employment. The question 'Can you take a couple of days off work?' clearly poses a choice between apparently equal alternatives. The person goes 'under the

*Dr Rogers believes that 'the purpose of medicine is the relief of suffering'. At the time he was also trying out the phrase 'patient management'. These phrases might be called pious and practical rationalizations respectively.

doctor's orders'. Then as a patient he is maintained. In fulfilling the therapy instructions the patient keeps himself going along the lines appropriate to his sickness. He is being maintained. And while being maintained he finds Dr Rogers less emphatic about health or illness. While he is being maintained a relationship is being constructed from regular, frequent visits, from knowing the exact name of the illness properly and volunteering circumstantial fact as to the welfare of the diagnosed sickness. In the event, the patient's problems are also the doctor's – though fleetingly. Dr Rogers will give advice, secure facilities and generally exert his influence on the patient's behalf.

Personal extras make the grace of the doctor. They also encourage the patient to feel affection towards him. Effective recruitment may in part depend upon the determination to give explicit orders and the patient's affective response to the doctor's showing an interest in them. Dr Rogers may have to elicit affection towards himself or, at the very least, facilitate its expression with a personal touch. In fact the maintained patient may become a problem to him. For as with the employer, discharge really depends upon the doctor. Dr Rogers has no problem if hiring, maintenance and discharge are compressed into his instruction that 'there should be a dramatic recovery in forty-eight hours'. But there is a problem if the patient is content in his career or cannot accommodate changes caused and symbolized by his illness. In this event, the patient is 'fired'; told to leave because there is nothing else; advised to change, to understand the change in himself.

The use of this metaphor suggests that the patient is necessarily engaged in choice and responsibility, and this is so. First then, we shall see how patients fit into Dr Rogers's routine and then relate to a sick career, mindful, of course, that their part is their part and likewise their function is their function.

From the patient to the doctor

To get into the doctor's movie and get something out of it the patient works out what he's got to say. Technically expressed, the fact is that the patient fits into the constructed reality (Emerson, 1970, p. 75) by making a rehearsal before coming to a consultation.

The effect of this rehearsal is to avoid the maelstrom of crises and get what is wanted out of the event. Conceptually expressed, this 'fitting in' is a process of accommodation to the event and its products. Consequently, accounting for action, as if from the patient to Dr Rogers, follows the organization of his routine.

To begin with, I wish to itemize some further assumptions that make the passage from person to patient comprehensible. They are:

1   The person has reason for being a patient.
2   The reason for being a patient is the reason for being in the surgery.
3   In a surgery you have to know what to do; a surgery is organized and its order established.
4   The person anticipates waiting, even if briefly, for his turn and moves from waiting to being a patient on instruction.
5   The person has an abrupt chronological time for being a patient.
6   The patient wants to know what his or her illness is, possibly by name.
7   The patient wishes to be healed, to have the illness taken away, to be a fit person again.

The concept of patient classifies a dependency. Independence has been usurped by illness and the dependence is upon healers. The illness has the shape of disease; body, mind and soul are troubled. The disease is overpowering and the patient needs to transcend the disabling of the condition.

The medical expression is, 'The patient presents a complaint.' But the tone of presentation is not that of complaining. Rather, it is the tone of being disheartened (Kline, 1969, p. v).

We begin again, therefore, with familiarization. Patients tend to report extreme pain and apologize for troubling the doctor.

> *'It's not so bad now. It's been like fire, doctor.'*
> —'And Dr Wilkins came last night?'
> 'I thought it was a heart attack. I haven't eaten anything.
> *My neighbour said I should get the doctor just in case.'*
> —'You did the right thing.'
> 'The backache's terrible. I can't bend.'
> —'Can you lift things?'
> 'No. I put it down to my nerves. I don't want nerve pills.'

She laughs.

> 'I don't know what I'm doing.'
> —'Where do you work?'
> 'St John's. It's not that.'

There is a slight pause in her voice.

> 'That's all I want and he's calling me an old woman. He meets me. He's daft. He's jealous. He's not beating me now though. He's insanely jealous. It's just him. He's sick. He's been needing treatment for twenty years.'
> —'You can have something to calm you down if you like.'
> 'If it's for my back and chest, is it?'

—'Take two an hour before going to bed.'
　'Thank you, doctor.'

The presentation of illness itself is most obviously rehearsed when a number of complaints accumulate to swell the consultation. The patient is then giving Dr Rogers things to diagnose.:

—'Ah hello Yvonne. How are you?'
　'All right thanks. *I've got a little list. I've got a wisdom tooth coming through. I feel a bit daft really, but my toe is hurting. It's nothing much really but it's a lot of little things.*'
—'Right, we'll have a look.'

Dr Rogers walks round to Yvonne and she stands.

—'Can you bend over?'
　'Ooh! it's when I get out of bed in the morning. I've had the pain for about three weeks.'
—'That's fairly normal when you are coming off the pill. You should really give it a rest. Do you feel depressed or miserable?'
　'Not really. My wisdom tooth's coming through and it does hurt.'
—'You could have arthritis in the toe. It may be worth expert advice if it's going to be worse.'
　'Should I get those shoes for myself?'
—'No leave it for a fortnight.'
　'I suppose they'll all get better.'
—'What about going to work?'
　'I was off yesterday and today.'
—'Do you want to go in tomorrow?'
　'Yes, I think so. It's difficult to know what to put.'
—'We'll just put dysmenorrhoea.'
　'Yes, thank you doctor, goodbye.'

With diagnosis, however, we might say that the patient is 'at sea'. It is the doctor's job to know what is wrong with you. The patient simply knows that something is recognizably wrong.

　'Yesterday my hands were all swollen up. They were itchy I could have scratched them off.'
—'Let me see.'

Dr Rogers approaches the young man as he takes his shirt off.

　'Look at them, all swollen!'
—'Well, all sort of things could have caused it, chrysanthemums, angora sweaters, it could be an allergy.'

91

    'I've been nowhere near them. I went out with a young
    lady, a friend of the family, on Saturday.'
—'Did you have a meal?'
    'I had a curry. I suppose that could be it.'
—'It's a histamine reaction. It's urticaria.'
    'Ur-tech-aria, urtitcaria; it must have been that Indian
    restaurant.'
—'We can give you some cream. Put plenty on, rub it in, it
should go in a week.'
    'I'll have a week then.'
—'Yes, come in next Monday if it's no better.'

It is evident that the patient is passive to diagnosis. If Dr Rogers
seeks a cause he will be helped but the volunteering of possibilities is
rather half-hearted. The name of the illness holds more interest than
the cause. After all, the patient has gone to the surgery to have it
looked at and have something done about it. The patient may be
passive in the knowledge that his presence alone will get some treatment from the doctor. In this case the rehearsal has probably been
that of actually attending Dr Rogers's surgery by appointment.

—'I'm sorry! We are twenty-five minutes late. I haven't seen
you since last July with your tennis elbow.'
    'I haven't been able to. I've tried. I've had a husband in
    hospital and going up there all the time.'
—'How many injections did you have?'
    'Two.'
—'It might be worth another.'

Dr Rogers moves to hold the woman's outstretched arm.

—'Are you getting pain on here?'
    'Yes, a lot.'
—'We'll give you one more injection.'
    'It's only when I pick things up.'

Dr Rogers moves back to sitting at the desk and begins to write.

    *Will you put through a knock, otherwise I can't claim
    anything.*'
—'Not through your age, eh?'

The woman laughs slightly.

—'Will you come with me?'

The woman stands quickly.

—'Right come on, Sister can fix it up.'

And yet, when it comes to therapy, the patient may have a clear idea of what he wants. He may prompt and steer the doctor with a list of rehearsed requests. The doctor dictates the diagnosis and then the patient negotiates the therapy.

Mrs M. and her daughter seat themselves.

> 'Alison has stopped her job. It was no good. She fainted yesterday in the market and an ambulance took us to Millway. We were there three hours. The Pakistani doctor gave her all sorts of tests. He said she had an enlarged heart and wrote her name in his black pocket book. She's fine now. She's always a bit funny when her father's home. He's at sea. He's back for a few weeks and then away for months. Well he's always getting at her. . . Anyway *she suffers terribly with her throat and she'd like some more of that medicine.*'

—'Would you like a note until Monday?'

> '*Yes.*' (mother and daughter chorus)

—'How would it be?'

> '*Well she's been off since she fainted and wants to get a new job. Next Monday would be right. . . .Can Jimmy have speech therapy?* I spoke to Miss Morgan and she said the doctor has to recommend it. Bill's having it already.'

—'Is it doing any good?'

> 'I think so but it's hard to tell. . . . *Can we have some more cough medicine? Last time Dr Wilkins gave us a little bottle and there's three of them and the oldest has two spoonsful.*'

—'I'll put it on Alison's prescription.'

> '*Can we have it on the paper for David George?* He's six and a half and that makes the mixture free.'

—'Right.'

> 'Alison's sadness has gone now and her father's back at sea. She'd only say yes and no, she'd never tell you what's wrong.'

Dr Rogers completes the four notes and hands them to Mrs M.

> 'Thank you doctor. *I'll be back about myself when I can. I don't seem to have the energy.* Say goodbye to the doctor Alison. Goodbye.'

Mrs M. 'knew the ropes'. She had rehearsed with Alison the duration of the desired sick-note. She collected a prescription for her children's winter colds. She had taught Alison how to behave with the doctor. But perhaps she would have settled for another little bottle of cough medicine. She would have settled for this providing the doctor had got the date on the sick-note right. For sick-notes are either right or wrong for the patient. Therapy is open to negotiation but the sick-note comes close to an open dictation by the patient.

—'How are you doing?'
   'I'm waiting for a hospital bed. *I wish you'd sign that, I gets another thirty bob a week.*'
—'When were you here last?'
   'The fifteenth I think.'
—'I'm not sure I was on then.'
   'It could have been the twelfth.'
—'I think it was. How are you feeling?'

Dr Rogers writes a note.

—'Totally incapacitated since lifting.'

Dr Rogers is reading the letter and Sister comes in saying, 'Could you look at Deborah and her bandaging?'
Dr Rogers leaves immediately and on returning:

—'Right. That'll see you through until the sixteenth of November.'
The right sick-note for the patient is the one with exactly the right timing.
   'It's my back doctor. It's better now but I still get a little twinge in the morning. If I could have one more week it should be O.K. *I want to start Wednesday,* Monday is a heavy day.'

Dr Rogers walks towards the man and he stands.

—'Can you crouch?'

The man makes to crouch a little at a time.

   '*Can I have a private note for the works?*'
—'Yes.'
   'Ah! thank you.'

The man's voice has dropped half an octave.

—'Here you are.'
   'Thank you very much, doctor.'

Dr Rogers turns to me.

—'The patient decides when to go back. You can't make them. I'll check his card and see if he's a shirker.'

And, later that same surgery, the shortest consultation I observed proved his point:

   'It's off.'

The man holds up a bare, crinkly white arm.

—'It's all O.K. then?'
   'Yes fine. *I'll go back Monday.*'
—'Right, take care now.'

Dr Rogers's consultation within a consultation (his 'holism') may, on the other hand, catch the patient unawares. In answering his questions on 'mood' or 'depression' the patient may be drawn into an account that had been rehearsed for and with others. Nevertheless his asking direct and confidential questions may 'cause the wires to cross'. He may then hear what was intended for someone else.

   'I usually come about this time of year. It's cystitis.'. . .
—'And it's stinging and burning.'
   'Yes'.
—'Right. We can give you some stuff to stop that.'

There is a pause.

   'I suffer with migraine a lot. I've a sister in Ipswich and she phoned and told me that the vicar's wife had some new pills. I've tried everything. When I've got migraine nothing can move me. It's like someone's got a shovel in my head. And hammering. . .'
—'It's all inside bottled up. Do you have any worries? Any personal problems, things like that?'

There is a much longer pause.

   'Ah well, I can tell you doctor I know it won't go any further. I work for a finance company. If you come to me for £100 I'd lend you it. Well I'd lend you £130 and you would pay it back with the £30 for me. I've loaned to a man, I've known him for years. He is buying this house and selling his own. He says he'll give it me. I'm sure he will, but he can't until he gets the money for his own.'
—'How much does he owe you?'
   'More than a thousand pounds.'
—'And you are worried that you might not get it back.'
   'It's my savings. I've only the one son. He's right of course. He always is. I shouldn't have done it I know. But there it is. I've given this man so much; I've just kept giving him more . . .'
—'Well, you will have to wait and hope he gives it back. I'll give you something to calm your nerves and perhaps they'll work and the man will give you your money.'

May I now repeat my argument? The function of Dr Rogers's

routine is to recruit patients: to recruit persons to a sick career. In its turn the function of the person's rehearsal is to be a satisfactory patient; to accommodate to Dr Rogers's placement of them in their career. This accommodation is obviously inevitable when Dr Rogers is hiring a person to a fresh sick career. As such the person is lifted out of his old job and while on the sick, he can look for other, more congenial work.

   —'What's the trouble?'
> 'I've got a pain in the testicles. Two months ago I got a knock at work. Yesterday I was chasing the dog and I kept getting pains all the time.'

Dr Rogers rounds the desk and the young man drops his trousers to his knees.

   —'Is it here?'
> 'No.'

   —'Here?'
> 'A little bit, it was up inside.'

   —'Here?'
> 'Not quite.'

   —'Well, I'll give you a note. . . .'

There is a brief pause.

> 'I've been labouring in this factory. I've got to walk right up the other end and carry these heavy boxes. I'm starting 'prentice motor mechanic after Easter.'

   —'Do you want to give in your notice?'
> 'I'm not sure.'

   —'Do you need a private note?'
> 'I think so.'

   —'I'll have to ask you for three bob for it. Are you going to look for another job this week?'
> 'I could do with more money . . .'

   —'and less boxes!'

The young man laughs and leaves with his note.

The accommodation may, however, be less full as Dr Rogers maintains and finally fires the patient. Maintenance may be resisted even if it is not opposed outright. Earlier a man with 'depression' wanted to be 'back at work within two weeks'. One woman's consultation was full of resentment towards her career.

> '*I thought I was bad before, I don't go out anywhere now except hospitals.*'

   —'How is the pain?'

'No better, he didn't tell me anything.'

—'I would expect you to do much better than normal. You haven't got diarrhoea and you're not passing blood. How much pain are you getting?'

'Quite a lot.'

—'What are you having?'

'I'm on Valium. Mr Richards has decided to give injections rather than the pills.'

—'What did he do?'

'Just said for me to come for injections. *I haven't been outside the kitchenette apart from hospitals.*'

—'We'll give you a course of this and if it's no better we'll send you to a consultant. It's a ten-day course of treatment.'

'*It's been going for months now.*'

Dr Rogers has three ways of relieving himself of a permanent patient. First, he can repeat over and over again that the person should find work and make the sick-notes out for decreasing durations. Second, he can put a patient on a maintenance dosage of tranquillizers that the latter collects from the reception desk. Third, he can 'kick the patient upstairs'; he can pass on a recidivist to a clinical or psychiatric consultant and thus declare him a hospital case. These tactics are nevertheless Dr Rogers's last resorts. As he says himself, he prefers and believes that patients discharge themselves. He guesses and the patient says when.

Consistencies and compatibilities have thus been detected from the perspectives of both doctor and patient. Dr Rogers's routine was identified by repetitions with different patients. The rehearsal of patients was identified by the definition of three mannerisms; sometimes illnesses were listed; sometimes therapy in the form of prescriptions was negotiated and sometimes sick-notes were virtually dictated. All this in Dr Rogers's effort to do what he had to and the patient's effort to say what he had to say.

The question I turn to now is how is consultation recognizable as a total situation? I mean, what do the relations of routine and rehearsal produce? In turn, then, from functional analysis to structural analysis. I refer now to the phenomenon of dominance in inter-class contact.

Meanings and contexts to the event

There is more than routine and rehearsal to be found in my observations. For there is content as well as form, there is the melody of detail and the genre of music to which it belongs. I refer, of course, to the fact that in ordinary language Dr Rogers is middle-class and his patients are working-class. And I refer to the fact that Dr Rogers is an agent of social control and his consultations can be appropriately understood as acts of social control. I mean, then, to explore what happened in terms of dominance (Aron, 1969, p. 187n), and by dominance I mean the way inequalities of power and privilege are maintained in face-to-face relationships where these same inequalities are found. I mean, more precisely, that Dr Rogers is a superordinate; that his patients are subordinates and yet the actions of both parties make freedom and benefits for each other out of this symmetry. To substantiate these propositions I need to be able to relate the participants' respective social class perspectives to the notation of the surgery situation. I must, then, move from the context of class to the content of consultation. I begin again, with the world, works and words of Dr Rogers.

Dr Rogers lives three miles away from the surgery in a £12,000-plus select residential development and has a continental car and a speed boat in common with his neighbours. He moved recently to the Midtown practice from one in a small country town some 200 miles away. His father was a GP, Dr Rogers has had extensive hospital experience and makes it his business to master, understand and use the latest developments in medicine as a physiological and biochemical science. He could be said to be at the top of his profession.

Dr Rogers is one of a select few. His patients outnumber him by 3,500 to one. He is a scarce resource in himself. His time as a doctor is perpetually precious. He is privy to knowledge that is necessary to the well-being of all. He is licensed to practise an art for which the punishment of unlicensed practice is imprisonment. And, in addition to being a scarce resource in himself, he controls access to a wealth of resources. He treats, prescribes and hospitalizes. He opens the door to the bounty of 'social security'; sickness pay; holiday pay; compensation and disability pensions. And, finally, he is an engaging resource. He brings his interests to bear in the patient's interest. He is one of the few who direct the person's interest towards himself (Simmel, 1950, p. 181). The dice are loaded, we might say, for Dr Rogers's consultations going largely his way. Somehow Dr Rogers's control of the situation is maintained as it is expressed, neutralized as it is made clear. And the clear expression of superordination is in the almost unobtrusive content of the consultation, in the details that Dr Rogers takes for granted, understands as natural after all these years.

When it is a patient's turn next, he or she edges on the bench watching the door and watching for the last patient to walk out. When it is clear, and any rivalry for the next turn has been resolved, the patient walks to the door and knocks. Dr Rogers calls out, 'Come in!' The patient then tries to answer all his questions and accept, by understanding, his diagnosis. During this time the consultation may be suspended by Dr Rogers making or receiving telephone calls or leaving for the treatment room at Sister's instigation. Meanwhile the patient waits. As the prescription and/or sicknote is completed the patient stands and approaches the desk to receive his paper. The patient says, 'Thank you, doctor' and leaves, As he draws the door to, Dr Rogers calls a word of farewell, his head bowed in completion of the patient's record card. And throughout all Dr Rogers's phrases have the confident tone of a boss.

Dr Rogers asks the questions and the patients give the answers. He is comparatively disinterested in the questions they ask him and slightly interested in the indirect answers they give sometimes to his direct questions. As a rule he refers to himself as 'we'. 'How can we help you?' he asks. And yet when he has determined therapy he assures the patient, 'I'll give you something now.' In using the royal 'we' his inquisitorial power is made more abstract whilst in saying 'I'll give you' he is altering an occupational obligation to the status of a gift.

Occasionally other regularities are evident. If the patient seems unsure that his complaint is sufficiently severe to warrant attention Dr Rogers assures him that his complaint is genuine and he did the right thing. If the patient's complaint necessitates contacting other authorities Dr Rogers says, 'I'll get them to "do whatever they think is needed" ' and less frequently he uses the patient's first name when asking a personal question. For example, he asked 'Terence' if he would see a psychiatrist. Dr Rogers had probably read his name directly from his record card.

In what Dr Rogers says, therefore, he conveys a wealth of practice in routine phrasing that enhances his power by direct or indirect use of its prerogative. And in what is unsaid Dr Rogers's superordinate position is also evident. Clearly Dr Rogers makes up his mind what is wrong and serves the patient to relieve suffering (Berger, 1967, p. 52). Dr Rogers also has his private views on what is wrong with the patient. He believes that some patients conceal psychological problems and that others manipulate him to get facilities or sick-notes or simply to get noticed. But he does not confront the patient with these opinions. In this way he avoids controversy and its attendant confrontation. In fact Dr Rogers is able to make up his mind about his patients and keep his thoughts from their view.* Thus, though

* 'If you show them authority they drift' (Dr Melvyn Davies). Or, more compassionately, 'The emotion of the relationship can begin by loving patients and end in hating them. Most patients are not likeable people, they are scheming and deceitful. Normal life is bizarre; each time there are the strangest personal details. The doctor must love his patients, if not he must like them; if not he must respect them; if not he must feel sorry for them' (Dr Julian Tudor-Harte).

they remain patients, he also sees them as people. Yet he only sees them as part-people. 'Doctors are disease-oriented, not patient-oriented.' A key point of the diagnostic routine is that the doctor does not descend to the person but rather pulls out the pathological condition for his own attention. The doctor is suppressing the unwanted baggage and looking for the operable parcel. When saying, 'I would say you were beginning to respond', he was largely making up his own mind.

The theme from Dr Rogers's home situation to what he says in his surgery is his confidence in a 'right to rule'. He has a natural super-ordination based on a superior background regulated by a practised routine. It is as though he possesses objective authority (Simmel, 1950, p. 183).

All Dr Rogers's patients are working-class. Their homes have already been briefly described. Their main concerns are money, family, and each other. They speak of 'saving a few bob', 'buying the best' and 'never having enough of it – it's all money, money, money'. They plan to escape with a 'big tickle', with winning the pools or at bingo. As families they live near each other, helping out as one or all fail to get by. They teach each other to live cheaply; to scavenge from waste and wreckage; to use their heads and make the job a bit easier. They build, maintain and demolish.

The working class mingle of necessity. This togetherness staves off a persistent and peculiar kind of poverty – if things get worse life could stop being worth living. As citizens – before being patients – the working class are weakened by inarticulateness, by a fear of being spotlit by authority and subject to special treatment. And in the surgery they are weakened by their illnesses (Zola, 1971, p. 7). Their physical condition makes them naturally dependent upon, and subordinate to, the doctor. The patient houses his own problem, Dr Rogers is his possibility of a solution. In fact the patients can be grouped by nature of their dependency. Each group needs the doctor's help to cope. Their clinical illness is close to their 'social illness'; they have been damaged by the world at large and are still trying to accommodate to it. These groups are:

Male

Young men, disoriented by, and at, work hoping for a change of employment.
Ageing men damaged by, and at, work hoping to keep at least some form of employment.

Female

Young women disaffected from work, not knowing what to do but able to continue.

Pregnant women, excited and fearful.
Young women with children unable to control their health and illness to others' satisfaction.
Mothers with teenage children caring for a whole family.
Ageing women with nothing to do.

The chronic sick

Young and ageing males and females accommodated to drug dependency, pendulating through physical and mental illnesses, unable and unwilling to change; paralysed with the fear of things as they are.

If you can accept the 'objectivity' of these dependencies it is obvious why patients rarely ask questions and rarely laugh. Dr Rogers's dominant position enables these groups of patients to tolerate their dependencies and even act upon them. It also enables patients to pass from one group to another.

In their speech they tell of their difficulties with life: 'It's him, he's insanely jealous, he's been needing treatment for twenty years.' And they tell directly of their treatment by medical authorities: 'I haven't had any letter from any department,' 'Dr Jones threatened me. He said don't interfere with the treatment I'm giving you.'

In sum, the everyday life and immediate complaint of working-class patients collaborate to make subordination to the doctor natural. And this is both cultural and physical phenomenon; throughout life there is deprivation and dependence upon employers, in sickness there is disability and dependency upon doctors.

The mutual determination to remain superordinate and subordinate forms part of the explanation of why Dr Rogers and his patients fail to relate to each other in so many instances. Both parties are busy getting something out of a highly compressed exchange. They suspend any conversational style they might have, to produce some results. The doctor 'gives' medication and the patient 'gets some relief'. And to say that confrontation is avoided is to make possible an alternative analysis of the consultations reported in this text. There were non-events within the events. Disbelief and simple non-comprehension were frequently present. But they were rarely checked. A consultation is not a conversation. And when 'real conversation' occurs, when the social relevance of the event surfaces it occasions laughter in either doctor or patient. Dr Rogers made a number of cracks, and through them slipped his awareness. To the child with a sore knee who coughed he said, 'Got a bad cold eh?' To the woman with tennis elbow who wanted it attributed to a knock he said, 'Not because of your age, eh?' And to the young man with a pain in the testicles that proved hard to find he

101

said, 'not heavy boxes, eh?' Dr Rogers joked with his manipulation by patients.

The most major manipulation in consultation was 'the recruitment to a sick career'. Classes are largely maintained by forms of co-operation within them and non-communication between them. And communication between classes is usually instanced by something going wrong. The working class have to go and see the boss if they are in trouble or to get their cards or to try and get another job.

Similarly they have to go and see the doctor when something goes wrong. The surgery is often the scene of significant biographical change (Zola, 1971, p. 10). The doctor does more than keep people at work, he helps them change jobs. The recommendation of 'light work' to an ageing labourer is a crucial event in his work biography. The doctor is instigating a discontinuity in employment. The longer the patient's 'sick career' the greater the likelihood of a change in his occupational career. If the patient is satisfactorily accommodated to diminished capability the doctor is naturally involved in 'sorting things out at work'. The doctor is just like a boss. If the patient is on a sick career he is as good as a boss. If the patient is to come off a sick career the doctor fixes things with the bosses he knows. In fact this rare instance of inter-class communication is made much less precarious by the bosses looking so much alike from the distance. The distance they keep from the worker-patient is the same.

It may be that the terms domination and dominance are still a little unclear. For though they have a provenance of usage in sociology their theoretical value has yet to be established in current sociological work. By domination I mean the structure of a type of relationship and by dominance I mean the nature of this relationship, necessarily inter-personal and necessarily productive.

To begin with, we all can say that in most contexts there are people above us, variously level with us and below us. This common-sense reasoning also suggests that some contexts are more pervasive in their positioning than others. But the more important aspect of common-sense reasoning is that there is a tendency towards congruency in people's experience of stratification. To put it crudely, on top is on top whatever the context. A king is a rose and seldom a briar. Dominance depends upon a prior structuring, it depends upon an implicit acceptance, or taken-for-grantedness of the social positions from which people enter, quite generally, a particular relationship.

Thus dominance concerns the recipes that two people, drawn as it were from above and below, use to catch the same train and yet keep to their stations. In the surgery Dr Rogers has his routine. He is 'businesslike'. He is direct, efficient and open. He helps people and makes sure they know in what ways he is helping them. The patient subordinates to this routine with rehearsal. Also the patient defers to Dr Rogers, he is respectful and uses 'doctor's' formal title.

And both routine and rehearsal help the relationship to be productive. There are definite consequences to consultation. And these consequences are peculiarly symmetrical. They are of mutual benefit and entail a 'little bit of freedom' for both parties. The doctor is being paid and the patient permits his preferred practice of medicine. The patient is being troubled and the doctor permits his preferred practice of sickness. They encourage each other to negotiate for what they want and help each other get it.

In summary, then, domination can be represented as a diagram:

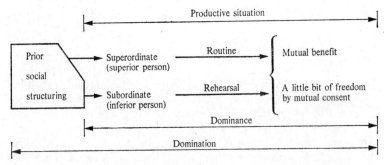

FIGURE 5.1   *The process of domination*

6   The qualitative method in theory

Introduction

The qualitative method is an act of faith. The believer begins with a
perspective, states his assumptions and arrives close to proving the
latter with his researches. The species itself is a recent mutation and
has three genera: phenomenology, symbolic interactionism and
ethnomethodology. It is these genera that have become the believers'
creed. Each has its history, heroes and sense of essence. Each has
already been developed by at least two generations of adherents.
And each is a gentle, if disturbing, world-view.

At the onset I must confess a profound antipathy to the qualitative
method, whatever its antecedent family of faith. For despite charming
dialectics and kind practitioners I am driven to screaming distraction
by the sing-song way it says what it means whilst promoting an
infantile philosophy. And yet I find this method more honourable
than the quantitative method. The honour comes from the integrity
of being able to admit that much is still a mystery. So though I
begin this account with an easy style its path still leads to damnation.
I begin with all that is good and holy yet I conclude by castigating
the method's transgressions. In my view, this style of sociology
has come to rest in purgatory.

Yet it can be validly countered that there is no such thing as a
style of qualitative method. There is rather a forming-field; a host
of investigators interpreting the social processes of interpretation.
The only way, that is, of producing a single focus is to make a list
of all the travellers upon the road and scrutinize their references
for passing gestures to each other. In any event, the qualitative
method is a flower that may soon bring forth fruit. For the long list
of practitioners includes those who are now bursting to write its
rules and propound its laws. Thus though there is enormous excite-

ment and movement in the field its pioneers are edging their ways to untold certainties. At this moment then, there is foment and the glistening attraction of being able to see back to the founders and forward to a fully formed position. So even though there may not be a style of qualitative method there certainly is a small army of sociologists thinking about meaning and doing their sociology with a large measure of observation. And this army still has the three main battalions mentioned a moment ago. Phenomenology is the intelligence corps, symbolic interactionism is the signals regiment and ethnomethodology doubles as light infantry and the occasional special-mission paratroop regiment. No doubt this characterization is an unwarranted slight on the serious and sincere nature of each inquiry. But in all honesty, it is just this ponderous self-deception that needs puncturing.

Let us begin this account with a survey of the 'field'. In other words, let us acknowledge the historical authenticity of 'the concern with patterns of communicative behavior' (Dreitzel, 1970, p. vii).

Dreitzel does his best to collect all the thinkers and themes in one sweep:

> One of the most puzzling recent developments in sociology is a new emphasis on approaches derived from symbolic inter-actionism – that is from the shared symbols and meanings of everyday activities – and in particular from phenomenological philosophy. This is probably best illustrated by a sociological movement called ethnomethodology as represented by Harold Garfinkel, Aaron Cicourel, and their students. However, the ethnomethodological approach is by no means the only sign of a renewed interest in the patterns of communicative behavior which underlie all social interaction. Peter Berger and Thomas Luckmann's widely read book on *The Social Construction of Reality* is an eminent example of phenomenological theorizing outside the realm of ethnomethodology. Both Berger-Luckmann's and the ethnomethodological approach rely heavily on the philosophical work of Alfred Schutz, a German émigré who was a direct student of Edmund Husserl, the founder of phenomenological philosophy. Interest in the work of Schutz is gradually becoming a countervailing undercurrent to the established mode of structural-functionalist reasoning in sociology.
>
> The symbolic interactionism of George Herbert Mead (the leading theorist of the Chicago School of sociologists during the Thirties), in contrast to this recent trend towards phenomenological approaches, has long been incorporated into

structural-functional theory, as formulated by Talcott Parsons. However, some prominent students of Mead – notably Herbert Blumer, Ralph Turner, and Tomatsu Shibutani – have always remained hostile to Parsonian theory and have thus been relatively isolated in the field.

Although there have been some contributions from social psychology, it is only recently that Berger and Luckmann's work, as well as that of the West Coast school of ethnomethodology, have cast a new light on the relevance of symbolic interactionism. Also important is the discovery that the 'social behaviorism' of George Herbert Mead has much in common with phenomenology and with what, in the European tradition, is called 'philosophical anthropology'. The discovery of similarities between these different schools is largely due to the studies of Maurice Natanson. An exceptional and isolated figure of recent symbolic interactionism is Erving Goffman, whose popular essays on interaction patterns in small groups are certainly within the tradition of G. H. Mead. Although Goffman has contributed much to renew the interest in symbolic interactionism, the popularity of his work may be attributed to the fact that his brilliant participant observations rarely amount to additional theoretical insights and that his methodological procedure mostly remains obscure.

Confronted with new scientific developments it is always useful to ask for parallels in movements in society itself. This is especially true for sociology; since interest in sociological studies is motivated by the problems of society, social changes are usually mirrored by shifts in sociological interest. Obviously patterns of communicative behavior have become a focus of sociological studies because more and more people are confronted with problems of communication. 'Alienation in Interaction,' as one of Goffman's essays is titled, is, indeed, a basic experience in our time. This social phenomenon has been reflected upon and discussed in numerous theories of mass society and mass culture.

Thus Dreitzel gives nearly an official history and makes use of most of the major terms. And if we combine this with Becker's personal account ('What actually happened was that I studied with Everett Hughes' [1971, p. v]) and with Weeks's (1972) account we get something like this:

Husserl→Schutz→P. L. Berger
Simmel→Park →Hughes →Becker
Dewey →Mead →Blumer

Any of the above in any order →Strauss
→Cicourel
→Garfinkel
→Goffman

And the main point of what might seem a facetious array of names and arrows is that the qualitative method is contagious; it is transmitted by enthusiasm and transformed by the ardent student. Morris says of Mead (Morris in Mead, 1934, p. vii):

> That he was not the writer of a system is due to the fact that he was always engaged in building one. His thought was too rich in internal development to allow him to get down his ideas in an ordered array. His genius expressed itself best in the lecture room.

And so we have a good reason for the *forming* nature of the method and the personal nature of its development.

Meanwhile any of the founders can be investigated for the deeper roots of his vision. Schutz's seems taken with Weber's worries over *Verstehen* (Zijderveld, 1972, p. 176 and esp. pp. 181–3, and Hindess, 1972, n. 7). If we can concentrate upon Mead once more for a moment, Morris (op. cit., p. ix) says in the course of an introduction:

> He belonged to an old tradition – the tradition of Aristotle, Descartes, Leibniz; of Russell, Whitehead, Dewey – which fails to see any sharp separation or any antagonism between the activities of science and philosophy and whose members are themselves both scientists and philosophers.

A little later (p. xv) Mead's achievement is that 'the individual act is seen within the social act; psychology and sociology are united upon a biological basis; social psychology is grounded upon a behaviourism'. And finally (p. xviii, n. 8) a more modern note is struck: 'Mead's behaviourism assimilates much of psychoanalysis, Gestalt psychology and existential psychology.'

In Strauss's introduction to Mead (1956, p. xi) he notes his personal contact: 'Within a week after my arrival at Chicago I was studying Mead's *Mind, Self and Society* directed to it by Herbert Blumer, who as a young instructor had taught Mead's classes after Mead's unexpected death', and then later, like Morris (op. cit., pp. xii–xvi), Strauss unravels the influences upon Mead of rationalism, romanticism and scientism. For example: 'But it is to Darwin and his successors that Mead is most indebted: he regarded Darwin as having provided the empirical underpinning for the Revolutionary, but inadequate, Romantic notion of evolution' (p. xviii).

Enough, I hope, has been cited to substantiate the impression that

107

there is a formidable provenance to any thread of the qualitative method and for the last three generations this has taken the form of a kinship bond. More generally, Berger (1963, p. 8) simply states: 'I have tried to be faithful to a central tradition that goes back to the classics in the field and I believe strongly in the continuing validity of this tradition.'

So be it. So far, however, the account has been replete with the necessary names, isms and ists. It is, of course, necessary to be more exact about content. In one sense, to do so prompts the following sections, but in another it may just be possible to gather, to corral a collection of rampant egoists. In fact this seems a good place to start.

1 All practitioners of the qualitative method have strong claims to having developed an individual approach. Little wonder. The individual *is* central in qualitative theory. To quote Morris again: 'Mead's endeavour is to show that mind and self are without residual social emergents; and that language, in the form of vocal gesture, provides a mechanism for their emergence' (p. xiv).

There is me, you, us, and the words we share. Cicourel (1970, p. 41) lists five rules that a researcher must clarify before making claims to 'objective' findings. Rule 1 says: 'Participants in social interaction apparently "understand" (by elaboration of verbal and non-verbal signals) many things, even though such matters are not mentioned explicitly. The unspoken elements may be as important as the spoken ones.'

In this way the qualitative method may have a therapeutic value, by putting people and their expressions first. No doubt its theorists can continually sort themselves out and push ahead.

2 All theorists of the qualitative method subscribe to a 'dialectical developmentalism'; whatever is happening, reflection is changing you and me and us. There is 'self-interaction and social-interaction' (Denzin, 1969, pp. 925–8). Every theorist is at great pains to make all these assumptions clear. All offer a general evolutionary fate for social phenomena: definitely for man, probably for his groups and possibly for society.

3 Qualitative theorists are generally only interested in society as the broad canvas whilst they busy themselves in the shrubbery down in the bottom left-hand corner. 'I conceive of society as collective action and sociology as the study of the forms of collective action' (Becker, 1971, p. v). The attitude is to produce a 'psychiatry of normality', to be a sociologist of the possible.

4 Qualitative theorists are all committed to the production of 'better theory'. They are usually successful. The qualitative method is generally viewed as intrinsic to its theory and vice versa.

108

Admittedly it is not the reader's problem whether what I call the qualitative method is describable as such. It is my problem to investigate a genus which I know to be so constituted but which produces such red herrings as each writer being an equal spokesman and a fully qualified individualist. On one point, however, all qualitative theorists unite: the quantitative method is a bad joke. The quantitative method is also the butt of the occasional light joke: 'The prominence of statistical techniques in American Sociology today, has, then, certain ritual functions that are readily understandable in view of the power system within which most sociologists have to make a career' (Berger, 1963, p. 21). This joke tells badly to qualitative theorists. Blumer, Turner and Becker have put up with a lot in their time. Only in the late 1950s did they begin to come in from the cold. And it was a cold created largely by the callousness of quantitative-method practitioners who had been literally licensed to print their own funds in return for services rendered. For most of the coming generation it must be enough that such men refused many forms of bribe and patiently taught what they knew to be true. And yet now I would argue their patience has been rewarded by being able to see the limits of the pursuit. I do not regard this as in any sense ironic. It is rather a fact that sociology cannot be pursued for sociology's sake – though admittedly undergraduates can be recruited to pursue it indefinitely.

We are coming, then, to the make or break of the qualitative method. In keeping with the prevalent evolutionism of the theory Zijderfeld (1972, p. 178) wonders:

In short, Schutz seems to represent a remarkable convergence between some 'classic' and 'modern' traditions, as well as between some American and European currents of philosophical and social thought. One might perhaps say that a scientific discipline reaches a level of maturity when some fundamental theoretical convergences begin to occur. If that is true, Schutz can be viewed as one of the first to have helped contemporary social thought to develop from the stage of adolescence with its necessary incoherence to the stage of maturity with some measure of consistency.

In effect, the qualitative method, its theorists and its theory could become a new dominant style of sociology on the ground that the quantitative method has become both applied and incomprehensible whilst 'it' is ripe for maturity. This claim should be seriously considered, not least because the implicit and explicit criticisms of the quantitative method are usually right. Further, the claim to mature synthesis could be substantiated by the few common interests that I have managed to draw out of the sprawl of writings.

And yet in the final analysis it will be the collective conviction of these practitioners that will bring the trial of maturity – the responsibility for dependants at all stages of capability.

I have tried to bear this 'historical tendency' in mind whilst devising the following sections. For whilst I see any synthesis as being produced by the 'objective relativism' of the style's proponents I have to accept that such opinions will produce real consequence for those that hold them. The section headings themselves, however, were also so named to answer the following questions:

Theory	What does the theorist think about social life?
Imagery	What devices does he use?
Activity	How does he go about his daily researching?
Substance	What has resulted from such studies?
English productions	Are there local products of this style?
End	What really does the future hold in store?

Qualitative theory: with the eyes of the overworld

Again the root problem is either to draw out various points of agreement or to list the achievements in theory of the many people mentioned in the introduction. I shall tend towards the former alternative and seek to convey the hum of the ethereal mood that can be found in qualitative work. For as one student has it: 'The older material historical and dialectical sociology of knowledge with its concern for politics and social structure has now been replaced by a one-sided idealism – ahistorical, apolitical and individualist' (Bryan, 1971, p. 326).

From this view we begin a kind of detective work. The writer refers to a sociology of knowledge, that implies Berger and Luckmann and that means the assessment is really of Schutz. In effect, most assessments of phenomenology are evaluations of Schutz's work whilst evaluations of symbolic interactionism are applied to that of Mead. Usually ethnomethodology is excluded from general criticism. In effect, the eyes of the qualitative method are taken – one each – from these two thinkers. They are not usually combined in one mind, so to speak, because both were very busy developing a language to describe what they were seeing.

Schutz's purpose 'is to analyse the phenomenon of meaning in ordinary social life' (1967, p. 44). This involves how actors make sense to themselves and others in processes of on-going 'typifications'. Unfortunately, it is impossible to simplify all of his descriptive attempts and terms. For one thing they are already simple; 'multiple realities'; 'taken-for-granteds'; 'stock of knowledge' and so on, and for another they represent signposts along the footpaths of folk wisdom (Silverman and Jones, 1973, p. 104) or 'the sociology of common sense'. It is not just that this theorizing is deceptively simple. It is more that man, the social actor, is so deceptively simple that his ways are wonderful and mundane.

Many would argue that Schutz spent his odd moments of intellectual life working towards a place from which to begin. To this extent his posthumously published volume is where he finished and students might justifiably start. Silverman (1972, p. 159) has kindly provided a succinct summary:

> Schutz argues that action and experience occur in the context of a system of 'relevances' which shape our reactions to the world. These relevances are drawn from the actor's biography (past experiences), his autobiography (reflections upon the former), and his stock of knowledge at hand.

'Topical' relevances inform the actor when a problematic object or scene stands out from his horizon of taken-for-granted phenomena – they provide the 'theme' of an experience. When the actor decides how to typify what has happened he refers to 'interpretative' relevances. These give an 'account' to the occasion and prepare the scene for future action. 'Motivational' relevances apply when one contemplates such action; they generate what we want to achieve (our 'in order to' motives) and how we view ourselves ('because' motives). Drawing on Husserl, Schutz notes that a double idealization operates in human existence. When applying a typification one says 'and so forth and so on' by assuming that a phenomenon has characteristics for which no present evidence exists (this is Garfinkel's etcetera clause). Second, when deciding future action, one naïvely believes that previously successful formulae of action will once again deliver the goods – 'I can do it again' (ibid., p. 159).

And, as Silverman continues, all this is well in line with what we might call the 'big-daddy dialectic', the Catch-22 of being conscripted for life: 'These systems are social constructs which are shared and *sustained* by the actions of others. Action and structure are thus dialectically linked; action occurring in the context of a pre-defined world but itself serving to re-shape that world' (ibid.).

It is this theme that most students grasp and then realize that its essential truth is a good corrective for structural-functionalist straitjacketing but difficult to do anything with. 'Ah well,' they sigh, 'I suppose it's true, it sounds all right . . . is that what sociology is?'

This is a fair and awkward question. For if one began where Schutz left off then his 'work is frequently said to have laid the foundations of a phenomenological sociology' (Hindess, 1972, p. 6). If this is so then one can begin to sort out the founding fathers to see if they are in or out of this species of sociology. So despite the years of laborious effort to make Marx a sociologist he is now put out again. Durkheim is in for his work on the 'conscience collective'. Simmel is a borderline case. And of course it is just this kind of imperialistic nonsense that has brought hoots of laughter from properly educated sociologists.

There is, therefore, the ticklish problem of whether Schutz's ruminations constitute sociology at all. Hindess asserts (ibid.):

> In fact Schutz's phenomenology involves a gross distortion of Husserl. Far from being phenomenologically founded, Schutz's sociology employs a phenomenological gloss to support its basic and unquestioned premise that 'the world of objective mind' can be reduced to the actions of individuals.

The use of his work, that is, may make sense in comparison with the available alternatives but this is hardly the stuff of a new and promising future for sociological soothsaying. It is inappropriate simply because sociology confronts man-made collectivities and their contents. Schutz is then a kind, old social psychologist.

Schutz did however engage in a debate with Weber's ghost. He spotted the methodological weaknesses in Weber's otherwise admirable formulation of ideal types. To use Zijderfeld's (p. 181) phrasing:

> Is there any guarantee that the artificial constructs of the social scientist contain some measure of stability, some kind of objective ground which provides the residual understanding of meaning with some measure of reliable evidence?

Zijderfeld's detailing of Schutz's criteria for typifications is highly recommended. It shows the distinct advantage of the scientist making use of his everyday knowledge rather than pretending that he has not got any. It also leads at least one 'ethnomethodologist' (Cicourel, 1970, p. 40) to draw an obvious conclusion:

> In the ideal the actor and observer-researcher employ different kinds of constructs and their procedural rules are distinct. In actual practice, however, the actor's everyday theorizing is probably not much different from the observer-researcher. Both employ the same basic rules and similar typifications, and neither may clarify (during interaction) the particular vernacular or rules used to communicate the domains of relevance each describes nor delineate the strata or layers of meaning intended or suggested by the linguistic categories and connotations used. Differences between our 'practical theorist' and an 'academic theorist' may all but disappear when both describe everyday activities.

Finally it should be said that Schutz's work may be suspect to some because of his occupation. Admittedly it sounds lame to put it as baldly as this but a man engaged in 'usury capitalism' must be affected by its taken-for-granted's somehow. Zijderfeld (p. 176) sees it to Schutz's advantage that he was 'free from academic fads and the controls of academic prestige':

> Schutz . . . was not a social scientist in the modern sense of the word. He was trained in law and pursued his thinking and writing in philosophy rather than empirical sociology taking Husserl, Bergson and Weber, and later in America, James, Cooley and Mead as his main field of discourse. Meanwhile, his writing and teaching were, like his music, never his profession. He seemed to have earned his living in the world of finances, engaging in philosophy and music as a sincere and true dilettante.

Hindess (p. 11) is rather more tart: 'If Husserl's ego is that of an ascetic mathematician that of Alfred Schutz betrays the indulgence of a banker with time on his hands'.

In fact the sociological impact of Schutz is probably not in his guesses about the making of meaning but in the operational truth that the mass of people are rule-bound, rule-making and thus law-abiding. It is a vexatious fact of sociology that the 'mass' is a normalizing, incorporating and accommodating collection of sleep-walkers. Schutz, of course, did not say so directly – to do so would be to contradict the mood of his musing. And further to do so would have brought a disturbing note of social criticism into his melody. Yet as Dreitzel comments, 'If the patterns of communicative behavior are the patterns of our everyday world, their study is an essential part of a critical understanding of the distortions and repressions of our everyday life' (1970, p. xxi).

We turn now to 'symbolic interactionism' and to the work of G. H. Mead. Again it is not possible to do justice to the man's 'span of thought' and 'brilliant insights'; Strauss's introduction (to Mead, 1956) does a very good job in this respect. And in piecing together the sociological theory of a pragmatic philosopher and social psychologist one is entitled to ask again why the man's full focus was upon the individual? What seems clear is that Mead developed the implications of evolution for man as a reflective and moral being and having done so was able to question the fixity of thought and institutions which he was making evolve and evolving within. As an evolutionary he argued the totality and temporality of all phenomena. Time and again the 'I' cannot be separated from the me that is looking at it; nor can they be wrenched from the 'significant' and 'generalized others' which precede them and yet are superseded by them in the context of reciprocally defining space and time. Like Schutz, that is, Mead is a full-blown theorist adding ramifications and refinements as he plunges into further puzzles. Again, like Schutz it is sweet reason that prevails, only it is the reason of historical fact and scientific fact. Examples must necessarily suffice (Mead, 1934, p. 243):

> I have stressed the point that the process of communication is nothing but an elaboration of the peculiar intelligence with which the vertebrate form is endowed. The mechanism which can analyse the responses, take them to pieces, and reconstruct them, is made possible by the brain as such, and the process of communication is the means by which this is brought under the control of the individual himself. He can take his response to pieces and present it to himself as a set of things he can do under conditions more or less controllable. The process of communication simply puts the intelligence of the individual at his own disposal. But the individual that has this ability is a social individual. He does not develop it by himself and then enter into society on the basis of this capacity. He becomes such a self and gets such control by being a social individual, and it is only in society that he can attain this sort of a self which will make it possible for him to turn back upon himself and indicate to himself the different things he can do.

As a pragmatist Mead saw his theory – and let us assume that for Mead *all* his thinking was an aspect of *one* theory – as a practical judgment upon the present stage of 'evolution' and a practical suggestion for getting to the next. Like most pragmatists, however, he allowed himself to believe that the next practical move would realize the ideal (1956, p. 282):

> What we call the ideal of a human society is approached in some sense by the economic society on the one side and by the universal religions on the other side, but it is not by any means fully realised. Those abstractions can be put together in a single community of the democratic type. As democracy now exists, there is not this development of communication so that individuals can put themselves into the attitudes of those whom they affect. There are a consequent levelling-down and an undue recognition of that which is not only common but identical. The ideal of a human society cannot exist as long as it is impossible for individuals to enter into the attitudes of those whom they are affecting in the performance of their own peculiar functions.

In truth, Mead is more approachable, less slippery and more erudite than Schutz. He continually weaves his practicalities and ideals, what he thinks man is and the way he thinks evolution is going, into one taut rope. With this rope he can pull evidence from history about social consciousness, evidence from biology about nervous systems and growth, and his whole sense of himself into the realization of 'the human social ideal' (1934, p. 310):

The human social ideal – the ideal or ultimate goal of social progress – is the attainment of a universal human society in which all human individuals would possess a perfected social intelligence, such that all social meanings would each be similarly reflected in their respective individual consciousness – such that the meanings of any one individual's acts or gestures (as realised by him and expressed in the structure of his self, through his ability to take the social attitudes of other individuals toward himself and toward their common social ends or purposes) would be the same for any other individual whatever who responded to them.

Strangely enough the 'liberal in the best sense', reformist essence of Mead's thinking has faded in interest in contrast to the mechanics of child development and reference-group theory. The whole has been separated into science and philosophy respectively so that it is the scientific part that has since become 'labelling theory' or provided 'playful-puppet' type definitions of the individual. The philosophy has been trivialized to statements like 'Everyone makes some contribution toward changing his community' (Strauss, in Mead, 1956, p. xxiii). But before elaborating these developments it is worth while to record just one comment upon Schutz and Mead generally, upon idealistic conceptions of social change (Schwendinger and Schwendinger, 1972, p. 12):

Upon writing about the materialistic conception of history, Engels noted that in the eighteenth century the scholars of the enlightenment were dominated by idealistic conceptions of social change. As a consequence, they envisioned a utopian 'kingdom of reason' wherein superstition, injustice, privilege and oppression were to vanish in the face of eternal truth, eternal justice, equality grounded in nature and the inalienable rights of man. However, 'we know today', Engels (1882, p. 142) added in 1872, 'that this kingdom of reason was nothing more than the idealised kingdom of the bourgeoisie; that eternal justice found its realization in bourgeois justice; that equality reduced itself to bourgeois equality before the law; that bourgeois property was proclaimed as one of the essential rights of man; and that the government could only come into existence as a bourgeois-democratic republic.'

I

Clearly these broad metatheoretical matters are of little interest to those who use some ideas and terms from these theoreticians' essays to guide their own research. Garfinkel makes great use of Schutz's 'textures of relevance' and other descriptive terms. In describing trans-sexed persons – an admittedly difficult categoric exercise – he accounts their feelings as procedures (1967, p. 118).

> They have as resources their remarkable awareness and uncommon sense knowledge of the organization and operation of social structures that were for those who are able to take their sexual status for granted, routinized, 'seen but unnoticed' backgrounds of their everyday affairs.

One has the feeling in reading this definition that, like Mead, Garfinkel was trying to get everything in, in one breath.

Goffman has made great use of Mead's reflexive act and produced an ambivalent and awkward theoretical individual (1961, p. 280):

> defining the individual, for sociological purposes, as a stance-taking entity, a something that takes up a position somewhere between identification with an organization and opposition to it, and is ready at the slightest pressure to regain its balance by shifting its involvement in either direction.

True to theoretical tendency, Goffman looks at the 'participant's', the individual's problems: 'I assume that when an individual appears before others he will have many motives for trying to control the impression they receive of the situation' (1959, p. 15).

Now any astute reader of such sentences can detect a theory of man, of social behaviour, of the social nature of motive and so on. For the qualitative method is replete with theory and explicit assumption; its practitioners honest as to what happens when you work outwards from the individual towards his operating milieu. Built into this theory therefore is an advocacy of generalized introspection. It is this method that helps the theory and vice versa. As Becker says (1971, p. 22):

> Since the subject matter of sociology is the social life in which we are all involved, the ability to make imaginative use of personal experience and the very quality of one's personal experience will be important contributions to one's technical skill.

In this way even the theory of qualitative theory is tight with its method. And in this fact lies much of its attraction. For even this, the briefest of accounts of theory, has flown through classical philosophy over theories of man and what he makes of himself to theories of thinking and thinking of theories. No doubt this account is too short for justice and too lumpy for quick digestion. One thing should be clear by now, though – the qualitative method in theory is not a bashful Boy Scout doing his first backwoodman's badge. There is enough in Schutz and Mead to keep a thousand miners happy. And all the time the student is within their thought, it touches upon most things beginning with himself and links all together as it reels away in front of him. Then there are the more recent definitional exercises of men who have continuously demonstrated the ability to use and rework theory. All use introspection, and so 'as it was in the beginning' lasts right up to the end. To repeat a previous point from a further perspective, the qualitative method in theory is honest down to its boots, such is the nature of phenomenalism. For as Rock says (1973, p. 20):

> It is imperative to faithfully reproduce the social world as it is sensed by its occupants. Any departure from this attribution of facticity to the occupants' understanding is both a distortion of primary social phenomena and a resort to mystification.

Imagery in qualitative theory

In formal literary criticism there are two comparative devices; namely, the metaphor and the simile. In qualitative theory we find initially the metaphor of dialectic and latterly speculations about the utility of the similes of careers, dramas and games. And behind these apparently different 'perspectives' there are the same 'root images' about social life.

The use of 'the dialectic' has been mentioned before; it says man is in society and society is in man. There is mutual affect and effect. Quoting Mead (1934, pp. 215–16):

> As a man adjusts himself to a certain environment he becomes a different individual; but in becoming a different individual he has affected the community in which he lives. It may be a slight effect, but in so far as he has adjusted himself, the adjustments have changed the type of environment to which he can respond and the world is accordingly a different world. There is always a mutual relationship of the individual and the community in which the individual lives. Our recognition of this under ordinary conditions is confined to relatively small social groups, for here an individual cannot come into the group without in some degree changing the character of the organization. People have to adjust themselves to him as much as he adjusts himself to them. It may seem to be a molding of the individual by the forces about him, but the society likewise

117

changes in this process and becomes to some degree a different society. The change may be desirable or undesirable, but it inevitably takes place.

This metaphor is what we might call the 'ungrounded dialectic'. For the determination of the two 'opposing parts' is not grounded in any prior theory of the productive forces of life. Or alternatively a dialectical process is said to pertain between man and his circumstance because these two 'parts' make the whole of the sociologist's sphere of interest. Generally speaking, the two sides are not seen as having equal strengths any more than, say, man being a ghost and society being a phantom. Nor is the dialectical process of synthesis seen as being the outcome of a tenacious struggle. In fact the synthesis is reasoned to be present, that the two sides are complementary rather than in conflict. And thus an ungrounded dialectic is a metaphorical device to depict evolution rather than revolution. From where we are now, so to speak, we are going to where we will be next. It is this mood – for what else can a metaphor without its root source produce? – that is referred to as 'relativism'. As such the relevance of the dialectic's use is didactic. It has a value for teaching purposes. The pupil can be brought to see two things in one vision. No doubt a comparison with the function of binoculars can be made. It would, however, be unwarranted to claim that theorists of the qualitative method use a dialectic simply for teaching their students a form of vision. Doubtless 'the dialectic' is held as a world-view: coherent because the individual is always on one side of the equation. In practice, however, the dialectic can come to represent most relationships between most phenomena. A recent example can be found in Jock Young (1971); McIntosh (1972) detects two in his study of drug use:

> There is a dialectic between the drug itself and the drug culture: the culture focusses attention on certain drug-induced effects and ignores others; the physiological concomitants of these effects are actually enhanced in the user's body. Thus drug dependency can only be understood in 'social-pharmacological' terms, in terms of the inter-related physiological, subjective and social levels.
>
> There is a dialectic, too, between patterns of drug use and experience and patterns of social reaction to drug use. The adverse social reaction is not against drug use in itself, but against the reasons why the drugs are taken. Bohemian marihuana use represents a 'subterranean world of play' – a world of short-term hedonism, expressivity, autonomy, excitement and disdain for work – a world which the dominant work ethic assigns to the peripheral place of play. Active social

repression in turn affects and develops the sub-culture and the nature of drug use.

The summary above makes it clear that a dialectic is an acceptable device and one which supposedly reveals seldom-considered truths.

Meanwhile the central dialectic has continued to provide a need for its own elaboration. Berger and Luckmann (1967) are the most elegant exemplars of such mainstream thinking. They have a way of developing the dialectic to being 'all we know and all we need to know'. Taking part of their 'man in society' theme, Emerson (1970, p. 75) relates:

> Berger and Luckmann emphasise three additional processes that provide persons with evidence that things have an objective existence apart from themselves. Perhaps most important is the experience that reality seems to be out there before we arrive on the scene. This notion is fostered by the nature of language, which contains an all-inclusive scheme of categories, is shared by a community, and must be learned laboriously by each new member. Further, definitions of reality are continuously validated by apparently trivial features of the social scene, such as details of the setting, persons' appearance and demeanour, and 'inconsequential' talk. Finally each part of a systematic world view serves as evidence for all other parts, so that reality is solidified by a process of intervalidation of supposedly independent events.

And in so doing Emerson made a most practical use of these identified processes.

Yet the mainstream of the theory of the qualitative method has come to have rather less importance than its tributaries. These slight trickles seem to have sprung from one or other of the sides of the dialectic. For the dialectic without a ground is little more than a formally expressed process: a reasoning of how things carry on is also an instruction to anticipate that they will do so somehow. Thus man being a carrier of culture is really more interesting than man being a creator of culture. After all, it is a bit of a one-sided struggle. Some would also say that the struggle has been to dump the metaphor in favour of the simile. Certainly the similes of the drama and the game have become the stock-in-trade analogies for many qualitative researchers.

Now yet another account of the pros and cons of analogies in sociology would hardly be welcomed. No end of nonsense is discussed under the headings of an 'heuristic device', a 'model' and a 'perspective'. It cannot be helped, I suppose, that to some the devices are as real as the subject matter and certainly more hygienic;

that every simile-user makes his own qualifications and reservations and that the terms 'drama' and 'game' both imply *homo normalis*, a calculative weasel under the delusion that he is clever.

Goffman (1959, p. xi) prefaces with what he means by theatrical performance and then notes three 'inadequacies'. Having made a book's mileage from the analogy he ruefully concludes: 'Now it should be admitted that this attempt to press a mere analogy so far was in part a rhetoric and a manœuvre' (ibid., p. 254). And apparently it was all to a single purpose: *homo normalis* in face-to-face situations is having a hard time facing the situation and holding his face: 'The key factor in this structure is the maintenance of a single definition of the situation, the definition having to be expressed, and this expression sustained in the face of a multitude of potential disruptions' (ibid.).

Garfinkel (1967, p. 174) is not too happy with this 'naughty' view from a practical point of view:

One may allow, in agreement with Goffman, the accuracy of Goffman's 'naughty' view that members of a society generally . . . are much concerned with the management of impressions. We may allow, as well, the accuracy and acuteness of his descriptions of this concern. Nevertheless if one tries to reproduce the features of a real society by populating it with Goffman type members we are left with structural incongruities. . . .

Goffman's theatre is to Garfinkel a 'clinical ideal' (p. 184). Gouldner is less complimentary: he pounds away at the callow assumptions beneath the whole edifice (1970, pp. 378–90). My point is, however, neither practical nor political. It is sufficient here to say that the qualitative method readily begets such analogy, for fieldwork may actually provoke it. The reason is simple: a theoretical process is interminable whilst after a bit of drama we can all go home. There is no indication in the 'big dialectic' as to what these little dialectics might look like. So it is no wonder that self-conscious (perhaps semi-conscious) puppetry has arisen and seems perfectly compatible with the big theory. Such an analogy is more mechanical and its applicators would readily agree (Berger, 1963, p. 199), but that is only because the process is broken down a little. Somehow the big theory is intact and enhanced.

Perhaps it is not quite the same with the analogy of the game. For one thing, the elaboration of what the game means can be interminable (cf. Garfinkel's succinct account [1967, p. 140]), and for another the game action can be downright playful. In *Strategic Interaction* (1969) Goffman becomes truly light-hearted. He has his hero, Harry, playing some very serious games. He puts Harry in hair-raising situations and 'listens' to his reasoning. As a pilot of a plane on fire Harry might pray 'having improved reception' (p. 91). When Harry in the jungle sees a lion that could see him at any moment, Goffman comments: 'I assume that by now Harry knows enough neither to dither nor pray' (p. 92). (And while on the subject of how a game analogy seems to put a sparkle in Goffman's humour his footnote about a 'nice Jewish girl', pp. 88–9, is highly recommended.)

Overall I suspect that Goffman knows he is taking liberties with qualitative theory. For as he has developed, his similes have been more outrageous if not absurd. I know that he keeps up his academic references but he seems to be happiest itemizing the stages of yet another process that he has just observed that fit within the analogy. A man who can account for a double bluff with consummate ease can manage a quadruple bluff with little effort.

Thus I wish to conclude that chasing these two similes of the qualitative method is a waste of time. It is taking a jest seriously and thus making another joke. Of course I do not mean that all users of the analogies of drama and game use them fraudulently, but those that do not, miss the chance of making up their own sociology and prefer instead to plod on through self-prompted problems.

The concepts of 'career' and 'passing' do, however, seem to have more serious intent. For drama and game define a situation where the moves have been made before.

With career and passing the moves have been made before but now we are concerned with how making a move irrevocably moves the individual (Goffman, 1961, p. 119):

> Traditionally the term *career* has been reserved for those who
> expect to enjoy the uses laid out within a respectable
> profession. The term is coming to be used, however, in a
> broadened sense to refer to any social strand of any person's
> course, through life. The perspective of natural history is taken:
> unique outcomes are neglected in favour of such changes over
> time as are basic and common to the members of a social
> category, although occurring independently to each of them.
> Such a career is not a thing that can be brilliant or
> disappointing; it can be no more a success than a failure.

Undoubtedly the exemplary use of this concept is in Becker's 'Becoming a marihuana user' (1971). Here Becker identifies three stages of usage – light, medium and 'heavy man heavy' – through which a user may pass and at each stage 'normalize' his achievement. Equally as undoubtedly this sort of imagery takes some getting used to. First a term is taken from an everyday process, it is itself an idealization, then it is idealized into its abstract or formal properties and then it is applied to 'weird' circumstances to reveal more regularity, more normality than is to be found in the original context. Still these are not problems for the users themselves.

Many other concepts could be given, traced to theory and application, all to show the strange dependence of the qualitative method upon its devices. Yet it cannot be proved that qualitative theory 'comes' from its imagery and it would be unhelpful to attempt to do so. Rather, I wish to make the prevalence of rich – and usually apt – imagery sensible. I want to conclude this section by a trip to the roots.

The keystone of the bridge of this understanding is the necessary intimacy of social life. Clearly this relies upon a permanence of both culture and types of association; that all forms and contents will bend but not break.

People are living together; talking with each other; making their behaviour a simple and yet supreme language. The image therefore of the context of social life is the family. It is in the reality con-structioning of the family that the hub of meaning is to be found (cf. Berger and Kellner, 1970). It is in the making of marriage; the rearing of children; the entanglements of relatives and the daily significance of all these things that is to be found the ideal image, a beautiful context for self and other development. It is obvious, therefore, that Mead's social interests are at one with his social psychological interests. He was concerned with the free and full development of children in school; that is, in as near a family setting as possible. His wish to reform education was his wish to form again the fragile force of love and trust between adult and encroaching child.

The meta-context of the family is the tribe. 'Community' is a self-denigrating euphemism for manifold, multiple networks upon any line you care to name. A sense of community is a pale shadow of the love for one's tribe. A tribe can rise up and slaughter its enemies, decamp and flee intact. For all the psychology in the theory, there is anthropology in the imagery. For 'significant others' read family, for 'generalized others' read tribe. Then it becomes clear from the imagery that the qualitative method is meant to be a micro-sociology; its broad context, its meta-context, is that of the tribe. Presumably its meta-meta-context would be the humid chaos of the jungle.

Thus it is in no sense fortuitous that since Mead the most famous qualitative studies have taken as their focus the anti-family tendencies of institutions. In medical schools (Becker *et al.*, 1961) and in asylums (Goffman, 1961) there are two distinct families, a neighbourhood of thems and us-es, of separate languages and survivals. These studies in fact take as their point of departure the chronic misunderstandings between people in apparently the same situation.

(I do *not* mean that this imagery was necessarily intentional, it was the fuzziness of the theory that made it practical: 'Incidentally, children of resident doctors were the only non-patient category I found that did not evince obvious caste distance from patients: why I do not know' [Goffman, 1961, p. 196, n. 68].)

Chronic misunderstandings: in less than ideal moments they could be the character of a family and customarily they could be the moments between the tribe's families. They refer to social prejudices which in some precise combination serve to maximize the smallest differences between life styles into qualitative differences in life chances. Jock Young (1971) has rightly gone straight to this fact with his reasoning that the police and others actually amplify the deviance of marihuana smokers. The 'amplification' is more than the giving of distortion, it is the preparedness to lie. For no hippy is inhuman, no drunk completely without rights, no student an absolute fool. And yet qualitative studies reveal lies told by one group about a group with whom they are closely related. In fact there is a relationship of dependency. As is so often said, teachers and pupils depend upon each other and so do all other semi or fully incarcerated groups of controllers and controlled. There is pretence. Sometimes the qualitative method is characterized as the sociology of fraud. The controllers pretend that the controlled do not matter and the sentiment is reciprocated. For both, the formula computes ego survival with group superiority. There is an active collusion to prevent the intimate understanding and mutual development of an ideal family. There is an antipathy towards the rolling stone of a 'community of interest'.

These revelations carry a tone of pathos out from the situation to the liberal reader's understanding. The crass cruelty of coercion (the frequently used last resort) comes to resemble the deep-seated problem of the persecutors, for the persecuted are already numb.

If the qualitative method has a theory of its result's effect, it is therefore to embarrass oppressors, to show up all those who exploit the unfamiliar, custodial way in which we usually live. This effect comes, I suggest, from the force of its imagery.

The activity of the qualitative method

How, then, does the qualitative-method style of researcher go about his business? Clearly he is not without a theory of social life and has the aid of its attendant imagery. Naturally these bring a refined sensitivity to his bearing. He has a great deal of respect for his subject matter. His listening is an integral part of his scheme. Above all, at the onset of his research he is not sure what he will find and has little idea of what he will finally say. Thus, along with a preparedness to wait and see, it is necessary to go further and further into the subject matter, to pull out from one side and then poke away at another. A qualitative researcher does his training 'in the field'. He has to be good at participation and observation. For he is entering another world, no doubt for most people an underworld; he is to bring back a map of the life there. So he cannot be satisfied with the odd trophy. He must make all that he has found clear – especially that which at first seemed confusing and contradictory. And so there is another feature in common with anthropology – qualitative research is in the nature of an exploration. The argument for the qualitative method is that this exploratory style produces 'better theory'. By better theory is meant theory that fits the facts and theory that sounds right.

Thus the books describing the appropriate activity for qualitative research are replete with the dual justification that it suits sociology and suits its subject matter: it provides 'a faithful rendering of the subject's experience and interpretation of the world he lives in' (Denzin, 1970, p. 10).

For the student, sadly, there are differences in emphasis, even disagreements, over how this good faith should be professed, the two main trends, at the moment, being towards eclecticism about the subject and conflict with actual subjects. As they are essentially different methods they will be taken in turn.

The advocates of eclecticism are Denzin (1970), Becker (1971), and Glaser and Strauss (1967). Goffman is indirectly an eclectic. Denzin, it should be said from the start, makes a mess of it. His eclecticism is little other than finding a place for everything. He produces a confusion; finding an equal place for mathematics and meaning and yet consistently preferring the latter. Nevertheless he does try to give the service of showing the procedures of interpretative fieldwork. For participant observation he prescribes: 'Smaller samples will be selected, documents will be collected, informants will be selected, unstructured interviewing will be done and descriptive statistical analyses will be presented' (1970, p. 12). This sums up a standard qualitative report; it also indicates that where to study is a problem neither of theory nor of activity. It has to be assumed that the subject is a world of people who can talk about it.

The problems for qualitative research are practical: the people may not speak (Cuber and Harroff, 1963, p. 141):

In the research we have conducted, we have focused upon a select group of subjects for the purpose of securing their conceptions of reality in the man-woman world, their strivings and apathies, and their own evaluation of the success or failure of their own *modus operandi*.

They did so with what 'could be described tersely as the unstructured, lengthy and intimate interview' (ibid.). It is worth following through their 'sampling procedure' and listening to the considerations (ibid., pp. 94–5):

> Such an undertaking . . . presumes that one can find subjects sufficiently self-conscious about their life-processes that they have intellectualizations worth talking about and second, that they are sufficiently articulate to be able to communicate such ideas effectively to someone else. [They chose a group of 'upper middle class'.]

> To insure further homogeneity interviewees were limited to an age span of 35 to 55 because we were more interested in mature reflection than in the immature projections of the very young and yet wanted persons, before, as a rule, serious health or disillusionment begin to presage senility.

> We sought a non-clinical sample . . . at least free of some of the manifest distortion-producing influences of a crisis-caught group.

Sometimes this clearing and cleaning of the universe for a good sample is called 'theoretical sampling'. In truth, the criteria of sampling can allow for most contingencies and are usually report-specific. That is, each report also says who provided information and the reasons for 'choosing' them. More important for the qualitative researcher is the interviewer's effect on the situation.

Denzin is very precise about the interview situation itself. He suggests that it is a hostile situation, that all matters discussed are contentious and that the interviewee is bound to be ill at ease. He recommends fieldworkers to 'dress in the mode of dress most acceptable to those being interviewed but employ a style that communicates who you are with respect to them' (ibid., p. 140).

Becker, too, is at great pains to draw attention to the observer effect (op. cit., p. 47); he believes it is as important as being able to recognize a lie and assess its evidential value (p. 29).

In this way the qualitative researcher is not fooled into thinking that it's just a matter of talking to people and writing up what they say. For as Becker puts it, 'My discussion refers to the kind of participant observation study which seeks to discover hypotheses as well as test them' (ibid., p. 26).

The 'traditional' qualitative method suggests the use of 'sensitizing' concepts. They are ideas that you start off with that are supposed

125

to make you sensitive to what you should know and then be receptive to modification, change or abandonment as appropriate. For Blumer's answer to his own question 'What is wrong with social theory?' was, in part, that its concepts were wooden and yet woefully inaccurate. Accordingly, he gave some indication as to how concepts might be sensitive in the field and the fieldworker ever sensitive to the extent of their appropriateness. Denzin puts this in his own perspective: 'The proper use of concepts is at first sensitizing and only later operational: further the proper theory becomes formal and last the proper causal proposition becomes universal and not statistical' (op. cit., p. 14). This, of course, is a continuation of Schutz's criterion of 'adequacy' (Zijderfeld, 1972, pp. 186–8). There is a problem as to where sensitizing concepts came from, the only answer being that as a creature of his culture the sociologist had a good idea of what was going on beforehand and anyway a sensitizing concept is only of prime utility as somewhere to start. Denzin's suggestion, after all, is not unlike Weber's call for inspiration: 'such techniques as introspection, the use of imagined experiments and the playful combination of contradictory concepts also serve . . . (op. cit., p. 14).

And for all the need of something to go in with there is the need to come out with findings clear and clean. This means that sleuthing in the field is double-checking, trying different angles and generally provoking subjects into affirmative statements. Thus Denzin favours the 'logic of triangulation'. 'The combination of multiple methods – each with their own biases, true – into a single investigation will better enable the sociologist to forge valid propositions that carefully consider relevant rival causal factors' (op. cit., p. 27).

Becker has twenty-seven stages of 'field analysis' (op. cit., p. 26) and also favours 'multiple observations' (p. 54) or a 'multi-method triangulation' (p. 58).

At first this 'triangulating' may seem impossible to achieve but if Denzin's opening remarks are still remembered he mentions checking documents; the neighbours; local radio and TV stations and any agile octogenarians. To be less sarcastic, the qualitative method may seem to be 'ideal' for participant observation but its proponents have been busy applying it as a strategy to a broad range of 'data'. It is this eclecticism of data source that has led to many a criticism from observers: 'There are limits to what can be mined from history and all too often these papers rely for data on newspaper cuttings and on the participant observation of the 'what I did on my summer vacation' variety (Sparks, 1973, p. 148).

No doubt this seems a harsh judgment to the book's authors. For life histories, documents, diaries are more than fair game; they are to be used to the full: 'Through his own experiences, general knowledge or reading and the stories of others the sociologist can gain data on other groups that offer useful comparisons. This kind of data can be trusted if the experience was "lived" ' (Glaser and Strauss, 1967, p. 67). In this way virtually anything vaguely connected can get the researcher started. But these are also data banks in their own right and though both Becker and Denzin offer some rules of procedure it is the 'constant comparative method' of Glaser and Strauss that is the most highly developed.

Now Glaser and Strauss do not just want better theory, they want 'broad, rich, integrated, dense and grounded theory' (op. cit., p. 256). For all that they engage in the pursuit of air, that which they want is soil. Undeniably anyone with their energies can check, double-check, sleuth, submerge and come round about again. Undoubtedly, too, their book covers almost every eventuality of every stage of research with many kinds of data. What they 'prove' is that communalities can be found and assayed as discerningly as can old gold: 'They seem to be suggesting that the concepts, categories and theories we seek are intrinsic to the phenomena we study and will be immediately evident to us if we look closely' (Rock, 1973, n. 21). To which Glaser and Strauss can reply: 'Our position is not logical, it is phenomenological . . . we arrive at results that potentially may be judged as successful' (op. cit., p. 6).

It's warm, it's happy, it works. Glaser and Strauss have indefatigability. They have married European humanism in the shape of phenomenology to its suitor – the all-American creed of unbridled, practical progress. They spell out a whole method and for each element there is optimism. They brush most distinctions and problems aside. In brief, they could claim to have staked the territory of the qualitative method by making its activity potentially all-embracing.

Glaser and Strauss do not, of course, enter into the finer details of questioning others and 'linking' where it is most advantageous to do so. Their activity seems genuinely hell-bent on theoretical elaboration. Still there is the matter of taking field notes and in contrast to the quantitative-method masters, no end of trouble is taken to work out the best and least disturbing way of doing things. As I have emphasized before, the core of the qualitative method *is* its pragmatism.

It is not necessary, however, for a practitioner to go into all the effects that he might have and all the ways he might approach phenomena and check his conceptualization. For this is implicitly the language of verification and some researchers are more concerned with how they can find out things than they are with how they can prove them to be so. As in quantitative research there are the 'logics' of discovery and verification. I quote Taylor (1972, pp. 24–5):

Even symbolic interactionists who might at least nominally be expected to concentrate upon talk have interestingly enough concerned themselves more with meta-communicational problems, with the meaning of paralinguistic utterances, with the language of gesture, posture and physical space than they have with what is typically said in conversations or chats. . . . For after all, one aspect of communication about communication, is that it is not thought to be so evidently under the actor's conscious control as is the communication itself. Meta-communicational signs are more given off than given and may, therefore, be regarded as somehow 'truer' indications of the actor's real purposes and intentions than are those communicational elements like his clothes and his conversation over which he is assumed to keep a more telling surveillance. The connection between *The Presentation of Everyday Life* and *The Psychopathology of Everyday Life* is not confined to the purely nominal similarity between Freud's and Goffman's titles; it is also to be found in the emphasis which both books adopt in looking for errors and slips in social interaction as clues to underlying processes. It is when things go wrong that we are said to glimpse the nature of man: embarrassment for the social interactionist and anxiety states for the analyst have a similar theoretical significance. They are occasions upon which talk breaks down, when accounts are no longer being given or being narrowed.

In addition to looking for slips, though, the researcher can do his level best to cause them. He can make his activity one of sabotage; consciously created rupture in the normal run of things. He can challenge his subjects. 'In the empirical applications of Goffman's notions one is continually tempted to press the informant with exasperation: "Oh come on now, you must know better than that; why don't you confess?" (Garfinkel, 1967, p. 174). Garfinkel does just that with Agnes – his justly celebrated trans-sexed person (pp. 121, 131, 137, 140):

Approximately 35 hours of conversation I had with her were tape recorded.

Time after time in the course of our meetings when I directed the conversation to homosexuals and transvestites Agnes had a great deal of difficulty, simultaneously managing her fascination for the topic and the great anxiety that the conversation seemed to generate. The picture that she would present then was that of a mild depression.

When I asked Agnes if there were any 'real bad things' that

had happened to her, the strain in her attempt to reply was so evident that I found it necessary to modify the question and asked instead for some things that were 'bad things but not such bad things'.

On the occasions with her [when] I employed the usage that she had been 'acting like a female' I would get one variation or another on the essential theme: I am a female but the others would misunderstand if they knew how I was raised or what I have between my legs.

Despite all this probing and prompting and 'despite a total of approximately seventy hours of talks arranged with the three of us ... there were at least seven critical areas in which we obtained nothing' (p. 163).

Perhaps Garfinkel was too gentle with his subject! With other subjects he has been more provocative: 'Undergraduate students were assigned the task of spending from fifteen minutes to an hour in their homes while assuming that they were boarders in the household' (p. 45).

students were asked to spend from fifteen minutes to an hour in their homes imagining they were boarders and acting out this assumption. They were instructed to conduct themselves in a circumspect and polite fashion. They were to avoid getting personal, to use formal address, to speak only when spoken to (p. 41).

These exercises produced despair and abuse in the respective families and (p. 118)

permit an appreciation of these background relevances that are otherwise easily overlooked or difficult to grasp because of their routinized character or because they are so embedded in the background of relevances that one simply is 'there' and taken for granted.

Gouldner (1970) has roundly condemned these schoolboy pranks for what they are. There are enough enemies about without making a few more. And if there is to be conflict in a method's activity let it be with those deserving opposition. For his more particular part Gouldner says (pp. 393–4):

The cry of pain, then, is Garfinkel's triumphal moment; it is dramatic confirmation of the existence of certain tacit rules governing social interaction and of their importance to the persons involved. That he feels free to inflict these costs on others, on his students, their families, friends or passersby – and to encourage others to do so – is not, I would suggest, evidence of a dispassionate and detailed attitude toward the social world, but of a readiness to use it in cruel ways. Here, objectivity and sadism become delicately intertwined. The demonstration is the message, and the message seems to be that anomic normlessness is no longer something that the sociologist studies in the social world, but it is now something that he *inflicts upon it* and is the basis of his method of investigation.

I tend to agree with Gouldner. There is a point to conflict methodology – but not to any old conflict that one can provoke (cf. Young, op. cit., p. 279). That is, a provocation cannot be justified on the grounds of what it discovers and nor can a sociologist displace his responsibility for the disturbance he inspires – unless the world is one of play and the sociologist just gives it a shove when it errs to leaden seriousness.

In addition to encouraging discovery by happening Garfinkel is quite scornful about establishment logics of verification. He regards them as erroneous and potentially dangerous (op. cit., p. 283):

It has been the purpose of this paper to recommend the hypothesis that the scientific rationalities can be employed only as ineffective ideals in the actions governed by the presuppositions of everyday life. The scientific rationalities are neither stable features nor sanctionable ideals of daily routines, and any attempt to stabilize these properties or to enforce conformity to them in the conduct of everyday affairs will magnify the senseless character of a person's behavioural environment and multiply the disorganized features of the system of interaction.

This disregard for scientism is certainly not shared by the other writers referenced in this section. For the qualitative method is generally judged to be on its weakest ground *as an activity*. Somehow the very fact of needing faith in the researcher seems to shake some sociologists to sickness. Time and again the same dull reasoning that the qualitative method is all right for micro-sociology is wheeled out and then the *caveat* is added that still one needs to be suspicious and of course it would not do everywhere. And somehow its practitioners have been affected by a criticism that comes from an ignorance of their own theory.

Glaser and Strauss (1967) go to great lengths to show how a researcher can get an ever-increasing purchase upon credibility and manage to convey it. Becker (op. cit., p. 109) is always concerned that researchers should do their best in selecting valid material. He, however, often holds high the ideal of science. His advice is simply how to come as close by as possible.

But it is Denzin who tries to prove that the qualitative method is scientific. He claims that 'universal explanations of human behaviour can be developed' (1970, p. 15), that 'a small set of very abstract and general principles can explain all human behaviour' (p. 17), and this in the context of symbolic interactionism. He finds support in Polanyi (1964) and Bridgman (1961, p. 322) to the effect that science is an imaginative art.

Thus muddled criticism has in part been met by a brave defence. The surprising thing is that some qualitative researchers regard their actual activity as their weak flank and then claim either that all science is something or other or that they are just as scientific by virtue of the things that they take into account. Perhaps it is that they find their 'relativism' just a little too relativistic in practice.

Substance: the meat of the matter

Understanding . . . is grasping the point of what is being done or said. This is a notion far removed from the world of statistics and causal laws: it is closer to the realm of discourse and to the internal relations that link the parts of a realm of discourse. [Winch, 1958, p. 115].

Closer to the realm of discourse . . . could this mean seeing and describing things in much the same way as anyone else would? The answer to this question is a qualified yes. That is, the product of qualitative method is generally readable, usually understandable and often 'interesting'. In fact the substance of the qualitative method is often unexceptional and has led one reviewer to ask: 'Why does phenomenology promise so much and deliver so little?' (McCormack, 1973, p. 23). The response to this rhetoric is simply that a qualitative researcher can see no more than is there (Cuber and Harroff, 1963, p. 141):

Perhaps our most important finding was not in the form of data about men and women or marriage, but a vivid and recurrent reminder that when the professional listens modestly, he can learn a great deal more from the subject than he would have had the wit to ask about, if he had approached the interview with a set of questions or hypotheses derived from prior experience. It seems to us that the most important part of this investigation consists of new concepts and hypotheses which apparently are quite familiar to the persons in this class but which for the most part specialists have not talked about or have touched upon obliquely.

Here the writers are complimenting themselves on their choice of activity on the grounds of 'learning more'. Thus they argue that they

K

have produced more goods. In fact they have produced 'a typology of marriages' and a 'realistic' conclusion. The marriages they observed could be classified as having relationships that are 'conflict-habituated', or 'devitalized' or 'passive-congenial', or 'vital' or 'total'. So (p. 145):

> To conclude, the overriding generalization of this study is that marriage is often continued out of habit, tradition, practical convenience or austere social relations and that what the mental hygienist might call a good man-woman relationship in marriage is the exception rather than the rule.

Most qualitative-method reports say much the same thing. They produce species – typical or genotypical categories. The whole is broken down to the sum of its parts. Each part is checked carefully to see if it is a sensible, substantiated and theoretical type. The 'data' are then reorganized in these terms and selectively given to typify the type – to play the part. As was argued in the section on theory the types produced are generally types of 'association'; interaction is almost always in the setting of a relationship.

Rarely do researchers aspire to Goffman's substance (Glaser and Strauss, op. cit., p. 136):

> Goffman is among the most prolific inventors of concepts in sociology. . . . These are integral to the development of his theoretical frameworks: He says of his *Stigma* (1963) framework: 'This task will allow me to formulate and use a special set of concepts.' Goffman typically begins his books by presenting his theoretical framework. From this he builds upward and outward. 'In logical steps'. He introduces categories one after the other, and simultaneously develops this framework by discussing their referents and the relationships among them. For instance, in *Stigma* we are introduced quickly to stigma itself, then to virtual and actual social identity, and other categories, also to relevant properties, conditions, processes, tactics, actors, and consequences.

Obviously there are many reasons for the variety of Goffman's terms. One is that in proliferating concepts Goffman has made light capital of those he has already endowed. Another is that his starting point is usually that man, the individual, is a calculative being and presumably most sociologists either disagree or cannot bring themselves to say (1969, p. 86):

> Individuals typically make observations of their situation in order to assess what is relevantly happening around them and what is likely to occur. Once this is done, they often go on to

exercise another capacity of human intelligence, that of making a choice from among a set of possible lines of response. Here some sort of maximization of gain will often be involved, often under conditions of uncertainty or risk. . . .

A further reason is that Goffman can see the significance of one observation for many contexts. Thus he does not simply work from his 'concepts' but because his concepts are both sensitizing and categoric (as far as one can tell) he can turn a piece of data about as if it were a wheel (1961, p. 192):

Another hospital example of working the system was scavenging. . . . Saucers used by staff as ashtrays in the hallways of the administrative offices of some services were periodically searched for usable butts. Open communities of course have scavengers, too, and it would seem that any large system for collecting and then destroying used objects will provide a way for someone to get by. . . .

[Footnote 60.] Compare concentration-camp experience (Kogan: n.d. 111): . . . there were hundreds who time and again tried to ransack the garbage pails in search of edible offal, who gathered and boiled bones.

[Footnote 61.] A significant part of the equipment that small-town boys use to build their world out of comes from refuse depositories of various kinds. The psychoanalytical version of these cloacal-like activities is interesting, but perhaps occasionally suggests over much ethnographic distance from the scavengers in question.

No doubt, however, others could model themselves upon Goffman's style and produce a similar substance. Presumably these neophytes would tackle similar, or even the same, substantive areas for their work. Presumably, too, they would accept that the qualitative method is most apposite in small-scale, face-to-face situations. For both originals and their copies such a move would be a mistake. It would be in error on two counts. First, there is an emergent conflict in the method that is becoming apparent as the body of literature grows. Second, ethnomethodological work is beginning to indicate that it has much more competence than seemed the case at first.

The conflicts in the method have been detailed by Rock (1973, pp. 18–19):

There is a constant strain towards micro-sociology on the one hand, and on the other towards the generation of ideas which do not even reach the heights of middle range theory. More recently this strain has been reinforced by a microscopic historicism which stresses the uniqueness of any cultural system.

And second (p. 20):

> A movement away from the close observation of rules-in-use
> to a rigorous discussion of the common properties and origins
> of those rules would involve an uncomfortable leap from
> phenomenalism to a more conventional sociology.

Just this leap is being made by a leading ethnomethodological theorist, Peter McHugh. Admittedly McHugh's style is difficult to broach at first because the problems he tries to answer do not seem to be sociological. The ways he goes about answering them and the overall answers are undoubtedly of sociological status. His speculative inquiries have consistently been concerned with the ascription of motive (McHugh, 1969; Blum and McHugh, 1971). This he argues is a process in which any collectivity engages as an evaluation of any activity: 'Our interest is in the production of the idea which makes any conception of relevant usage itself possible [as a] stipulative exercise in legislating the use of a "concept" ' (1971, p. 98).

So far it is difficult to tell whether or not this form of the qualitative method will draw adherents from other forms, attracted by philosophical vigour rather than yards of field notes. Further, McHugh's work is complementary with that of Garfinkel. The latter does focus upon whole persons and 'on-going accomplishments' (op. cit., p. 167). Of all the qualitative method's substances, that is, those which hold attraction are still those which demonstrate the fullest faith in the maker of meaning and do strive for exactitude.

In looking to the forms of qualitative research by way of their substance mention has already been made of claims to being 'a sociology'. The substance of this work does seem to indicate that the qualitative method produces a special or sub-sociology.

A peculiarity of this possibility is that whilst social psychology sections are prohibited in the American and British Psychological associations they have recently become accepted parts of the respective sociological associations. Thus we might say that there are grounds for thinking that there is more sociology than psychology in their make-up. A further professional issue is that in both countries qualitative researchers have busily established sub-professional associations: namely, The Society for the Study of Social Problems and The National Deviancy Symposium. From this it would appear that qualitative sociologists exhibit a tendency of their theory: to go micro and have a good interaction.

An examination of the literature, however, reveals a desire to be two things; sociology proper and a special sociology (Glaser and Strauss, op. cit., p. 18):

> We focus on qualitative data for a number of reasons: because
> the crucial elements of sociological theory are often found best

with a qualitative method, that is, from data on structural conditions, consequences, deviances, norms, processes, patterns and systems; because qualitative research is, more often than not, the end product of research within a substantive area beyond which few research sociologists are motivated to move; and because qualitative research is often the most 'adequate' and 'efficient' way to obtain the type of information required and to contend with the difficulties of an empirical situation.

Goffman tends to find that each of his subject areas is so conducive to a special sociology (1963, p. 174), that his concepts transcend and transform hitherto separate substantive areas (1969, p. ix). 'My ultimate interest is to develop the study of face-to-face interaction as a naturally bounded, analytically coherent field – a sub-area of sociology.'

Berger and Kellner (1970) are also sociologists, and sociologists of something in particular (op. cit., p. 70):

We have used the case of marriage for an exercise in the sociology of knowledge, a discipline that we regard as most promising. Hitherto this discipline has been almost exclusively concerned with macro-sociological questions, such as those dealing with the relationship of intellectual history to social processes. We believe that the micro-sociological form is equally important for this discipline. The sociology of knowledge must not only be concerned with the great universes of meaning that history offers up for our inspection, but with the many little work-shops in which living individuals keep hammering away at the construction and maintenance of these universes.

But this issue, as to whether the substance of qualitative research is proper sociology, or a proper little sociology or somehow both, is of more concern to actors than it is to audience. For what the substance does reveal is that qualitative research is still very much a matter of personal quest and may only now be becoming an organized search for the Holy Grail. Whatever its practitioners find, the messages they are sending back are beautifully clear, modest, pictures of what they have seen. Above all, the substance of qualitative research is to be prized as prejudice rectifiers, as contradiction spotters, as sympathizers in the pathetic struggle of small people. The substance of qualitative research shows its authors to be brave people dedicated to the lucid expression of matters most complex.

English productions

There have been two generations of English qualitative-method researchers. The earlier one was influenced by indigenous anthropology. The current one is operating under the guidance of American

135

masters. Whilst the earlier exponents gained respect the later group are gaining actual ground. Already the National Deviancy Symposium has been treated to premature glory and carping criticism. For the problem with both generations has been the scale of their operations. Somehow no really extensive research has been undertaken and no one has emerged as a creator of this alternative culture. This is not to say that there will not soon be a sizeable report on a discrete milieu or that some poor writer will not have every paragraph picked to pieces with desiccated aggression. The problem for any development in English academic culture is that of acceptance by those who have no intention of using developments and contributing to them. For a small academic sphere English sociology is full of able critics but disabled creators, so neither generation has been given a chance or felt able to romp away without one. Admittedly the younger generation can still win a part of English sociology simply because it has undergraduate appeal whilst quantitative methods have students groaning in their chains. Begrudging acceptance is, of course, cunning condemnation. This concealed condemnation emanates from those who have a hand in dishing out funds. So qualitative researchers scratch a little and assemble small-scale reports. Thus the slight support and sparse funds are justified in the eyes of the threatened and crabbed defilers of English sociological development. All in all, English qualitative researchers have suffered indignities similar to those of their American counterparts. And like the latter, book for book, paper for paper and page for page their work has had double the merit of their detractors' own efforts.

I am now writing on substance. English efforts have been less self-conscious and so less theoretical. This is partly because the earlier, more likely generation, was under the impression that their work was an anthropology of modern societies, an investigation of the rituals of urban industrial tribes. In this group we put the work of Willmott and Young (1957) at the Institute of Community Studies. Two other tribes are miners (Dennis, Henriques and Slaughter [1956]) and fishermen (Tunstall [1962]). A second reason for the virtual absence of theory is the related belief that the facts speak for themselves, that theoretical discussion obscures the real issues. This we can only say is the most English of notions and is used as a haphazard defence rather than as an articulate article of faith. So it is in keeping that a philosopher (Winch, 1958, pp. 23, 51, 84) developed the rationale of the qualitative method and is rarely referred to:

A man's social relations with his fellows are permeated with his ideas about reality. Indeed, 'permeated' is hardly a strong enough word: social relations are expressions of ideas about reality.

The analysis of meaningful behaviour must allot a central role to the notion of a rule: that all behaviour is meaningful, therefore all specifically human behaviour is *ipso-facto* rule-governed.

Those rules, like all others, rest on a social context of common activity.

The rare referencing is directly attributable to Winch's status as a philosopher. An Englishman would not ally himself with a philosopher unless he was absolutely sure that he understood him. (Americans quote Wittgenstein but very few Englishmen would dare to.) Winch also makes it difficult to 'do' sociology at all: 'The central problem of sociology, that of giving an account of the nature of social phenomena in general, itself belongs to philosophy' (ibid., p. 43).

Two sociologists of this 'generation' have not been deterred. Both, as it happens, have taken critical questions as their foci. Madeline Kerr's *The People of Ship Street* (1958) and Jackson's *Working Class Community* (1968) take virtually the same perspective: How do most of the working class come to accept being working-class? Why are the ones that get out exceptional? Kerr's thesis is that the experience of the working class is to be socialized by a mixture of 'violence and indulgence'. 'The deprivation of Ship Street people lies in the fact that their arrested maturation leaves them unfitted to play complex or more discriminating roles, even when these are offered to them' (pp. 10–11).

In effect, she assembles an impressive array of evidence to prove that in terms of their experience of each other and the world the people of Ship Street are just right as they are.

It is this note of appropriateness that characterizes the National Deviancy Symposium's products. They do not 'normalize' deviancy or make it sound acceptable. Rather they show the farcical, fudging pomposity of law agencies and the persistent intelligence of lawbreakers. Cohen (1971) has called this a 'sceptical' approach (and has made clear the group's indebtedness to Becker). It is strange scepticism. The group's work is either scandalized or supportive. Society is on trial and is generally guilty of wanting everything its own way. Yet here again is the English attitude that the facts speak for themselves; that law agents are bloated and often vicious hogs whilst crooks are getting by as best they can. The point is simply that the members of this group have not felt it opportune to come out into open opposition. They are biding their time and building their forces. From how they write (which bears the marks of a good, cool style) they might one day be prepared to storm the Bastille and release the prisoners. To those for whom 'all property is theft' the imprisonment of a thief is a politically repressive act. So far being sociologists has dissuaded this group from being practical politicians. To be fair, they have had more of a problem with the portents of repression than they have had trouble in developing a programme. In their substance they are more 'political' than their American models. They have organized groups to help their victim subjects.

'Criminology' or 'deviance' can be modelled directly from America. Organizational and medical sociology, too, take very similar forms. In medical sociology the work of Strauss, Sudnow, Fred Davies, Julius Roth have found favour in the medical sociology research centres of Aberdeen, York and Swansea. Garfinkel, Cicourel and McHugh are the absentee teachers at Goldsmith's College.

The most obvious feature, then, is that English qualitative research has had one generation in 'isolation' and a subsequent generation of purely American parentage. Further, this latter generation has not fully gone into production, nor does it have its own theorists, nor does it have the scope and size of its American counterparts. In one area, though, it has a little more punch and if the National Deviancy Symposium does continue as the hub of qualitative research then there is a good chance of the English workers in this field going voluntarily to the barricades.

An end to theorizing

In qualitative sociology the 'methodology' is very nearly the 'theory'. That is, qualitative sociology is a way of studying and producing theory. As such there is not now a separate strong social or political theory. To put this another way, qualitative sociologists are not generally concerned with making statements to the effect that 'that's the way the world is'. Instead, they prefer to work at a very limited number of assumptions about 'the way people are'. These assumptions have a sing-song circularity for many scholars' tastes. Yet when dialectically and formally expressed they synthesize relationships between culture and structure. (When simplistically put they might read, 'When two or three are gathered together in their own interests they hash up some working agreements.')

The declining use of an intrinsic theory is yet more evident when we turn to the question of why qualitative sociologists do what they do. For questions of purposes are questions of politics. And qualitative sociologists have usually produced a politics of truth-seeking. They rightly claim that the truth is usually masked by myth. And they often argue that demystification is political action enough. They have, as it were, come to find all organization inequitable and hence iniquitous. Becker has worked through this theme in 'Whose side are we on?' (1971) and with Horowitz in 'Radical politics and sociological research' (1972). In this latter essay a sentence contains this assertion: 'the most important fact of our times: the need for a social scientific judgement of *all* available political systems' (p. 53).

Page after page of quotations could be given which state that qualitative sociology is scientific, or that sociology needs to have a scientific method – which is qualitative because of the subject matter —or that qualitative sociology is as scientific as any other sort. Denzin's (1969) opening chapter is replete with such themes. Glaser and Strauss's (1967) opening chapter also makes it clear that qualitative sociology is in the 'truth business'; that it makes and markets facts as good as anybody else's and without fear or favour.

The claim of radicals that this method is a self-indulgent trivializing of one's time – an ego-trip of a lifetime's proportions – is countered by the argument that truth-seeking *is* conservative (Becker and Horowitz, 1972, pp. 57–61). No qualitative sociologist makes any bones about it. He sifts a slag heap of minute data. He works fastidiously at every 'obstinate fact'. He believes in patience more than he believes in politics.

All in all, politics and sociology are necessarily separate for the qualitative sociologist. He may believe that his facts have the critical 'implications'. Goffman (1961) has not deleted all his impolite adjectives (p. 9), Cicourel (1968, pp. 243–73) has insisted that juvenile offenders from poor and rich homes will not get the same treatment.

An Open University course book describes the work of Atkinson (1971) on coroner's reports as sceptical. And, without going into the nuances of following the 's' with a 'c' or a 'k', it could be claimed that a tonal range from dejection to derision can be found in most field reports. One such account deals with how sex offenders account for their actions in court. Characteristically they claim they were off their heads. In conclusion the author clearly and coolly spells out his doubts (Taylor, 1972, pp. 367):

It may be disturbing to some when 'abnormal' ideologies are increasingly articulated but at least we can argue with their advocates. Perhaps the more disturbing alternative is to go on accepting that a large section of our society is subject to sudden blackouts and irresistible urges over which they lack any control.

Doubt may well be the product of the 'politics over there and sociology over here' attitude. For if one has been close to a group for a while, all seems reasonable except the lies they tell and are told 'to keep the peace'. Politics, of course, is more than doubtful about concealment in dishonesty. For politics as an activity is undermined by untruths and mistrust. Clearly, then, a qualitative sociologist does not see every act as a political act. When Becker (op. cit., p. 10) advises that 'anyone who buys a secondhand sail boat should never throw away any piece of junk he finds therein . . .' (and the advice gives several lines of reasoning), the 'taken-for-granteds' of having the money and leisure whilst others are undernourished and driven like slaves would not escape a political reasoner.

I do not wish to pursue this point to that of apoplexy. It is enough to say that politics to qualitative sociologists is usually that which:

1 Some militants shout about
2 Some people do in their spare time
3 Most people can argue about
4 A ritual of figurehead replacement
5 An academic study corridors away from one's own
6 An ugly nuisance

To repeat, politics is simply not a qualitative sociologist's business; he seeks only the truth. And so the political content and purpose of qualitative sociology may be *ad hoc* and muted. In these days when slight dissidence is marked 'militant' the 'leftish' tendency of myth-subversion may have to be championed. For, in conclusion, qualitative sociology is only now coming in from the cold. Its practitioners have been unified in their pursuit of acceptance and in the dignity with which they have damned the quantitative method's ignorance of meaning. Now, coming to the fore, leaving an older generation of quantifiers to flounder on the journeys between funding agencies and professorial chairs, qualitative sociology is likely to polarize in itself. It is likely to be drawn towards the scientism of ethnomethodology or interaction-spotting and towards the politics of dissent (Cohen, 1971, introduction). No doubt this will push qualitative sociology to a contemporary supremacy. My fear is that this form of aesthetics always flowers before its imminent decay. It is as though there have been cycles in its fortunes from Simmel to Mead to Becker. On each occasion the intense public recognition and academic interest has been overtaken by the shatterings of war. And then characteristically a qualitative sociology can take no part. It neither minds the machine nor masters the conflict. Qualitative research is therefore practised and developed in the interludes between wars when economic struggles force nations into collaboration and occupations into isolated jeopardy.

7 The practice of qualitative research

Qualitative methods are as American as popcorn. I mean really getting into it; digging the data; free form baby right on down to where it's at, zap, it's a west-coast seven-day wonder.

Imagine, please, a post-graduate briefing session being given by a mid-Atlantic acquaintance. 'It all starts with an interesting situation. It's just gotta be *inneristing*. Get real people doing their real things. Catch 'em. Catch 'em right at it. Go where the action is. Go where it's happening. Fill your head with what is going down. And BAM you've got data! An exposé. Everyone wants the truth. Tell them what the pigs are doing. Risk a little and tell it all. It's all there waiting for you. Just be neat, clean and cool till it's all on your pad. And WHAM you've got a paper pouring out of your pen!

'It's all a microcosm. You've got a little system there. People just don't realize how representative they are. Their thing is everybody's thing. Every day they're doing it. They're holding themselves in tight and blowing out their blues. They just can't help it. It's normal. You've got straights, crooked and heads. All normal. The straights hate, the crooked are on the run and the heads are high on the sea's breeze. They've got their worlds. Shucks to society man! There's all these worlds going down and that's in one society! Get into a world. Build yourself a hut on the edge of the tribe's village, fiddle with something and they'll come and tell you everything! Telling tales, lies and what's happening. Stick by your hut and they've just got to find out what you're doing. You know everyone wants a friend. Well, soon the whole village wants you as a special friend. Man, you just can't keep up with the data. It's coming from all sides. So let it. Get a part of the action. Get into a dance. Show them a bit of respect. They'll love you for it. And for God's

141

sake open your heart a little. Say what you think now and again. Just keep them going till you've got some questions.

'And then fire, man, fire! Get those questions rolling out just as soon as you've got someone to answer them. Let 'em flow. Good ones, bad ones, little ones and ones you can't say. Keep going deeper and further. It's all in your mind now. You're taking them over. It's truly amazing! It's all going in! It's all making sense!

'So it's a plot. It's a jigsaw. It's a piece of freaking music. You're getting those concepts generated quicker than a typewriter can jingle. You know it's coming. It's coming all over in bubbles and bangs. It's going to be a blasteroo!

'And BANG! The metaphor. The idea has come. It's a process. It really is. This happens, then that happens and splits up all sorts of ways; these splits keep going right until the end, and then it all comes together again. Like a river to the sea. Like the sun in the sky. Like a choir in a dome. They've got their careers! They keep right on going. Marching through Georgia man. It's all in everybody's mind. Sameness and difference. The moon and the tide. It's all so tight and spacious. There's room for all I say!

'Everyone in the tribe is making out somehow. They're getting by. You can't count it. You just know it. Those meanings they've got are real. They live by them. A web of motive. Spinning, spun by each little spider. Everybody uses the same thread. They all make a web. And catch themselves in it. That's the catch. It's their secret. Caught up in worlds of their own making. Everyone is a spider, a web and a fly. That's the reality! Leaping out of their mind, through eyes into the streets and then just jumping back inside again! No wonder it's so complicated. Man is just so busy with his web, grooving around mending and making threads every day. Just get the picture. Remember high school. Talking about teachers, winning the game; passing the test and saluting the flag. You just can't stop busy man from doing his thing. He's into it! Get into him!

'But remember now. KEEP YOUR COOL! It's no use ranting and blowing off. Just lay it on the line. You're not going to change the world. Tell it how it is. Don't start a war. That's what they want. Stand tall and unarmed. Just tell the truth. It's big enough. There's enough of us doing it now. The message is getting through. All men are equal. EVERYTHING SHOULD BE FREE! But if you get political you'll lose your job. You'll waste yourself. Keep going and sending those vibes out. Go down Skid Row. Swim the sewers. Stay with the blacks if you want. And let us know how you're going.

'O.K. you're stuck in a school of nursing. Well get into the operating theatre. Put a gown on and go. Of course they'll let you in. They're interested. They're bored. You're a nice guy. You ask good questions. The dean of the faculty likes your style. You're in there talking with his boys. You're not afraid. And he can read what you write. He really can. It's all so interesting it fits together. Dig, man, dig. Use your situation. Tell your graduate students. As Jerry says, "Do it!" Right. Be hearing from you! Don't let reality get you down!'

The criticism of qualitative method is that of a fashion rather than that of a form. We have difficulty in naming the style. The approach caricatured above is a mix of symbolic interactionism and ethno-methodology. It does not contain direct reference to either searching for shared meaning or breaking rules to see how they work. And this amalgam is intentional. For the qualitative method is a con-spiracy against the quantitative method which thus gains strength by mustering forces. As a fashion the qualitative method is a norm of an 'in-group'. As a force it represents the emergence of a new orthodoxy, a potential victory of nomos over numbers. As a method it is certainly vital and attractive. But more than that it is easy.

Dithering at the edge of the field is reduced to a minimum. The researcher thinks while he is researching. He thinks out what he is researching. He reflects on his own methods and the rules and exceptions he has found. He sleuths his own sureness. He goes to work on his problem; and he is helped by everything in front of him being a fact. The facts fit together because people do and people use these facts to be together. There's no action without interaction; no movement without meaning; no man who can't see himself and no group that cannot grow. The researcher knows all this anyway. That's why he goes from there. He doesn't need to prove it but rather to make good use of it. The truth is that if you get into a system then you can get round it in no time. There might be a lot to it, but you know it does not go on for ever.

And that is why a qualitative method works in a 'bounded situation'. What makes it successful, though, is its optimal use of scarce resources. Every researcher produces something and has his own field. It's like anthropologists having a tribe each. Every researcher goes for the interesting: the times when selective control of people is obvious; the ways people elect to be different and get it together their own way. There is no such thing as messing about with a hypothesis that might work. Qualitative method is guaranteed to produce something if only because it lets informants speak; gives weight to their own words; lets them be whole people making a lot of sense.

The content is thus doubly interesting. People speak in their own words and their voices come across social barriers to reveal truths from the pits of life. And all this intrinsic quality is enhanced by literary style. Qualitative method takes, or makes, a good writer. Its dominant metaphors demand fluency and simplicity. A status passage is an escalator for a willing passenger. A man flows through situations as easily as their saliences flow into him. The literary style and linking metaphor bring the dramatic quality of a narrative.

The qualitative method tends to be interesting, fluent and convincing. For the research has proved exciting for the researcher. Everyone was helpful. The voyage of discovery was largely one of turning different corners, coming upon patterns by a new path. Occasionally, towards the end, the 'making sure' did involve a little repetition. But by that time the end was in view. The paper was as good as written. The qualitative method is cheery work.

Yet, standing against this joy and fruitfulness is doubt. The research report is interesting but it is hardly important. What is produced is some sort of social psychology of a situation. This psychology concerns the ordinary in life. It concerns the survival of a simple people; small in themselves; sociable in their ways; stuck in their ruts. Little is happening in their world. They typify; negotiate; manoeuvre and gesture. It all comes the same in the end. People are determinedly narrow, holding their piece of social space like a solitary soldier on the ramparts of a ruined castle. Obliquely, the folly of man is his humourlessness, his stuffy, near stupid, pomp as he paces his patch.

Perhaps this is why the political message of the qualitative method is so muted. Perhaps the anarchistic aims remain covert not simply to preserve the researcher but because he is unsure of the maker of his data. From the perspective of the qualitative method there is nothing stopping man being free but himself. He messes up his own chances with perverse formulae for playing the game. And so the political message is for more researchers to join in and enjoy the fun. Man might be peculiar but from this perspective much of what he is up to is downright funny. We can look together, play together with besotted man.

In the trivializing of man and the social conditions the qualitative method degenerates to a voyeurist's phantasy. The subject slides from man at work to children at play.

part three

The method of social criticism

My inclination towards critique in sociology

A research report is a statement of findings, a letter to erstwhile friends and an argument about what should be done. Yet it is the quality of argument that determines the report's appeal. Unless the researcher has developed a tough reasoning his report reads like a shopping list.

As a child of May 1968, I was challenged to face the 'relevance' of my work. Did I care about what I was doing? Did I really want to know anything? Did I want my work to have more significance than another notch on my belt? During the ensuing times I learned to get angry and control this anger to some purpose. At first my noises resembled the growls of impotence. Then they changed to barks of rage. But who was my enemy? Was I to protest at everything?

I began to develop a different style: a popular sociology aimed at issues and evils of the day. Whilst working in industry I was also exploring the phenomenon of humour. I realized that I had the choice of arguing explicitly and wrote 'Fool or Funny Man' as an experiment. I thought I had risked a lot but people only said, 'Oh, yes, that's interesting.' Later I felt I wanted to comment directly on the diseases of managers and did so in 'The end of management' (1973).

Whilst engaged in critical writing I have found myself urging others to think hard, speak out and take sides. I have found a willingness to risk censure because of a determined responsibility.

In a polemic every word counts.

8 Fool or funny man: the role of the comedian

An introduction to the central theme: people paid to make others laugh may be understandably miserable

Recently rumours have hinted that some comedians are remarkably unhappy. This unhappiness, rumour alleges, is not because of normal stresses and strains (Sayles, 1969). Rather, it is suggested, some comedians are under-active; they are so lonely and confused as to be suicidal. Paul Ferris (1969) gave an article on the fun industry a sinister tone; he titled his account 'The Deadly Serious Business of Being Funny'. Now business is a serious business and being funny is a way of life. To have the job of 'being funny' could be to entertain a 'deadly' contradiction.

To come straight to a particular point: Tony Hancock and Lenny Bruce might have been the victims of an occupational hazard. Neither died with a smile on his face. Ferris's presentation has implications which suggest a theory big enough to link the death of Hancock – an archetypal little man, a clerk from East Cheam – with that of Bruce, a vitriolic loner, a satirist from Brooklyn. There has always been a suggestion that their deaths were opportune, terminating lives saturated with frustration and, in this sense, suicides. They may be the examples that prove the rule. Hancock and Bruce may have been pushed over the edge by a funny business.

For us, the audience, such notions are doubly disturbing. Ordinarily, within the humour that is part of our daily fare, we believe that the joker is smiling too; we share a smile. He jokes because he is a happy sort of person; he can see the funny side of life. And he is naturally so, these jokers are known as 'born comedians'. Can paid comedians be so different from comics met by habit and by chance? Is it all an 'act'? Are we merely 'an audience' for professional comics? And, just as these speculations might sadden

L

us, do such thoughts make comedians a little weary? Disturbing thoughts of comedians and the pleasurable nature of comedy are obviously incompatible. It is more comforting to feel that comedians must be happy people and contrary rumours are nasty. Comfortable thoughts for the audience may chill the comedian, particularly when this belief is expressed in its doggedly hedonistic form (Hunt, 1969); 'We want to laugh, we have paid to be entertained. Go on, *make* us laugh.'

The business of making people laugh is a single-minded task. 'A joke a minute' is a considerable production rate. And in the cause of production other thoughts must not intrude. Bad taste, such as tantrums or drunkenness, must be repressed. Nevertheless encapsulating people into jobs that can be painful encourages regression to childishness and resorts of mindlessness. Unnaturally, then, we return to this introduction's theme: why should having the job of being funny be painful? My reasoning is that the job of being funny alienates both the praxis (Sartre, 1963) and product of humour. The praxis is to *act* funny, to take a theatrical role, to script that which the comic and his audience try to believe is personal to the comedy. The product of humour is laughter, well-being; the memory of a glimpse of another world. In entertainment the desired product is the more particular well-being, that of a cash return. A good comedian is one who attracts a good-size audience.

Entertainment is a specific context of humour; one of industrial processes and commercial values. Such a context has consequences for the subjects of humour and the skills of comedians. These consequences may be more problematic for a funny man than they are for those he entertains.

A context for the theme: the phenomenon of humour as an act and an experience

Humour is an everyday experience, and as such is a symbolic event and a social affair. From any one of man's languages symbols are drawn, combined, juxtaposed, and by virtue of this juxtaposition prove volatile. The image explodes and laughter erupts. A simple presentation of such a process would use the terms of Gestalt psychology (Koffka, 1935). In a joke carefully and gradually a scene is set and peopled with characters: the 'ground' is laid. Then action is intended by these characters, they find themselves in a tricky situation and appear to be well and truly trapped. But a character twists and suddenly turns. He is out of the situation by a radical change in perspective or irredeemably into the trap through his own actions. This 'figure' devastates the 'ground'. The punch line re-arranges all that preceded it. Laughter comes from the joy of the revelation that the devastation produces (Thouless, 1925, pp. 208–11). Joy on one's own is amusement. Joy shared with others is fun.

The full humorous praxis is the social situation in which a revelation is shared and enjoyed; enjoyed because it is a revelation *and* shared. Simultaneously then, in company, a joke, its devastation and revelation, and its joy, can be both a liberating and unifying experience – a burst out of a carefully laid perspective and an instigator of pleasurable companionship (cf. Koestler, 1964, p. 43). Thus for fun, whilst something is shared at the end of a joke, a frame of reference has to be shared at its beginning. Each must believe that all are compatible, and in comparable situations (nervousness prevents laughter and produces its own symptom – nervous laughter, which asserts that everything could be a joke). So within a shared frame of reference there is a shared awareness of devastation and a shared will for, or acceptance of, its revelation.

Humour is a particular outcropping of seeing and sharing. Things are seen afresh, revealed by a creative change in perspective. This is joyful and doubly enjoyed when it is shared amongst others. As a creative act we know humour to be rare and difficult. As a matter of faith everyone believes that they are just that little bit funny. As a social experience humour is a most appropriate creation: a creation involving story-telling, actions and an essential humanity; without these properties the joke falls flat or becomes sick (cf. Radcliffe-Brown, 1945, pp. 95–105).

So the joker is pictured as a warm and generous man, with eyes for detail and attention towards far-reaching implications. He is both interpersonal and theatrical, he is relating to us and acting out a pungent drama. His reward is our laughter which he can accept, but cannot claim. Perhaps, too, his reward is that as it was initially funny to him he finally has verification from others.

In entertainment humour is both emphatically theatrical and calculatively concerned with the production of laughter. The audience becomes a matter of response so the calculations must penetrate and pattern its frames of reference. Comedians, here, are preferably actors and possibly linked with a specific audience; a market – the type of laughter on which their livelihood depends. As we know to our cost, to act is not necessarily to be ourselves, and to act funny can be a strain when our livelihood depends on it. This emphasis on acting and a cash criterion of success means that entertainment is an industry like any other industry. It is the consequences of having to be a 'natural' in an industrialized role that are troublesome.

149

Elucidation of the theme: an industrial and commercial context of humour particularizes and polarizes the praxis and product of everyday humour and this puts strains on to its productive employers, the comedians

Let us now consider the theme in terms of carefully selected illustration (Becker, 1963, p. 46). First, I shall construct a composite career for a comedian through semi-professional status to the lean years of a 'cabaret comedian' and culminating on the top with the 'television artiste'. Second, I shall try to show the 'separations' that advancement in this career implies. The development demands separation of the comedian from his audience, from his jokes and ultimately from his identity or self.

A semi-professional told me how he started to make money out of his act. 'I was asked to be the master of ceremonies at a family wedding. It went quite well because I knew nearly half of them – and the other half were just as drunk! Then neighbours and friends asked me to do it for their twenty-first parties and weddings. I got around £2 and was expected to make the rest up in drink like everyone else. When an agent asked me if I would like some club work I was relieved. I could get out of the local stuff, go to a town where nobody knew me, earn £10 a night and whip there and back in an evening in time to have a hot chocolate with the wife. I've no hangovers now!'

Each weekend he visits two clubs between 50 and 100 miles away from his home. His agent takes 20 per cent and he has the option of not working when he wants a break or considers a club uncongenial. The clubs are the social club variety, a small semi-resident band, a visiting act per night, with a regular and local clientele. Had this semi-professional wanted 'to go full time' his work would probably have consisted of a blend between rare but valuable private work ('compere' at a businessmen's strip-show as part of an annual night out or product promotion), the ever-growing night-club circuit and holiday camps in the summer.

Looking back, four comedians found several facets of Butlin's 'Redcoat' experience to be important (Carpenter, 1969, p. 9). Dave Allen worked at Butlin's, Skegness, in 1955, 1956 and 1958. He found fame 'hard work'. 'You can't get away once they know you – unless you lock yourself in your chalet. If you put on a moustache and dark glasses they'd think you were doing a stunt.' Roy Hudd's lesson was indefatigability. 'Well, you're sitting there at the end of the day', here his mouth curves downwards, 'and a happy camper comes up to you with "Hallo, knobbly knees!"' Hudd's mouth flips up, his big eyes light, 'well, you've got to smile, haven't you?' Des O'Connor recommends Butlin's to anyone who wants to be a comedian. 'You've got this captive audience, you see. All the shows are free – or they think they are. No worries about the kids or the last bus home; so they laugh that much easier.' Jimmy Tarbuck saw his experience more as a technical training – learning to be an all-rounder. 'It's the only way to learn. You've got all these people to entertain and you've got to make them like you before they'll laugh. You learn to use a microphone, to meet people, to turn your hand to anything.' And Tarbuck said, 'It's better training than the pubs. You can't rely on dirty material.'

Butlin's serves, then, as a crash course 'on the boards' – that trying time between being 'on the bottle' and 'on the box'. Four currently successful comedians learned to take fame, reply with a switched-on smile, from a captive family audience. These comedians have arrived on top and can now be called entertainers. The entertainment industry for them is comprised of live performances in pantomime and summer shows, television series (in which they perform songs and sketches linking guest artists) and the recording industry which attends to their audience's music. Thus there is an annual cycle to which entertainers can aspire – a cycle which utilizes the interdependence of the entertainment industry to full advantage. This cycle is shown with annotations in Figure 8.1.

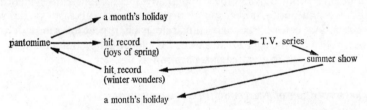

FIGURE 8.1 *An annual cycle for comedians-cum-entertainers integrating themselves into the interdependent industries of entertainment*

This cycle keeps the entertainer in the public's eye through a different emphasis on each type of medium at any time. During the television series the 'latest record' is sung – as it is during the summer show and pantomime.

For most comedians the status of a nationally recognized entertainer is the peak of their career, as humour is culturally and linguistically bounded. The next rung down is the same cycle without his records where the comedian is a 'charactor actor' with his television series in the autumn; the cycle of Charlie Drake, Harry Worth, and the late Tony Hancock.

Both entertainers and character actors work within a production process on stage and before the camera. The skeleton of this process is shown in Figure 8.2.

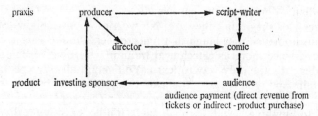

FIGURE 8.2 *The production process for a show in which entertainers and character actors are employed*

For the purpose of simplicity, entertainers and character actors can be called comics; their purpose is to get people to enjoy themselves, or, as Ken Dodd preferred in an interview to 'encourage them to laugh'.

I now wish to show how this career is fraught with separations, separations that entail an accumulating series of divorces between the comic and the complete process of humour. For it is to these separations that I wish to attribute frustration and any 'suicidal tendencies'. I have taken the liberty of arranging these separations in terms of an increasing alienation from different aspects of life; of being estranged from others and finally oneself. I have no evidence that such a series, an accumulation or simple increase, actually occurs. As before, the data illustrate each aspect of separation. Theoretically, though, such a series could add up, but practically it is convenient to treat each separation as discrete.

The separation of the comic from his audience

In entertainment those who share jokes with the comic listen to him *en masse* as a distinct audience who respond to him with laughter. Thus the milieu of the comic's humour becomes a problem for him. Somehow he must enable those he does not see, and cannot know, to laugh. In militaristic terms the audience is not a problem, it is the enemy – it has to be got over to the comic's side.

Tony Hancock experienced considerable strain whenever he started such a battle. 'When I was compering the Blackpool Show on TV this summer I would stand in the wings shouting: "Get on with it, you idiot! What the hell d'you think you are doing? Pull your finger out, you nit!" The stage hands thought I was insulting them at first, and got pretty narky. But I was talking to myself, out loud, insulting myself. It was my way of getting up steam, reaching the right pitch of self-confidence to face the audience' (Ottoway, 1966, p. 62).

A semi-professional told me that the enormity of the audience was one of the reasons that he went no further with a career in entertainment. With smaller audiences he could size up the situation and manipulate them into laughter. 'The first five minutes is warm-up. There is all the tension of selling yourself. Before you go on you try to find out who was at them last time, yesterday, or last week, something like that. Then you try to remember what his style is and drop the same sort of jokes. Next you need to know who is celebrating. Better still, are there any celebrities? If there is a table with twenty or so shining faces round it you can aim some of your slightly blue stuff at the motherly-looking one. Hopefully she's the VIP for that party. If she giggles, the rest will shriek with laughter. Really, it's at her letting herself go, but the audience think it's the joke and get warmed up to the next one. Once the mayor and I were there for the first time. The whole lot giggled away all night and paid me double at the end!'

The full-time comic may be a celebrity in his own right. His problem is not that of spotting the social groups out for a good time, but of re-establishing his persona and capitalizing on it. The formula involves his own clichés – 'Dodgy' from Norman Vaughan, 'Well, really!' from Frankie Howerd – with the universal clichés of 'Not you, madam' and 'Thank you, sir' for direct reference to people in the audience. The personal and occupational clichés revitalize 'the old comedian, the one you all know and love'. Nevertheless a failure could be an omen, a death-knell for a particular persona; the end of the act. Like any of us, the comic strives to avoid failure as well as achieve success. His success is his popularity and the audience can withhold its support each time he entertains. To sustain their support the comic continually reviews and then revises his 'gags' or 'patter'.

The separation of the comic from his jokes

The comic seeks new, quality jokes which he can enact within his established range of routines. There are many standard retorts in 'cross patter' performances (establishing repartee with hecklers) but the 'stand-up' comic (loosely linking gags around themes) must first catch his joke. Two professionals suggest that there are problems of both recognizing and revising a funny thought. John Cleese knows the problem of devising a personal cliché: he doesn't think you can consciously create a catch-phrase. 'I'm sure the person who thought up "I've arrived and to prove it I'm here"', he said, 'couldn't have known how successful that would be. You have to keep on plugging something before it gets well known. Right now we're obsessional about ferrets and by the time we have got fed up with them, in six or seven weeks, everyone else will just have

caught on' (Melville, 1969, p. 585). And then the comic can listen
to others talking, searching for raw material. Billy Russell thinks
that a comic has to work hard on a raw joke. 'A great deal of the
humour is evolved from some native utterance which has struck the
listener as comical and the originally unintentionally "comic"
saying has been trimmed, doctored, and rephrased to make a good
joke with a punch' (Gough, 1968, p. 8).

As something of a consequence, good jokes are precious. A semi-
professional uses personally compiled gag-books and the works of
Obern. He also hopes that he does not have to go back to the same
club too often. In earlier days a few jokes could be borrowed from
the radio, but now the media have too blanket a coverage. Now,
too, there is built-in obsolescence – or television. The 'sample'
audience is virtually the 'universe'. Norman Vaughan said that for
the first six weeks of being compere on 'Sunday Night at the
Palladium' he was on probation and had to use his own material.
On the sixth Sunday he ran out of gags, but passed the test, and
was awarded the services of two script-writers.

Being scripted, having your act written for you, separates the
comic from the comedian and creates a character actor *at* whom
people laugh. The comic becomes a clown. This is a circumstance
of dependence for the comic; the script-writers have to make him
funny. In a television series this can involve a determined exploitation
of the ex-comedian's psyche. Hancock said to Robert Ottoway
(Ottoway, op. cit., p. 63):

> I have to feel that the material reflects me. I see Green and
> Muir practically every day. We discuss what's going into the
> new series. But the important thing is that they should get to
> know as much as they possibly can about me. Delve underneath.
> Burrow into my psyche. Sort out the inner man. They have
> to know how I put things across in conversation before they
> can project the right sort of stuff for an audience.

There are many parallels with psychiatric processes and Hancock
certainly saw the processes as being, in part, therapeutic. But the
outcome is a funny man – a hilarious persona who does not joke.
His actions and views are a joke. He gets in a tangle with a television
repair man (which should play on the viewers' fears), he bitches
with the next-door neighbour, or martyrs himself as a blood-donor.
He sees everyday life as a joke, our lives as a joke, but it makes him
a clown, a fool. We could laugh at life, instead we laugh at him.

In this dependence situation the comic is doubly dependent:
there are two script-writers against one actor. This is not to claim
that a dyad team of writers gangs up on the actor, but rather that in
structural terms they are a coalition (Caplow, 1968, ch. 3) which

makes the comic an isolate. Eternal triangles are notorious for neurotic dynamism. This must reinforce the comic's dependence and the script-writers' capacity to explore his psyche and give him a funny part.

The separation of comic from self

Under the conditions of a scripted act – as a compere or character actor – the comic can be dominated by the persona. This persona was created for him and emphasizes some of his personal qualities. Nevertheless these qualities are usually those of expression rather than thought. The persona ties the comic's means of expression to the character of a link man or of an outrageous fool. Hancock saw this special form of type-casting as a series of repetitions: 'I've always been against a routine. You know, the comedian who used to come on with a funny hat, a tight jacket, and a revolving bow-tie, saying "Hullo, hullo, hullo!" I've never heard anything on the way to the theatre, only me stomach rumbling! And that's why I gave up the East Cheam character. Boredom. I'd lived with him for too long' (Ottoway, op. cit., p. 60).

The created character can have immense potency for its makers, media and actor (Ferris, op. cit., p. 71):

> A series can become a monster. This happened with Johnny Speight's 'Till Death Us Do Part', which became a national habit because the fearful Alf Garnett's prejudices and blasphemies touched heaven knows what in the national soul. His subjects have traditionally been the stuff of blue comedians' patter: God, sex, race, and family strife. But Garnett didn't make jokes about them; the joke lay in the way he flaunted his prejudices. . . .

But Alf Garnett fought back. His actor, Warren Mitchell, persistently denounced him on a promotion tour of Australia. Mr Mitchell was also involved in minor altercations with those who congratulated him for the courage of his convictions. Thus the comic can be exploited by his own act. And it is part of mass media's folk-lore that each actor has his great character part, preferably in a series running very successfully for a number of years.

These separations originate in the specialization of industrialization and the cash nexus of commercialization. That which is separated is the praxis and product of humour and that which could suffer as a result is the comedian. The comedian is pared down from a person to a highly specific role. The comic is the genus for two species: the compere (all-round entertainer) and the character actor. For the comic the audience is the enemy and each performance is an appraisal of his act. The more of an act his art becomes, the more finding new jokes takes him to the door of two script-writers, who can exploit his psyche to make him funny and leave him with a definite dominant persona that is carefully anchored in many of his characteristics. The friendly stranger (Simmel, 1950, pp. 492–508) can be turned into a friendless stranger to himself.

Variations on the theme: exceptions refine or refute a rule; semi-professionals and satirists may avoid, or render inevitable, strains within the industrial structure of fun

Exceptions, of course, seldom prove rules. They are exceptional in the sense of being outside or transcending the formulated rule. Those outside a rule provide a basis for its redefinition. Those above a rule can be in a position to destroy it. In entertainment there are many content with moderate success. There are many support comedians or 'feeds'. There are also those to whom success is irrelevant. They define their own frame of reference; their own awareness and script. Satirists do not have a market.

Some comedians do not seek success

The semi-professionals I talked with were horrified at the thought of going into show business. To them it meant an accumulation of inevitable anxieties; hundreds of miles' travelling; being exposed to recognition on the streets; leaving the family to the wife and supporting many employers and employees (agents, secretary and road-manager). A semi-professional is a hit-and-run comedian with a steady job and a regular home life.

Derek Guyler and Sheila Staefel are feeds. They act in sketches and provide the comic with the grounds for his punch line. Guyler turned down a show at the Palladium and both have regularly rejected the suggestion of their own television series. In an interview they said that they did not want the strain of competing with other comedians and the consequent privatization. Interestingly, they suggested that the separation of a comic from other comics would be the most painful for them. Privatization would be indicative of turning yourself into a business and of fearing one 'company-comedian' copying your product too closely and challenging your market percentage. Hancock was wary of the act and the abnormalities of success (Ottoway, op. cit., p. 63):

> The kind of comedian I want to be must be funny for a reason.
> He has to have a home to go to, and a bed to sleep in – so
> that the audience can believe him when the half-hour is over.

Too many comics can be turned on and off like taps. They have their place, of course, but it's not mine.

Some comedians work against their jobs

Satire and invective destroy the social construction of normality. The process involves the creation of an invalid syntax; a mad 'ground' on which 'normal figures' are projected. A clutch of chartered accountants return from a day at the office to their commune and do their own thing; some leather-tanning, sitar lessons, and potted plant cultivation. This image suggests that chartered accountants are hippies and that hippies are conservative conformists. What is left of the image?

Lenny Bruce battered away at the reasonableness that surrounded him (1966, p. 42):

> If I talk about a chick on stage and say, 'She was a hooker', an uncontemporary person would say, 'Lenny, you are coarse and crude.'
> What should I have said?
> 'If you must be specific, you should have said "prostitute".'
> But wait a minute . . . the word has become too general. He prostituted his art. He prostituted the very thing he loved. Can he write any more? Not like he used to – he has prostituted his work. So the word 'prostitute' doesn't mean any more what the word 'hooker' does. If a man were to send out for a one-hundred dollar prostitute, a writer with a beard might show up.

In satire the syntax is more or less attacked and thus more or less imaginatively destroyed. Whilst wit tickles or punctures an everyday logic, satire damages it for its absurdity. A whole style of life or section of society can be devastated with economy and without retort. Bruce did not script himself. He learned to control his patter, his style (op. cit., p. 103):

> When I talk on the stage, people often have the impression I make up things as I go along. This isn't true. I know a lot of things I want to say; I'm just not sure exactly when I will say them. *This process of allowing one subject spontaneously to associate itself with another* is equivalent to James Joyce's stream of consciousness. I think one develops a style like that from talking to oneself.

The satirist, then, confronts his audience, scripts himself and expresses himself. There are no separations in his role, whatever his success. But the court jester is no longer immune from the anger that he creates. So whilst the character actor enfeebles himself, the satirist knowingly exposes himself to risk – an exposure which flushes out his opponents.

The social context of the theme: humour has relevance for social continuity and change. Wit is conservative and satire radical. Entertainment encourages types of wit and satire. Some comedians will be the casualties of change in the industry

It has been argued that wit and satire are remarkably different forms of humour. Wit, like death, is a great leveller. The joke is human folly; people taking themselves too seriously, getting a bit above themselves, pushing their roles too far. A mother-in-law is only a mother-in-*law*. Her legal claims on the husband are dubious. He already has a mother. Witty jokes accept the *status quo*. In mother-in-law jokes the institution of monogamous marriage is accepted. The twist is that people do not always conform appropriately. Poking fun at them taunts them; challenges them to come out from behind their act, attempting to puncture their postures. Then we are level; rendered accessible and equal by wit. The issue is the humanization of humans. Humans too big for their boots; too stereotypical to be taken seriously or too deviant for their own good. Wit and wit-in-miniature, irony, are in conclusion proto-reactionary perpetuating social structures and the social structuring of roles. Wit opposes change as being deviance and demands stability by insisting that we are all human, all fallible and all too often foolish.

Satire and its virulent form, invective, attack the *status quo*. Positions and everyday meanings are ridiculed. Lenny Bruce attacked modern life because he believed it obscene. As a result his attacks were categorized as obscene. The *status quo* to a satirist is a juxtaposition of prejudice and piety. Prejudices provide stereotypes and stigmas which are valid targets for wit; targets that should not talk back. So Bruce, like Swift, groaned about his stigmas and battled directly with the prejudices designed to keep him in his place. Simultaneously satire attacks piety; that demarcation of sacred topics and rituals. Satire praises nonconformity and praises such acts as those of courageous innovation. Satire suggests forcefully the radicalization of society; that only a revolution will make the slightest difference to everyday life. Satire is, in sum, proto-revolutionary: if the audience accepts the satirists' view the world can never look 'normal' again.

Yet both wit and satire are only suggestive of stability or radical change; they are *proto*-reactionary and *proto*-revolutionary. The joke is not a prognosis for two reasons. First, because it does not contain the desired alternatives, it is enough to mock people into humanizing themselves and to ridicule society into radicalizing itself. Second, the joke is fun; there is the liberation of a laugh and the joy of sharing laughter. They differ basically because wit is a joke at 'them' – at others. There is ease of laughing at others. Satire is disturbing – the whole society is its subject; no holds barred, no subject debarred. There is the dis-ease of laughing at ourselves.

Entertainment places primacy on wit and on a wit with mass appeal. Such a breath of appeal demands considerable research on the appropriate subject matter. Fiona MacCarthy (1969, p. 7) sent back this report after a day's trip to the capital of the summer shows:

Blackpool's jokes have a strict formula. There is a certain ruling on what is and what is not funny. A nudist is a laugh; a black pudding is a laugh; and so are kilts and coffins, pregnancy and farting, brassieres and toilet paper, constipation and false teeth. Peeping Toms are good clean fun, and nuns can be hilarious, and foreigners (particularly cannibals) and harems. And the greatest roars of laughter greet the mother-in-law syndrome and wedding nights, adultery and poisoning your wife.

The jokes they like in Blackpool are also very localized and feature Sheffield blondes and Burnley men and Cardiff dames. A Leeds doctor who admitted that his favourite sport was sleighing. A Manchester butcher boy who got a little behind with his orders. . . .

All the locations are urban conurbations with a high proportion of working-class people. Miss MacCarthy could also have noticed the use of puns on television commercials. Such commercials create an appropriate subject matter and conveniently change every so often. In brief, good clean family entertainment. This is stand-up comedy linked with songs and other acts. Repartee, and the role of irony, are not possible, as entertainment relies on strict timing, minimal audience participation and scripted comics. The old cross-patter experts Ted Ray and Tommy Trinder, for example, are consequently less successful – integrating the second media level of the radio and quality night-club circuit. Nevertheless entertainment encourages its form of wit directly and discourages satire indirectly.

British television has produced a novel form of satire. It is arguable that politicians were considerably embarrassed by the satire at the turn of the sixties. It is evident that Independent Television screens a show a night and no satire spots. And it is interesting that a zany, timeless surrealism has replaced the weekend satire shows. Varsity club radicals, self-script expensive programmes with export potential.

Paul Ferris (1969, p. 69) called this hybrid 'comedy of the absurd' and reported a piece of planning.

We cut out Lochinvar and the Women's Institute applauding. Then a quick shot of the nose-blowing contest. Then there's a sheep flying past, and a jump-cut to the Epilogue – the wrestling match to decide the existence of God. *So the existence of God has been proved by two falls*, with the Women's Institute applauding.

As they write their own script, their show is their business (ibid.):

Money was often referred to, especially their hopes of 'residuals' – fees for repeat transmissions and the elusive overseas sales. . . . At one point Eric Idle suggested a sketch where every character had the name of a footballer. Cleese frowned and said, *'That'll* be good for our American sales.' 'Oh well, if you're going to say that about every sketch' said Idle. 'Every *other* sketch', said Cleese.

It is possible that the producer-controlled 'family show' and the comedian-controlled 'mad show' are the two forms of wit and satire to be sustained and developed in entertainment in the 1970s. The family shows will feature either the comic as compere or as lead in a domestic comedy series. These comics can be recruited directly and shaped immediately to suit the programme. Disc-jockeys and pop singers are more used to linking acts or performing with some dancers and a guest. Simon Dee and Tony Blackburn are interchangeable as compere comics. For domestic comedies actors can be recruited directly from drama school or repertory. They are less likely to take the part personally, they are trained to act and can be replaced in subsequent series.

The 'mad shows' are likely to move further away from topicality and link more with sophisticated wit. Gradually I suspect that wit's target, ever-present human folly, will be the message from such shows. Satire's force and *cri-de-coeur* will be seldom seen or heard. The script-writer–actor–businessman will soften somewhat towards fellow script-writers, actors and businessmen.

In such an age when recruitment is more closely related to the sorts of comics required, unfortunate unhappiness can be avoided. It is in this period of transition from development of, to dominance by, a medium that indicative incidents can occur. Those likely to suffer are comedians who have trained in pubs and clubs, arduously and assiduously established themselves and are then employed at the peak of their careers as comperes or actors. The satirical comedian is excluded from entertainment because he is incapable of separating his act from himself and thus is under his own control.

Slowly satirists may increasingly be labelled as undesirable and placed in the heretical category for their insistence on going against the grain.

Both the club comedian and the satirist must be aware that entertainment is the provision of a particular form of humour; that of ease-creating wit. The comic should become as reactionary as he considers his audience to be. This factor may provide a final perspective on the problematics of the comedian role. A comedian considers how things are related and how enervatingly different things look if differently related and then laughs at the results of this imaginative enterprise. When this skill is no longer demanded, or its constructions considered undesirable, what is often called a 'tragic vision' may become a personal tragedy for those comedians who see no way out of their skills and insights.

9 The place of class in contemporary sociology

The concept of class has prime utility in studies that range from our own society to our own situation. But somehow the concept usually slips through the user's fingers. By some means sociology undergraduates miss the concept's meaning and become bitter towards problems of definition. By chance, it seems, good sociology goes bad and having done so is best set aside. To many the concept is an antiquity and an embarrassment.

I find the concept's lack of use, understanding and emphasis something akin to a conspiracy to deprive sociology of its left foot. I wish to account for this with a superficial résumé of the concept's career.

The concept of class has suffered a peculiar fate in British sociology. From Marx to Booth it was clear that there was a working class, enslaved, diseased and checked by crippling poverty. From Rowntree to Marshall the working class were next to a middle class, and the latter were simply ordinary people with conspicuously better manners and chances. And from Lockwood to Bernstein the working class couldn't be middle class, they impediment themselves with a hand-to-mouth addiction to money and a snatched phraseology sensible only to each other. British sociology has depended upon there being a working class and there being partisan sociologists publishing their vitality and deprivation.

In fact the concept of class has suffered because of the attempts to squeeze status in as a definition of middle class. American sociology, it seems, from Park through Linton, the Lynds, Warner, Merton and Blau has sought the finer distinctions within 'middle America'; social rank, socio-economic group, reference group all lace the hierarchy: the hierarchy from dustbinman to circuit judge and bank president that is dominated by white America.

Both British and American sociology have been shoved back into place by rare writings of pointed quality. Westergaard's *The Myth of the Withering Away of Class* is a gem in its refutation of fancy with plain fact. Gordon and C. Wright Mills have piloted back to a concern with the qualitative detail in the lives of the poor, rich and those getting by. But now yet another trivialization threatens our sanity. Blau and Duncan's *The American Occupational Structure* (1967) muddies every conceivable distinction with measurement. They begin their opus with 'In the absence of hereditary castes or feudal estates, class differences come to rest primarily on occupational positions and the economic advantages and powers associated with them' . . . and so 'unless otherwise indicated all tables refer to all men between the ages of 20 and 64 in the civilian non-institutional population of the United States in March 1962'.

This looks fair enough until we wonder about the running equation

class differences = occupational positions = adult male
workers

The authors are in fact sliding from sociology into demography because of the data they used. In keeping with a disregard for class and a fascination with reaching middle-status levels, they refer to theories of stratification and make mobility their 'dependent variable'. Mobility, or failure to make it, is then made the object of the inquiry *and* the determinant of class. All men are individuated and within their occupational groups. Their classes come to resemble huts into which they have been herded: 'The patterns of mobility reveal the existence of two class boundaries which divide the American occupational structure into three classes – white collar; blue collar and farm'; and then they give their criteria: 'Each boundary limits both intergenerational and intragenerational downward mobility between any two occupations on either side of it to levels below theoretical expectation but permits upward mobility in excess of chance' (op. cit., p. 78).

Thus though Blau and Duncan see strata they never depict stratification: it's all a matter of how things affect mobility. Some do and some don't but do not expect surprises.

For example (op. cit., p. 359):

Some of the results reported in this chapter depart little from what might be expected on hypotheses generally accepted in the sociological literature. We have, however, been able to specify and support them a little more clearly than is sometimes the case. We found that being reared in a broken family is a handicap for subsequent status achievement.

The mobility they examine is every form of movement. The cause is always the same; the drive for success in the USA. Blau and

M

Duncan really catalogue what holds the unlucky ones back – like being a southern Negro from a large broken family, share-cropping out in the scrublands.

Yet still they use archaisms like class and status. It is as though this most contemporary of texts was compelled to curtsy to tradition. But in so doing they mock their heritage and leave it in disarray. For all their labours the message is trite: 'The job world is one big department store and when you are in it you travel by escalator going up, down and around.'

Nevertheless their work is impressive. And, in the confused state of current thinking, occupational structure might just be class structure made easy to get at; mobility may be just the peep-hole we need. And I know that many sociologists are entranced by the deft manipulation of statistical tools. But it cannot be said strongly enough, *occupation is not class*. Occupation structures are, by definition, simple hierarchies. Class structures are segregated milieux. It is easy, to the point of being facile, to 'prove' an occupation structure. It is difficult, to the point of being worthwhile, to identify the organs of the body politic.

In this paper I wish to argue that the concept of class is theoretically vital even if current researchers are not sure what to do with it. If one take the usual 'indices of stratification' a neat structure is virtually guaranteed. But the price of the guarantee makes the commodity worthless. Class is a concept that encompasses the poor, the filthy rich, the military and the institutionalized. These groups are the class structure itself. Their existence is a political fact. And the concept of class is the sociological use of political fact when considering the future of social forms.

I begin with a slight proof of my first assertion; with a re-analysis of someone else's data.

Class as classification in a social structure

There is, to be sure, a sociology of stratification, as if a suturing of second ribs from our founding fathers. From Marx comes the differential distribution of power, a polarization from the means and relations of production. From Weber comes status, the styles of living, the chances of life, and the honour of social positions. Whilst from Durkheim comes the differential distribution of task from the dividing and sub-dividing of labour. Each thinker envisages a structure clear enough to be able to identify the forces of its structuring. The problem now, though, is getting to the structure rather than the forces. If there is a rational pecking order, a relentless gradation from have-alls to have-nothings, in what ways is this structure to be depicted? For in some sorts of structure even the simplest factors get complicated. And these simple factors have little to do with Marx, Weber or Durkheim directly. Rather, occupation, education and property are taken as structural factors because they are structured anyway. To be honest, class is no longer a problem. Neither is status or even position. All that matters is what the structure looks like.

I was fortunate, in arriving at the end of a study, 'to find the structure'. Margaret Stacey and 'her team' had undertaken all the fieldwork for a replication of her community study. Everyone agreed that the data looked interesting but there were not many significant differences to be had. In wondering why, it seemed obvious to consider the extent of similarity first.

Method

Banbury's interviewers asked a number of questions on birthplace; education; occupation; domestic circumstances and voting. The answers to these questions were separated and given mathematical values. In the process 517 interviews proved usable in that they contained recorded answers on all the selected questions. Thus the subsequent analysis is of a sub-sample of the survey sample. The operation produced nineteen bits of data and their descriptive statistics are given in Table 9.1.

Table 9.1 can be read from left to right. The first column simplifies the data and indicates that the features have been transformed into variables. The description and coding can be read together. Generally the variables are simply a matter of the presence or absence of an attribute and so treated as '0 or 1 variables'. Nine variables have been constructed to the usual format. In this way their variations are based upon the range found at the time of survey. Amount of earnings, for example, varies from less than £10 to more than £40. And so at this early stage it is clear that no distinction is made between the 'affluent', 'rich' and 'plutocratic'.

Continuing now to the distributions found, it is clear that every variable varied. The ranges go from minimum to maximum value; the averages are roughly in the middle and the standard deviations show normal distributions with very few exceptions. The survey centred upon men in full-time, wage-earning, skilled manual jobs, who rent their homes. The edges of the study touch housewives who did not vote at the last election and professional people who had fee-paying education and now live on profits and own their own homes. From the descriptive statistics we might say that those surveyed were the normal spread of people who work for a living. In essence from a glance at both the measures and the means we expect consistencies.

165

TABLE 9.1 *The class data as variables and their distribution (cf. Bechhofer, 1969, pp. 112–14)*

Analytic title	Description	Coding	Minimum	Maximum	Mean	Standard deviation
BORNBY	Born in Banbury	No: 0, Yes: 1	0	1	0·414	0·498
BREDBY	Bred in Banbury	No: 0, Yes: 1	0	1	0·466	0·499
LEFTSC	School-leaving age	15: 0, 16: 1, 17: 2, 18+: 3	0	3	1·329	0·671
FEDUCT	Fee-paying education	No: 0, Yes: 1	0	1	0·095	0·293
HIDUCT	Higher education	No: 0, Night school: 1, Tech. col: 2, Teacher's training: 3, University: 4	0	4	0·286	0·884
HOUSEY	Housewife	No: 0, Yes: 1	0	1	0·015	0·124
FULTIM	Work full-time	No: 0, Yes: 1	0	1	0·781	0·414
PARTIM	Work part-time	No: 0, Yes: 1	0	1	0·199	0·400
RGCODE	Occupational group	As customary*	1	7	3·830	1·740
HJCODE	Status group	As customary*	1	8	3·335	1·663
INCOME	Source of revenue	Wage: 1, Salary: 2, Fees: 3, Profit: 4	1	4	1·333	0·666
WEEKLY	Amount of earnings £	less than 10: 0, 10–15: 1, 15–19: 2, 20–24: 3, 25–29: 4, 30–34: 5, 35–39: 6, more than 40: 7	0	7	2·702	1·581
DAD JOB	RG code	As customary*	1	7	3·603	1·621
NO VOTE	Voted or not	No: 0, Yes: 1	0	1	0·994	0·076
LIBERAL	At last general election	No: 0, Yes: 1	0	1	0·066	0·248
LABOUR	At last general election	No: 0, Yes: 1	0	1	0·520	0·500
TORYTT	At last general election	No: 0, Yes: 1	0	1	0·414	0·493
RATEHM	Rateable value of home £	less than 50: 1, 50–74: 2, 75–99: 3, 100–24: 4, 125–49: 6, 150–7: 7, 175–99: 8	1	0	3·485	1·240
TENURE	Form of occupancy	Job: 1, Council: 2, Rent: 3, Mortgage: 4, Own: 5	1	5	3·035	1·161

* See Bechhofer, op. cit.

We seek consistencies between variables by the simple conviction of correlation. Correlation asks: 'Does an increase in the holding of one property vary in a way similar to an increase in another; sufficiently strongly, that is, to reject a null hypotheses?' A correlation matrix is offered in Table 9.2. This table is a full matrix of all the correlations 'above a 99 % confidence limit'. Correlations, that is, above a 0·01 level are all recorded. This convention enables me to draw up the matrix directly, and enables the reader to find any interesting 'isolated' correlations he may seek.

It is open to anyone to chart his own path through the correlation matrix. The path I have chosen was mapped by considering structuring as an accumulative biographical path. The path is plotted in Figure 9.1.

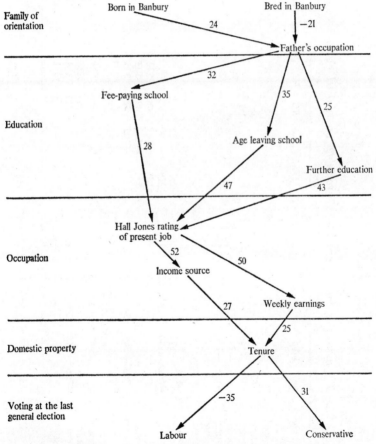

FIGURE 9.1 *Some correlations selected to chart a biographical path*

TABLE 9.2 The matrix of correlations between variables above 0·01 significance level (Garrett, 1947, p. 455)

Analytic Title	Born	Bred	Left	F.e.	Hi.e.	H/s wF.	FITM.	PtTM.	RG	HJ	Income	Weekly	Dad job	Lib.	Labour	Tory	Rates
BORNBY																	
BREDBY	·876																
LEFTSC	−155	−146															
FEDUCT	−151	−130	521														
HIDUCT	−126	−136	599	396													
HOUSEY																	
FULTIM						−237											
PARTIM							−197										
RGCODE	−184	−172	442	256	362		252	−235									
HJCODE	−202	−186	478	285	428		219	−200	924								
INCOME			293	156	220		180	−162	482	522							
WEEKLY			273	136	270		531	−507	439	503	490						
DAD JOB	−243	−209	347	320	255			−105	329	323	166	205					
NO VOTE																	
LIBERAL			−164	−152					−196	−221	−265	−142	−156				
LABOUR			150	157					197	228	259	153	166	−276			
TORYTT									311	338	245	220	201	−191	867		
RATEHM	−206	−219	236	204	242												
TENURE			252	229	194				263	291	276	253	218	—	−355	313	286

Figure 9.1 suggests that the stratification forces come into play at different times in a man's life. More generally, the correlation matrix and diagram both suggest that there are but differences in degree between the sub-sample's respondents. In brief, the survey looked at the same sort of people. They might even be the same class. For it would be very difficult to argue that there are two or more classes evident in the data. There is no empirical guidance as where to 'cut off'. The data indicates only that the man is within the same structure.

Moreover, matters of consciousness, relationships and culture have not been subject to scrutiny in this analysis. The reader is entitled to ask 'Where is the concept of class?' Where is the breadth, for example, of the following definition (Gurvitch, 1955, p. 345)?

Social class is a grouping: 1. suprafunctional; 2. vast in its membership; 3. permanent; 4. non-localized but dispersed; 5. factual (not voluntary or coercively imposed) in its emergence and existence; 6. open; 7. unorganized but structured; 8. combative in its orientation; 9. ordinarily resisting its penetration by the all-inclusive, global societies (except when a given social class is dominant in its power); 10. radically incompatible with other social classes; 11. exercising only conditional control and constraint over its members.

Class is more, therefore, than individuals having characteristics in common. Class is about the behaviour and beliefs of groups.

And so I would not claim to have analysed either social class or social structure. This is an analysis of upbringing; occupation; domestic property and political behaviour in a working population. We might have anticipated its findings once we knew its subject population. To use the concept of class we must move a little beyond the accessible. Studies of mobility and property in a normal population approach neither class nor society; they merely describe the mechanisms of the lives of 'ordinary folks'.

Class as a social phenomenon

From where should the sociologist sight his eye? At the bottom, in the middle or on top? Or is it possible to somehow stand at the side? Does the sociologist know enough of what affects his own life to know where to stand?

What is painfully at issue in the sociology of stratification is the sociologist's problem of where to put himself. A sociologist is a man of property; his few possessions secure him in his pursuit of interest. His few possessions being this important, the sociologist counts and counts again his small hoard of treasure and his little heap of coins.

In fact the sociologist is the sociologist of the middle level of stratification, his own level; from the lowest paid worker to the employer.

The sociologist makes the finest distinctions about those around him. By his calculation he is not very far from the top. He registers neither degrees of poverty nor shades of aristocratic riches. The poor are a category apart and it is unseemly to pursue the rich into precise details of their wealth. In this way the sociologist can produce a hierarchy with some degree of success. The remaining inconvenience is that of naming the levels.

So let us being with naming names. Let us say there are three classes in our society. There are masters, hirelings and slaves. Capitalism did not overthrow feudalism – it corrected it. Once there was a master, hireling and slaves. There was a king, 'his' barons, knights, squires and mercenaries, and then the toiling guildsmen, freemen and serfs. Capitalism corrected the dependence upon the qualities of the king by replacing him with committees. The masters are now many.

I wish to argue that the working- and middle-class juxtaposition in sociology is a gutless acceptance of the permissible. We are seeing a polarization of two classes in themselves – the masters and the slaves – and the encirclement of the hirelings into a further class in themselves. This is an historical trend recognized by Mills (1956) and Djilas (1966) as being the phenomena of 'élites' and 'a new class'. Hirelings are those who deal directly with slaves *en masse*, using the rules as their reason and obedience as their virtue. I am not saying that these are the classes of the world or of all states. I am saying these classes are relevant in Britain today. The relevance comes in the future necessity for hirelings to dissemble and defect to the slaves – leaving the masters to do their own dirty work. There may be analogies with other western capitalist countries but I find it necessary to separate out the British situation by virtue of the perpetuation of feudalism's fibres through its capitalist epoch.

The dominant models of relationship in this country are still the master and the slave – the good and the deferential. The hymnist sings of the rich man in his castle and the poor man at his gate – the bailiff doesn't get a line. And this, I think, is a peculiar feature of British culture: the hirelings are very busy amongst themselves making fine status distinctions and codes of conduct. They approach their inherited task with honour.

I come to identify these classes by noticing the spread of titles amongst industrialists; by lumping doctors, lawyers, managers and teachers together and by living amongst people struggling to stay alive and to die. I thought to check on this categorization by considering each class a sphere, as separate realms of experience:

The masters co-determine.
The hirelings collaborate.
The slaves are in conflict.

To be more specific, these are forms of enaction, they are the qualities of relationships within the classes. They are also the forms of explanation used by 'members' of these classes to account for each other's actions – as if an understanding of life itself. The masters co-determine and think the slaves do as well – but when slaves try to do so they constitute a conspiracy. There is, in brief, projection from class experience to another class's motives. The hirelings do deals with each other through extensive contact. The slaves squabble interminably.

Class as a social phenomenon is the depiction of a domination structure. It is the collision of property base and relational culture that produces the structure (and its incoherence if approached as the distribution of the same factors). A domination structure indicates that there are very few inter-class contacts and that these are probably handled by class members who ape the class to whom representation is being made. A domination structure makes exploitation acceptable by being *apparently* mutual.

Class as a societal phenomenon

If master–hireling–slave depicts the main structure what can be said of social deviants and society's jailers? Each class produces its deviants. There are those who realize that they can be different by copying another class's ways. There are those who fail to cope with their own class's ways. There are those who see the structure and prey on its weaknesses for egoistic and atavistic reasons. There are endless crises in a domination structure. For each class contact is yet another test of strength, but more basically there is no intrinsic reason for anyone in any class to feel happy, secure or successful with his lot. For the content of each 'class culture' is individualistic – it is what a class member may expect of a fellow class member. A slave expects conflict, a hireling expects a deal, a master expects more property. The class member who is contacted is trouble for the contacting class member. There is a crisis of trust – of doing something together to get something out of it individually. This crisis of trust is the production force of class deviants.

For all deviants can be located in a class by the nature of their crime [and their subsequent retribution (see Table 9.3). A fine is a caution. An imprisonment is an expulsion. Hirelings are demoted to slaves. Slaves are demoted to unsheltered slaves as gipsies or simple fugitives.

TABLE 9.3   *Simple deviance and justice*

Class	Crime	Punishment
Slaves	assault each other	fine
	thieve from hirelings	imprisonment
Hirelings	assault slaves	fine
	thieve from slaves	
	assault each other	imprisonment
	thieve from masters	
Masters	none	none

Gipsies are the most general 'extreme class', the permanent, propertyless poor who survive by cleaning up society's waste as a co-operative effort. The poor inherit the slaves' waste and so on 'up the structure'.

A deviant is one who objects to either his class's lot or its mode of waste. If the objection is practical it leads to the crimes and punishments itemized in Table 9.3. If the objection is passive it leads the deviant to sickness. In both cases the punishment prolongs the crime. The deviant is made to be the crime for the duration of his punishment.

Thus the groups administering punishment are precious hirelings. Characteristically the legal and medical professions are regarded as being outside society, rather than vital to the control of its self-generated deviance. So too, are the military and para-military 'professions' which arrest and subdue deviance. These hireling groups are in fact 'encircling' society and have internal master–hireling–slave structures as if to be beyond society. It is their hireling mercenary function which gives their class position. It is also their right to use instruments of terror and near random use of them which makes it plain that their job is to police within and between the hirelings and slaves. The slave class recognize them for what they are. The hireling class is ambivalent, hoping for collaboration but finding conflict.

Class and social change

I have spent most of my effort arguing that the middle class loosely conceived is, in fact, the hireling class and rather tightly organized.

Sociologically I am talking about one structure in a structured milieu. Thus politically I am speaking of the false and real class potential of hirelings and slaves. Politically I mean that there can be a polarization of administrators and administrated – and this would make the existence of the masters, the poor and the deviant more visible and more necessary in social action.

I guess that the uniting of slaves, poor and deviant would constitute a revolutionary change in consciousness. As if the working class of Marx was moving from a class-in-itself to a class-for-itself. I have developed these concepts because of their implications for action.

Sociology is about people having the natural right to a free and equal voice, to being man or woman or citizen. Hirelings of the world retire. Distribute your privilege. Name your masters. Prepare to lead a new class.

Thus I am in no way suggesting that there is no middle class. Rather the opposite. There are hirelings: the problem is to see them as a class and to have them see themselves as a class. For if the polarization of master and slave is to be effective in cracking the masters' rod it must be because of a rupture in administration; it must be because the hirelings have moved off as a defunct class to put their skills at the disposal of the slave class. The hirelings are well situated for this work. They have homes, land and enough fat to live on for the duration of their task.

10   The idea of social criticism

Introduction

Social criticism in inherent in sociology. In fact there are so many
perspectives from which method or material can be criticized that it
is difficult to be exact as to the proper subject and course of such
criticism. For these perspectives derive from dialectics of being:
dialectics that have been widely explored by qualitative theorists.
And these perspectives characteristically entail evaluation; what is
happening is good or bad. Every perspective involves an author
making it plain where he stands.

So much for perspectives. There is no one school of social criticism.
There are social critics. There are significant individuals in a social
movement. A social critic is usually a socialist, a humanist and an
agnostic. His work is usually a contemporary statement of historic
truth. The critic himself will probably be periodically persecuted. He
is usually well ahead of his time.

All in all, social criticism is an act of explicit responsibility.
Every critic is deeply aware of his debt to dead men. He is also aware
of all the virtues that are needed to make life worth living. Thus a call
to arms – the unsheathing of revolutionary zeal – is a cry for historical purpose. The call being for men to awake and distinguish dream
from nightmare.

Why does the responsibility of the social critic thus extend to his
feeling responsible for his society? Presumably the answer must lie in
his purposes: in his work having real and symbolic significance; in
his work being an assessment of something in itself and another blow
for the cause of criticism.

Perhaps this cause is to the highest ideals of life – currently to the
many forms of communism. Perhaps all social critics are just sneaky
Reds with loud voices for bellowing about their bleeding consciences.

Perhaps they pompously assume that they have charge of the torch of culture, the flame of civilized being, and thus they should pronounce as a priest. And so perhaps social criticism is no more than a self-justificatory idea; a convenient illusion for frustrated men.

I would suggest that though it is tempting to discard or embrace social criticism it is better to consider it as a method. No doubt, since any words on this subject will offend some, it is better to cause such offence as quickly as possible. So I must confess to being a practising social critic who is therefore less sure of his grounds than his own critics. And if this chapter on the 'idea' dissatisfies the reader I can only refer him to many accounts that I consider superior to my own, to Bottomore's *Critics of Society* (1967) or Stein's 'The poetic metaphors of sociology' (1963) or Bandyopadhyav's 'One sociology or many?' (1971). For rather than claim social criticism to be based on an impeccable theory or to be a plateau of contented consensus between practitioners, I want to claim for it the status of an inspiration for method and an instruction to evaluate this method. Thus the idea is the guiding light or the traveller's constellation of stars. It is, and represents,' the existence of a social movement towards the new. It should be remembered, if nothing else is retained, that all social critics ride upon the tides of history; they are contradictions in terms; they are committed intellectuals.

In this chapter I rely on the analogy of the universe; the North Star and Orion's belt. I wish to make the mental set explicit because it is important to me in organizing a mass of writing. To be honest, I see this chapter as unlikely to dispel all the confusion that surrounds 'political writing'. I hope, rather, to make manifest how one traveller orients himself. All I wish to prove is that action speaks louder than words.

Problems, programmes, projects or purposes?

A full sociological vision must include the following concerns:—
1) concern with the interpretation of the history of modern society; 2) concern with interpreting major modern crises;
3) concern with developing decisive value judgements leading, when possible, to effective action; and 4) concern with systematic ordering of concepts, propositions and techniques to stimulate further enquiry. [Stein, 1963, pp. 177–8.]

It may be remembered that qualitative and quantitative methods presuppose a 'kind of data' and thus a 'sort of problem'. Social criticism starts with its problem – and most certainly not any old problem or what the sociologist 'happens to be interested in'. There are real problems – it does not matter how one describes the rest. Of

175

course these problems are not questions to which one tries to put various answers. There are problem areas – as indicated by Stein's second criterion. There are crises and a sociologist should engage himself in their interpretation.

Gerth and Mills (1954) give four 'master trends'. Such master trends are problem areas, loci of crises and inter-related crises for social life. They are:

1 The co-ordination of political, economic and military orders (pp. 457 60)
2 Psychological aspects of bureaucracy (pp. 460–4)
3 The decline of liberalism (pp. 464–72)
4 Character structure in a polarized world (pp. 472–80)

These problems for sociology can be expressed in one general concept (Cuzzort, 1969, p. 134):

> Mills was concerned with one aspect of society which never loses its significance – the question of power. His work remains centered on power – the nature of power, the distribution of power, the uses and abuses of power, the man of power, the power of organizations, the myths of power, the evolution of power, the irrationality of power, and the means of observing and comprehending power in the vastness of modern society.

Having come so far, from real historical problems through contemporary crises to power as the central phenomenon, we come to a place of bewildering choice. For a problem cannot really be stated in such terms; the terms are also the method of approach.

One choice is to define the theoretical 'problematic' (Hirst, 1972a, esp. p. 224). This path is rarely taken, as very few know how to follow it. A second choice is to articulate the cause of groups in conflict with 'authority' (Paul, Jimmy and Mustafa Support Committee, 1973). A third choice is to consider the audience of sociological work as being anyone who can read: 'Big range sociology is a public sociology – open to inspection, subject to criticism, anxious for improvement' (Horowitz, 1964, p. 19).

For my own purposes I let the master problems slip by (cf. ibid.). I take as my problem that of being actively involved in current struggles to study and develop consciousness. Huey Newton (1972) says:

> That's the only way you are going to get people organized. Anyway, it is to try to show them you're sensitive to their needs and you're doing something about contributing to their general move to alleviate themselves of the burdens they have in their daily lives.

It may be felt that such a statement of intent slithers uncontrollably from sociological problems to political purpose; that this is an easy way out from being rigorous and scientific. For there are other choices to be made between purposes. One is to ignore the rattle of gunfire and get the science right. See Hirst (op. cit., p. 224):

> The weakness of modern sociology is first and foremost a theoretical weakness, a weakness that can be remedied by no amount of ideological transformation, political radicalization or change in background assumptions. If we listen to the sound of guns or of pneumatic drills for that matter, it is because of the emptiness of our heads.

In contrast, I am not greatly disturbed by any 'weakness'. Sociology is quite strong enough for my purposes. For I should admit to having ideals, or in Worsley's terms (1964, p. 328), to having an ancient problem as well as a modern one:

> It is not the war in Viet Nam that we should be engaged in, but the struggle to identify and eliminate the causes of that particular war, and the wider World War IV which it threatens to spark off. This would be a serious human task to set ourselves, for we have as little real need to destroy the world, or starve its people, as we have to conquer space. We do have an overriding cosmic need to solve a very ancient problem: how to make two blades of grass grow where one grew before.

I see this as the expression of a practical problem. Thus I regard many of the 'philosophical' expressions of purpose as unimportant: especially when couched in terms of purposes themselves. For example (and out of the context of the paper), '. . . One of the basic intellectual traditions of the West – the dialectical exploration of the fundamental purposes of human life' (Gouldner, 1964, p. 202).

Generally speaking, therefore, there is a big choice between politics and philosophy as an author of purpose. The political purpose generally referring to the overthrow of the many forms of oppression as a step towards liberty and the philosophical purpose being a glorification of this liberty and attendant joys: 'a wild sociology which sings of family, of habit, of folly, and the resonance of history and public life' (O'Neill, 1973).

Reisman (1950, p. 23) has his feet on the ground:

> Speaking for myself, I have always felt it important to think on two levels simultaneously: a middle level area of reformist concerns and possibilities where one works within the given system, and a more long-run Utopian concern with fundamental

transformations. It would simplify both action and understanding to merge these two levels into an uncompromising attack on the status quo. . . .

So in choosing the political and practical I engage in projects. Admittedly the choices implied in this section's heading may strike the reader as a matter of the hair-splitting semantics of the left. I have touched upon problems and purposes; I now wish to work inwards and choose between programmes and projects. As my work is usually of short duration, limited (or shallow) interest and concerned with a partisan's answer to a group's question, 'What do we do next?, I refer to my enterprises as projects. I do so particularly because of the absence of a plan and thus a programme cannot be scheduled.

No doubt I have made light of the raging issues about the choices. Having made my own, I am seldom concerned with retracing my steps. All in all, the idea of choice being between known and freshly thought alternatives is the most important for me. I take this from Sartre's teaching on engagement (see Bondy, 1970). I further assume that a man must be a rebel before he matures to a revolutionary. Finally I assume that there are no personal solutions to personal problems. It is in this way that I draw round, back to Mills: 'Perhaps the most fruitful distinction with which the sociological imagination works is between "the personal *troubles* of milieu" and the public *issues* of social structure' (1959b, p. 8). With Mills I would suggest that there is barely an area where there is not a worthwhile problem. But it is just this compartmentalizing of areas that has made problem statements difficult to express. Life does not occur in the same segments as examination question papers. And it is for this reason that any sociologist will find himself finally drawn out into matters of history and international relations. For all that I have expressed politics and philosophy as optional, history is mandatory. Or rather, the sense of the historically relevant and the good sense to avoid the historically irrelevant are within the idea of criticism as a science.

History and sociology

History was discussed as integral to a sociological problem statement. Historical analysis is thereby vital to its solution. Of course we are discussing social criticism and as such more than explaining or describing how things came to be. As critics we are concerned with how things could be. In Fox's words (1973, p. 231):

> Sociology as a discipline confers its greatest strength when it helps us at least to some limited degree to reduce our dependence on the blinkers of our own social conditioning and thereby to escape from self-fulfilling prophecies of 'what is must be'.

So at least part of the 'historical aspect' of social criticism is 'futurism'. This may take the form of anticipating the demise of 'late capitalism', or it may consider the production of new forms of relationships. Thus Reisman (op. cit., p. 28):

> The power of individuals to shape their own character by their selection among models and experiences was suggested by our concept of autonomy; when this occurs, men may limit the provinciality of being born to a particular family in a particular place. To some this offers a prospect only of rootless men and galloping anomie. To more hopeful prophets, ties based upon conscious relatedness may someday replace those of blood and soil.

Prophecy is not prediction. As Merton illuminates, if knowledge is held about what could happen, such knowledge-holders can reflect upon it and fulfil or negate the consequences. Though it is not quite as simple as that, for there are a number of ways in which prophecies can be made. If they are extrapolations of a present tendency, then they are a cheat; that is, they are ahistorical. If they entail *pre-science* then they are a lie in that the imaginative fetch is only justified by the relief into which the present is thrown.

But of much greater interest than futurism is the proper historical method – that elusive erudition that elucidates the dynamics of master trends or gives a context for events. The master historian being Marx, sociologists are saved the task of entering history proper. They can read *Das Kapital* and learn how to study the genesis, maintenance and fall of classes across many centuries. There is no end to dispute over reading *Kapital*, however. Much of it centres upon 'the nature and conditions of the problematic' (Hirst, 1972a, p. 225). But as those developing these ideas are antagonistic to the ideas of social criticism (and favour what might be called the science of critique) their work is tangential to my subject. (See Hirst, 1972b.)

So far, it seems, there is very little sociology in social criticism. The problem may have a sociological 'flavour' but where, one might ask, is the sociological theory? It must be admitted that the quotation from Hirst above is correct. Sociological theory is a remarkably undeveloped field. Generally it offers two related axes; that a problem should be seen in its context and that both are structural phenomena. Rex (1961, p. 189) says:

> What is required is an attempt to relate particular specialized problems to some sort of theoretical model of the total system of interaction of which they form a part. An overall theoretical model of the particular society which he is studying is an

essential tool if he is to see particular problems in perspective. Given continued argument about the general nature of the social system which we are studying particular problems, even of a personal kind, take on a new meaning and real sociological significance.

This, of course, is barely different from Mills's formula for a proper subject. It is, however, more concerned with the 'social' and as such implicitly directs attention to structure. It could be followed by: 'In our view, providing it is linked with the ideas of social conflict and social change, the idea of social structure is *the* lead off point, and the anchorage idea of sociology' (Coulson and Riddell, 1970, p. 43).

So from history come tradition and event, and from sociology come structure and process, but obviously they are more than conveniently related for the practice of social criticism. Obviously, then, there must be an ambivalence of relationship and of usage. To some definite extent we should expect a social critic to dislike what he finds and the lenses through which he sees his subject. We should expect him to be dissatisfied with the adequacy of the history and sociology that he is using to 'make' more history and sociology. To land in the field of operation for the first time is to observe the social critic criticizing his own theory (Bensman and Vidich, 1960, p. 120):

> Commitment to one school or theory means, in most instances, commitment to selected levels of data. These forms of commitment prevent the research worker from criticizing his findings from alternative points of view and may blind him to the exhausting of his own favored approach.

Thus social criticism is historical, sociological and self-critical in action. Therefore social criticism is critical of the irrelevant forms of these fields that are plainly in the majority. Much of our present history is a verbal circus – of scandal, espionage and stunt. But it does not matter. It is 'noise' in the system. It would matter if it were not manipulated, hysterical hypocrisy. And as for contemporary sociology . . .

Mills (1959b), Stein (1963) and Gouldner (1970) have given considerable thought to their sociologies of sociology. They are usually humorous and generally condemnatory – 'fat-cat sociology' stinks. So I will not toil away behind their efforts (and I have made enough harsh judgments elsewhere in this book). It should be clear by now that Gouldner's adjective 'reflexive' fits Mills's own 'imagination' well. For the idea of social criticism is but the centre point of a spread of criticism that goes from one's self and work to one's world and its apparent futures. In this sense social criticism is much more a passion than a reason, it is art and rarely science. And of course the counter-criticism is very much grounded in these facts. As Glaser and Strauss observe, 'Much of C. Wright Mills's work, we believe, is exampled with only little theoretical control, though he claimed that data disciplined his theory' (1967, p. 5). Naturally the very self-criticism of the social critic makes this sort of pin-prick much easier to land.

Exceptions and an example

By now it is yet harder to pretend that there is anything other than a gang of rampant individualists landing swift kicks on the Leviathan and demanding that it – whatever it may be – change, *radically*. And, we might say, why not? The answer must be that there are instead generations of social critics living in different countries and influenced by different scholastic forms. Perhaps the last factor is most important. Abendroth, Birnbaum, Marcuse, Arendt are consciously European scholars. Either each is exceptional by virtue of subject or historical approach, or they are simply exceptional people. Or perhaps, as with quantitative and qualitative researches, many full friendships are contained in any list. Certainly many related acknowledgments can be found – there is a unity of trust.

It is, of course an arid question to ask whether or not there is a school of social criticism or if a convention has been devised to guide a method. And all the more so when each is also committed to his own responsibility and each regards his method as an intrinsic part of his problem.

It is better, therefore, to seek a few full examples than it is to draw lines between examples. One painstaking study is that of Laing and Esterson (1964). Their introduction is a masterly example of a clear problematic; a general account of fieldwork; limitations of the study and purpose expressed as relevance (pp. 27, esp. 23):

> We have tried in each single instance to answer the question: to what extent is the experience and behaviour of that person, who has already begun a career as a diagnosed 'schizophrenic' patient, intelligible in the light of the praxis and process of his or her family nexus?

> We have tried to develop a method, therefore, that enables us to study at one and the same time (i) each person in the family (ii) the relations between persons in the family (iii) the family itself as a system.

Pages 23–5 discuss the interviews and the researchers' criticisms of their method. Their last paragraph (p. 27) states their claim:

181

We believe that the shift of point of view that these descriptions both embody and demand has a historical significance no less radical than the shift from a demonological to a clinical viewpoint three hundred years ago.

Social critics in sociology

It is only in societies which have become literate, possess economic reserves, have developed an urban life and in some measure a professional intellectual class, that any sustained criticism of the working of society is possible. [Bottomore, 1967, p. 9.]

It is clearly possible to list all the sociologists who have engaged in issues of their epoch and establish that the 'old tradition', the writings of the founding fathers are all characterized by at least reformist concerns within institutions. To a great extent the question of the history of social criticism is that of the social role of the intellectual; the engagement of an intelligentsia in more than their class interests; the sharpening of the pen with a sword. For in the last hundred years two classes have combined to make a great deal of history: the peasants and the intelligentsia. Their combined force has demanded the emergence of a standing army to contain them. Prior to their combination social criticism was 'incestuous' in pillorying the manners and madness of aristocrats. We might call a whole school of social criticism that of art and literature: from Goya's cartoons to Swift's satire. And we would have to agree with Bottomore that in recent times a theory of society has underpinned the social aspect of criticism; that there has emerged a social scientific mode of engagement even though the class with which an intelligentsia is to combine is still far from clear. To quote Bottomore again (p. 119) for an historical setting:

Social criticism is not science, but in modern times it has been very much dependent upon the social sciences. In earlier ages it was often religious movements – the 'religions of the oppressed' as they have been called – which led the way in social criticism. Somewhat later it was the schools of philosophy which largely assumed this role in Europe. But from the end of the eighteenth century most of the movements of criticism were based upon some theory of society. The utilitarians, the Saint-Simonians, Compte and the positivists, the various schools of socialism, and especially Marxism, all combined in their teaching a theory about the nature of human society, a criticism of contemporary society, and a plan for its reorganization.

Thus if it can be accepted that social criticism may well have been philosophical and literary but is now deeply influenced by a social science which it fathered, then the proper issue is science versus ideology. For some would justify their social criticism because it attacks the rich and champions the poor. But really the highest ideal of social criticism is that of science – a pure problem of simple truth. And so a dilemma takes shape: to be on the right side and on the side of truth. When we express it as bluntly, or as badly, as this there is obviously no real dilemma: social criticism can be anything a critic likes, only the claim to scientific truth is wrong. It may be correct, fully correct, if the social critic begins the other way about.

Presumably the dilemma comes from the continued success of the literary tradition. William H. Whyte, Vance Packard and Paul Goodman in the USA have touched the nation's soul while a dozen sociologists were fingering the wrist for a pulse. This literary style is essentially liberal and yet it is complementary to the scientific work of Paul Sweezy (1953). It is complementary, that is, because its subjects are similar. Nevertheless the two approaches are as alike as chalk and cheese. Both are successful, researched and readable and have suitably embarrassed sociologists in the same field to learn a trick or two.

Further there have been strong pressures upon sociologists to go inter-disciplinary or at least to work with another discipline for mutual benefit. As Ariès has it, 'It is the interface of good sociology and another good strong discipline that provides rationale of argument' (1963, p. 5).

This expression says that joint disciplinary work aids argument. Of course this is often true. For argument is a vital skill and is often impeded by the self-evident assumptions of a single discipline.

A second force for inter-disciplinary work is grounded in the idea of real problems and the widest possible audience. Rosenberg and White (1957, p. 5) put it this way:

it seems to us that this area of study cuts across the artificial boundaries that so often serve as a barrier keeping scholars of like interest from speaking to each other. We hope that this Reader will be a step in the creation of an interdisciplinary focus on problems common to everyone who takes a serious interest in what is happening to this aspect of modern civilization. Although the book was compiled essentially for students of popular culture in university communities, we trust that it will be read by many other interested observers, particularly those within the media profession themselves.

So we might argue that the milieu of American enterprises is the centrality of 'the European tradition' with peripheral impact of the successful and socially responsible. And it is very strange how different British social criticism is in comparison: 'In England, for example, sociology as an academic discipline is still somewhat marginal, yet in much English journalism, fiction and above all history, the sociological imagination is very well developed indeed' (Mills, op. cit., p. 19). In effect a literary influence is felt in Great Britain that is very much that of a heritage. Victorian and Edwardian novelists abound in 'acute insight' and 'rich description'. They also made their consciences clear. In a 'stable democracy' an intelligentsia feels at least as much guilt as it does anger. So the mood of these writings was of the pitiful destitution of the poor. Thus the first generation to follow the Webbs and Rowntree was that of Titmuss and of Simey (1968). Reformers clear in their egalitarian values and particularly clear that 'values' played an essential part in social science. Phalanx upon phalanx of social worker marched forth with this song in their ears. But then came sociology.

A second generation arose, a generation of conflict theorists. These men pulled the discipline back to its scientific base: the reforms would have to wait for the bases of conflict to be marked out. The European tradition was surfacing again. Rex, Banks and a host of LSE graduates had Marx and Weber so close together as to make them the two pillars of the same portal.

And so many choices have been made for the present generation. They can make their novels at least as interesting and portray sociology departments as centres of absurdity as do Malcolm Bradbury's *People Are Not For Eating* (1963) and Jo Martindale's *Dry Mass* (1969). They can take the road of social reform down to Shelter or squatters. They can criticize most of sociology as ill-disciplined good intention; as a flash in the pan of egotism. Or they can try to pretend that social criticism has no place in sociology – that 0°C ethnomethodology is all criticism and all fact. Or eventually they can face the choice of their American counterparts who admit that social criticism has got into sociology and thus forced sociologists to accept a qualifying adjective.

The adjectives convey a similar range of meanings. Sociology is to be critical, radical, reflexive or socialist. Thus Gouldner (1970, pp. 489, 502):

a reflexive sociology is and would need to be a radical sociology. Radical because it would recognize that knowledge of the world cannot be advanced apart from the sociologist's knowledge of himself and his position in the social world, or apart from these efforts to change these. Radical because it seeks to transform as well as to know the alien world outside the sociologist as well as the alien world inside him. Radical

184

because it would accept the fact that the roots of sociology pass through the sociologist as a total man, and that the question he must confront, therefore, is not how to work but how to live.

The historical mission of a Reflexive Sociology is to foster a critical awareness of the character of contemporary liberalism, of its hold upon the university and upon American Sociology as well as of the dialectic between welfare and warfare policies, and of the liberal sociologist's role as a market researcher on behalf of both. Reflexive Sociology premises that the character of any sociology is affected by its political praxis and that the further development of sociology now requires its liberation from the political praxis of liberalism.

And so on as the theorist gets himself together. Become a man of action, commit your sociology to the cause of freedom and see how different knowledge looks then.

Not all writers are quite so heedless of sociology. Birnbaum and Stein indicate what part sociology can play 'in being critical' and how this strengthens the discipline. But we must return again to Hirst's criticism of the paucity of theoretical structure. What has been written is more of a language structure – a range of words representing real and unwelcome conditions – fact is fused with value. Such a vocabulary includes concepts of responsibility; alternative; struggle and development. Generally the combined force of these concepts is the description of a revolutionary condition. They also permit the contrasting image – the state of peace beyond the coming war (Williams, 1962, p. 160):

Many of the measures proposed are radical. All need further definition. But already, at the level of theory, we have broken the deadlock which is so obviously damaging our society. We can conceive a cultural organization in which there could be genuine freedom and variety, protected alike from the bureaucrat and the speculator. Actual work would be in the hands of those who in any case have to do it, and the society as a whole would take on the responsibility of maintaining this freedom, since the freedom of individual contribution is in fact a general interest.

In large measure being a 'man of action' – an existentialist man in action – is more a part of the theory than is a 'problematic'. That is, 'heroism' is part of the theory of method as distinct from the theory of theory. Gouldner is most emphatic upon courage as being *in* reflexive sociology (1970, pp. 504, 509):

A reflexive sociology insists that while sociologists desperately

185

require talent, intelligence and technical skill, they also need courage and valour that may be manifested every day in the most personal and commonplace decisions.

For the sociologist is to engage in

a reflexive sociology as a central part of its historical mission, the task of helping men in their struggle to take possession of what is theirs – society and culture – and of aiding them to know who they are and what they may want.

Thus a sociologist is also to have the courage to liberate himself from sociology and liberate sociology by transformation. Social criticism in sociology comes to an apocalyptic crescendo.

The reasoning here is that sociologists are generally corrupt and so their products are worthless. Nothing would be lost by clearing them out. Even if we are left with '10 per cent of the literature' at least it will all be worth reading. And certainly Gouldner is right that hired hacks dominate research and make their work unreadable to all but their chosen masters.

Yet still sociology is seen as a threat in all but its most applied forms. The paymasters and university chancellors have rightly recognized the inherent resistance of sociological thought – and sociologists – to total subservience. So the critical sociologist (let us call him) has something of a problem. He has adopted a 'confrontation strategy'. He wills conflict as necessary. He moves to open hostility with his employers. Some older academic set-ups may well approve of a few brilliant teachers. But they will not welcome 'a department of critical sociology' whose manifesto is to turn students on to combatting the evil in the very town or city whose exploitative practices paid for the university's foundation and pay many of its members to this day. Is then, this social critic to become less local, less vocal and more academic in his work? Will he not say:

It's a job
I get paid for it
I get long holidays
and the chance to get away from it all.

After all, does not Gouldner's fire put the sociologist at the centre of revolution when his true place is at the edge? How are we to compare the heated honesty of the man with what he can do as a cool analyst? Thus Mao Tse-tung (1926, p. 1):

Who are our enemies? Who are our friends? This is a question of the first importance for the revolution.

To distinguish real friends from real enemies, we must make a general analysis of the economic status of the various classes in Chinese society and of their respective attitudes to the revolution.

Mao identified the following classes:

1 The landlord class and the comprador class
2 The middle bourgeoisie
3 The petty bourgeoisie
4 The semi-proletariat
   a overwhelming majority of semi-owner peasants
   b the poor peasant
   c the small handicraftsmen
   d the shop assistants
   e the pedlars

The income source, sub-division and political attitude of each class is given and as the Publication Committee observes this analysis solved two problems:

Comrade Mao Tse-tung pointed out that the peasantry was the staunchest and numerically the largest ally of the Chinese proletariat, and thus resolved the problem of who was the chief ally in the Chinese revolution. Moreover he saw that the national bourgeoisie was a vacillating class and predicted that it would disintegrate during the upsurge of revolution, with its right wing going over to the side of imperialism. This was borne out by the events of 1927.

This small paper may well be the obvious example of purposive, scientific social criticism. And should the sociologist determined upon social criticism not find himself in so fortunate a position he may care to take Alfred McClung Lee's (1972, p. 23) advice:

Radical and humanist sociology is a constant struggle. Its devotees often have a rough time of it or at least rough periods in their careers. I have often urged students of mine who are sincerely interested in working for a more useful and creative sociology to develop a secondary occupational skill, and some of them have found it mighty useful to be able to fall back on their ability to do journalism, carpentry, printing, housepainting, copy editing for a book publisher or dealing in second-hand cars or antiques. To others such a secondary occupational skill gives an added sense of independence.

Critical sociology: in conclusion

We could easily carve each other up and probably I have been too rude to many quantitative and qualitative researchers. In fact in these perilous times – where great change is needed and imminent and yet many cannot see it and others realize the horrors of domestic repression – personal frustrations can 'build up' and be partially drained off in interpersonal acrimony. For it is clear that any establishment compromises for its own survival and its productive workers simply groan under an increasing load and waste of work. Becker and Horowitz (1972) make a very sensible appeal against factional gangs assassinating the characters of establishment members. They refer critics to the cause of science and a cool head in times of stress. They are right that discipline is needed – in criticism more than in any other branch of philosophizing. But they are wrong in appealing for a truce. Now is just the time when all the false directions can be jettisoned with little loss. In another decade upwards of a quarter of a million willing students will have been misled into thickets of confusion and there lose hope, happiness and any semblance of ability. Just at this time any decent teacher can make a course worth while by challenging the epistemology and ontology of all our orthodoxies. Why wait until a poor 'tool' is irreparably broken? Surely we do not need to prove uselessness before we reject the choice?

11   The practice of critique

A critique engages its author to the extent that his ideas clarify while it is being written. A critique makes changes in its author. This change comes through the fire of his words. The subject matter is broad, the topic is urgent, the concern is immediate. The whole tone is one of brittle brilliance. A critique demands an author who will respond to matters of the day because they will matter all the more tomorrow. The author becomes something of a 'nowist'. His problem is to seal an epoch; to reveal a truth and to make a private trouble *his* public issue. A critique takes courage.

For in being partisan, creative and belligerent the author is as comforting as an Old Testament prophet. He is speaking of virtue, the good life and more especially a moral sociology. In writing a critique the author is claiming a right to speak. He is, in the process, damning himself for an opportunistic use of data; a glib use of words and a strident note in his breath. The author in standing out is exposing himself. Having done detriment to his sociological style, he is risking his career in sociology. Only intellectual giants can move the size of stone he seizes. He may earn posthumous fame but he is given a helluva life now. How dare a man claim to be one of a few?

I can only assume that an author pens a critique because it is the best thing he can do. He needs very little data. He can criticize his own usage *en route*. He can deploy old memories. He can cast asides at many things that irritate him. He can be like the sociologists of old and pronounce. Once he has the combative style, is careless of his reputation and is driving ever on through his feelings, his message has a constancy: look, see and seize.

The man is a bundle of action. He no longer worries what sociology is. He is a sociologist. The author of a critique is a sociologist in action. For in effect, each new phenomenon he 'studies' becomes fresher for his attention. He makes his readers think. He is naturally

189

original and his aim is clearly to have more people producing more variety. It is as though he is demanding that sociologists themselves reverse their emphasis in the dialectic of man being created by and the creator of his society. His manifest skill is an example of his demand: the responsibility of man *is* to recreate his world, start today!

But despite the author's use of chance data, anybody's concepts and no theory his critique smacks of socialism. He is taking sides; saying that the oppressed *are* oppressed and yet noble. The man seems to have moved from pedagogue to demagogue. His literacy is a thin cover for his creeping communism.

The problem has always been where do you put Marxist sociology? Marxism is stronger than sociology. It is antipathetic to other 'sociologies'. It is dialectical. It is critical. And it's very difficult to practise.

The author has got his sociology mixed up with Marxism. He has been unable to restrain himself. Let himself be political and slide from sociology into Marxism. This gives his work its cogency. With deceptive simplicity he charms the layman in us all. For it is true that he has confronted 'real' social problems. His own responsibility cannot be denied. What is at issue is whether or not this is responsible sociology.

For the author, however, a social critique and a sociological critique are much the same thing. A social critique is directed at policy – say, class and race prejudice in education. A sociological critique is directed at the policy-making institutions. Whose ends are served by classism and racism? Where will these policies take us? Why should we have no real choice? For the author, that is, a critique is a criticism from within and he has definite feelings about being 'in' society. His work is just the series of events with which he took issue throughout his life. He defended some rights and attacked some obligations. He has been busy all the time in an abstract evaluation of the age in which he is caught and the directions he is trying to influence.

To the author, it seems, his critique is as much a matter of history and philosophy as it is sociology. The sociological axis is the 'data', the groupings in which people are to be found, the mechanisms of normality and the damage they cause. The author's big problem was stopping his immediate concern long enough to shape a coherent commentary. From this perspective his note of doom is inevitable. He closed an epoch to observe it. It now matters to him that many are still trapped within it.

It is this historical sense that makes his critique futuristic. He is a watchdog – jealously guarding the quality of life. He can see that things cannot go on as they are. He can see the present as history. So he raises the spectre of hope and makes light of his despair. But as well as an ideological, or ideal, purpose for saying how things could be there is also a practical purpose. The juxtaposition of the real and the ideal reveals that which is reactionary in the real; that which has a vested or partial interest and that which will abuse its power for its own survival. Why cannot it be so? is a good question if used to ask what is stopping it. And how can these stoppers be removed? This refers to the dialectic in the practice of critique which concerns social time. The present is suspended between past and future, making both real – and yet unreal to each other. The dialectical method in a critique is to prise open this transformation. To examine choice in the light of new directions. In this way a critique is much more than a fascination with future forms. It is the author's stand in his own historical time, scanning what he can, demanding a conscience in sociological work.

In making this stand the author is, of course, making a claim for his sociology. The claim is for the necessity of humanism, scepticism and concern with the subject of sociological inquiry. In the process the author comes to a realization if his critique is any good, if it has fired his own imagination, that he has produced a manifesto. He had determined upon a programme of personal commitment.

12 Postscript: theory and practice in the light of sociological method

Each of the previous chapters has a style appropriate to its method. On reflection, the sociological convention is one of language faithful to its tradition: methodologies are truth-invoking rituals; theories are truth-provoking inanities.

The account of positivism is that of a harassed clerk. That of symbolic interactionism is of a hippie screwing a life-size rubber doll. That of 'critical sociology' is a culture-hero defying his despair. The methods have been made human; discussed as the researcher's experience. There are the trials of doubt. It is this doubt that helps to put so many projects to ruins.

Sociological theory is often regarded as being distinct from its diverse methods. It is as though theory were immune from the diseases of its practitioners. So the problem I wish to address in this chapter is the old one of the relationship between theory and method. I do so largely by way of a comparison between the methods.

I must emphasize that I am not discussing either all sociological theory or all sociological method. I am discussing theories in the light of the methods accounted. I have long envied friends engaged in historical analysis, biographical analysis and content analysis of current affairs. But I have long since realized that only a saint or a stool-pigeon would get any funds to practise these arts. Thus I am accounting 'hack research', the endeavours of those who must publish to survive; where the subject cannot be allowed to determine the exact approach. Nevertheless I am still concerned with the most glorious aspects of theory. I am convinced that fledgling sociologists repeatedly try to fly into the mind's eye and out across valleys rich with daily life. So I have asked two questions to make some comparisons and link theory with method. The questions are:

1 What is a sociological problem?
2 Is there a 'true' path of research?

What is a sociological problem?

It is tempting to answer this question by saying either that sociology has no problems of its own, or that its problems are those of the host society at the time. For if sociology has no real problems we could readily understand why so many sociologists devote themselves to administrative issues. And if social problems were the main concern we could readily understand why so many sociologists are needed (every institution 'needs' a sociologist for its social problem). Beyond institutions there are the four horsemen of the apocalypse riding through the land. Poverty, famine, disease and war have always 'threatened' society; as if they were in the nature of things, as if they were the nature still to be conquered. It could be said that there is so much wrong at home and abroad that sociology has little need of its own problems.

Of course, this is not true. Much of the fun of being a sociologist is arguing over the nature of the discipline with other sociologists. There is a delicious confusion from having to speak of the subject as if it were a discipline; recognizing a plurality of approaches and accepting that it's the subject matter of these sociologies that makes them interesting. A key problem for sociologists is containing this confusion and concealing its force from outsiders.

To be facetious for a moment, the problem within the city walls is that sociology is a feudal estate. There are factions of barons; noble warriors; foolish wool-gatherers and ancient mumblers. The young knights need a King Arthur who will give a lead to their chivalrous deeds; who will give their round table its social problems.

For if there is to be a proper sociological problem there must be a *sociologicality*. Not a 'study' of something or other but a logic of discourse. And this is obviously not put together like a science (or like a transcendental philosophy [Luckmann, 1972]). This discourse is in the process of being made up. To be sure, there are epistemological problems and ontological issues. It is a fact that continuous efforts are being made to establish a theory of knowledge and a theory of man. But sociology has a built-in inhibitor to easy answers. Sociological knowledge is about groups of people; there is not a great deal of interest in man. Groups are an invention that hold more fascination than their inventors. In fact the sociological terms for man are an embarrassment; they convey the bit the particular sociologist is interested in. Man is an actor; an informant; an incumbent or simply a member. Most sociologists wince when confronted with these 'concepts'. They say that they are studying what happened, or what is happening or what will happen.

Sociologists are students of time. Space and time are the axes of sociology in the making. Sociology is emerging from a century of

193

secular preoccupation with the patterns of social space and social time. The discourse does not have a dilemma or crisis beyond needing brilliant speculative practitioners – a race of Gandalfs for their hobbits. The point is quite simple. The way the discipline is developing is to demand that its disciplinarians be wizards with a spread of intellect from ants to the Alps; from fossils to future forms. I suspect that this demand looks like a challenge and vision to the embarking student. I also suspect that the galactic, microscopic search lays large numbers of students out with delirious exhaustion. I know that many settle for a 'personal' method as respite and then come to loathe the way in which they must argue that either quantitative or qualitative or critical methods *are* sociology. (That others are impostors posing beyond the responsibilities of validation, understanding and involvement.) Paradoxically, bickering over methods really saves a lot of sociologists from being crushed by their own mediocrity. If they were not experts in the detail of their method's moves and picking at another's nonsense they would be strung out speechless across the wastes of space and time. They would have little to say, less to teach and nothing to test. The tendency of sociology, the drive of its discourse, is that of the metaphysic. The disposition of those resolutely resolving this logic is monastic: making a song to the beauty of life; a hymn of thanks for its variety; a chant for its ceaseless strength. The problem for the sociologist, then, is to develop his art to the most pleasing form. The sociological problem is the essence of human nature.

Is there a 'true' path of sociological research?

A 'true' method would resolve three distinct difficulties for its practitioner. It would

1 unify theory and method
2 focus upon the 'true' problem
3 commit a sociologist whole-heartedly to its practice

In brief, there would be a path for the sociologist to follow; his mode of engagement would be unequivocal.

I have argued that there does not seem to be a precedent for sociology and perhaps I should substantiate this. There is no unit of analysis: no indisputable focus of analysis. There is no theory of causation: no distinctive way of relating actions to outcomes. There is no body of literature: no agglomerating mass of findings. Instead of all these certainties there is idiosyncrasy. There are men calling themselves sociologists keeping a commentary upon what is happening in 'their discipline' and referring to other sociologists in warm and cool terms. It seems that sociology demands engagement: that there can be no sociology without the efforts of these men to engage in their world and in a debate with their predecessors and contemporaries. This is the source of the demand for the 'true' path of research – if a sociologist is not whole-hearted he is down-hearted.

Quantitative sociology gets as far away as possible from theory 'in order to' test it. It has an 'objective' emphasis. This emphasis means the researcher has to accept a power relationship. He is above or below the subject studied. His manners are therefore those of dictation or deference. He is working 'within' the structure. The tones of this power relationship are more perceptible in the manner in which he approaches 'his respondents'. He is either 'nice' or humble.

Qualitative sociology has an affair with theory. It has a 'subjective' emphasis. The theory, or rather the parts and their patterns, are revised in the light of fresh data. This data is gained by being on everybody's side but somehow being an independent person. The tone of this intimate relationship is perceptible in the reported statements. The informants make confidential and near-conclusive remarks. The researcher is merely honest in his appraisal.

Critical sociology, or rather a critique in sociological form, has a 'combative' emphasis. Its tone is the militancy of its writer. It is a matter of his own relationship with the data. He sees neither respondents nor actors but rather ciphers. His protest is guttural. The researcher's tone is one of profound unhappiness.

Each method has a different criterion for theory. They are explanation, understanding and advocacy respectively. In effect different theories are advanced about how it works, what it feels like and what it's worth in the quality of life. Each theory and method are roughly compatible and there are, in fact, certain compatibilities between them. The quantitative and qualitative methods are compatible. The qualitative and critical theories are compatible.

The mutually supportive use of quantitative and qualitative methods is ppropriate and indicative. There is a prime concern to describe: to have the reality 'out there' accounted for. Both describe: the setting they describe comes 'as it is' – one gets coverage of the respondents, the other gets their confidence.

'As it is', conversely, is the critical researcher's nightmare. He knows how strong a grip 'common-sense reality' has upon its puppets. He has that much in common with the qualitative researcher. He respects 'what is' as his sleep-walker subject's terms. He wants, however, to wake them up rather than trail their paths.

Both quantitative and qualitative researchers are largely uncritical of their methods: the latter need refinement, improvement or 'systematization'. The critique, in contrast, is also an indictment of its own method. Whilst qualitative and quantitative researchers make the most of what they have got, the critique asks questions that reveal a glaring ignorance and stretches a little data into many dark corners. In effect, there is a shifting of emphasis through the three approaches. If the quantitative approach is a method fetishism, and the critique an obsession with theory, the qualitative approach emerges as the more level-headed, down-to-earth equivalence of the two. If the rhythms are compared the quantitative method is a tedious, harsh shuttling back and forth between its own fixations. The qualitative method is a tenacious, lush ebb and flow between its changing images. The critique is a tough, lashing spiral spinning up and out towards new forms of social imagination.

Each form has its 'political implications'. The quantitative method has a vested interest in how things are: in conserving as much as possible until the publication is out. The very process of quantifying itself takes so long that there needs to be a stable equilibrium. Prediction does not refer to what will happen as a consequence of the collision of mighty forces but what will keep happening over and over again. The quantitative researcher cannot have too many things happening at once.

The qualitative researcher is much more relaxed. He does not care how much change goes on. He knows it's not real change because the people are still in the same situation: they are just shuffling about in their skins. In fact he does not mind what the hell happens. He cannot really get steamed up about it: to him the game is a joke taken seriously and the players are putting flesh on a hollow frame. The qualitative researcher would not personally have anything to do with it. The qualitative researcher is a libertine in contrast to the conservative quantifier.

But neither take their research especially seriously. It may express a hard-won skill. It may be an outright allegiance. It may have untold interest and implications. But it need not matter. Both researchers study 'other people' – they have other homes and lives to go to themselves. They put part of themselves into th r job – and it may be the best part – but they are damned if they are going to put their all.

There is nothing immediate about quantitative or qualitative results. No one is waiting for the answers, no one is going to get fired when the report has been read. Their social 'effects' 'filter down' or 'ripple through' or offer an 'interesting perspective'. The world is not shattered even if the researcher is.

The keynotes of quantitative sociology are ameliorative conservativism and of qualitative sociology are laissez-faire anarchism. The tones emanating from a critical researcher are less easy upon the ear – he is pacing back and forth between his personal rebellion and his most recent call for social revolution. A critique is socialist. Democratic and humanitarian; dictatorial and economic are nuances in contrast to the definiteness of socialism in the work of critique. The problem 'chosen'; the data 'borrowed'; the manner adopted; the audience that includes the researcher himself; the continuous drive for the simple language that inspires social movements. There is no doubt in the researcher's mind: it's his problem too.

In conclusion

I have not answered this chapter's questions with direct argument. For I have learned that you cannot come to sociological theory through method. Perhaps this is only because a researcher gets woefully out of touch with theory as it is more generally understood. Perhaps this also is because a researcher has more need of a theory of sociological action. And, in keeping with a popular hope, I would say that a research sociologist would do well to be sure of his 'paradigm'.

My own preference for the method of critique is obvious. The model I have 'taken' is C. Wright Mills. I have rejected arse-licking empiricism and bland theory in favour of his 'new sociology'. Mills did create a new method, theory and subject area with each substantive work. I do not think that the new sociology is, in fact, new. It seems to be a traditional sociology surfacing in yet another generation with its very modernity coming as a shock. Mills united his sorrow, anger, knowledge and dignity in his sociological imagination. He did his very best. 'The true radical is dateless, without chronology, no sense of time, or fitness, or demand for result: only the theory of appearing to oppose the unjust' (Hodges, 1971, p. 69).

I have a wish for fellow researchers; make Mills your model. A few years ago to do so was hopelessly old-fashioned. Now it looks difficult. And whenever I have been stuck in a piece of research the trap has been sprung by reading his advice 'On Intellectual Craftsmanship' (1959a).

Appendix 1   Statements and correlations

Variable 1   Profession of the Protestant ethic.

Dimension 2   Belief in salvation through hard work

Scale 1   Hard work as a general value
  1 A man must find his own way through his own efforts no matter what the difficulties.
  2 A man finds himself by accepting honest uphill work.
  3 The most important thing in a man's life is a sense of challenge.

Scale 2   Hard work in national affairs
  1 Welfare legislation makes people soft.
  2 Planning feather-beds the country unnecessarily.
  3 More state activity should be involved with tackling the problems of unemployment.*
  4 Most poor people simply have not tried to improve their lot.

Scale 3   Hard work in industrial affairs
  1 The man most worthy of admiration is the chap who went it alone and, after years of hard work, has emerged a success.
  2 A period of recession is beneficial because it toughens a man to take control of himself and struggle for an individual solution.

Correlation matrix of the items

	11	12	13	21	22	23	24	31
1211								
1212	.200							
1213	.217	262						
1221	.073	255	.200					
1222	−.116	−199	−071	−105				
1223	−.021	177	300	−095	−034			
1224	.194	244	170	152	029	009		
1231	232	335	318	145	073	090	290	
1232	268	102	259	267	069	048	−025	326

*A question to ask of the opposite view: built into the test like a 'lie-detector'.

Dimension 3   Belief in thrift

Scale 1   Thrift as a virtue

Sub-scale 1   Thrift as a general value

1 'Putting a bit by regularly' is an essential habit.

2 The first thing a boy should do when he starts to earn is open a deposit account.

Sub-scale 2   Thrift in national affairs

1 The government should actively prevent people spending up to their last penny.

2 The state should limit hire purchase commitments.

3 The government should set an example of thrift and economy.

Scale 2   Money as a means to an end

Sub-scale 1   Money as a means to an end in general terms

1 Thrift is an outmoded virtue.

2 An overdraft is no disgrace.

Sub-scale 2   Money as a means to an end in daily life

1 Money is only really important in terms of the things it can buy.

2 It is better to buy what one needs than worry about where the money is going to come from.

	11	12	21	22	23	31	32	41
1311								
1312	.338							
1321	176	087						
1322	153	159	413					
1323	207	180	009	087				
1331	−.252	−118	−138	−034	−260			
1332	−.092	−054	−180	−177	−045	073		
1341	271	030	−096	042	203	−074	−069	
1342	−.076	038	−116	−123	−162	447	136	−008

Dimension 4   Respect for property

Scale 1   Belief in the sacredness of property

Sub-scale 1   Sacredness of property as a general value

1 Property merits most consideration in life.

2 A truly moral person would always have a deep respect for property.

3 Vandalism is inexcusable.

Sub-scale 2   Sacredness of property in legislation

1 Crimes against property should be more severely punished.

2 The state should spend more on the protection of property.

Sub-scale 3   Sacredness of property in industry

1 Employees should be punished for damaging equipment.

Scale 2   Belief in the sacredness of the person*

Sub-scale 1   Sacredness of the person as a general value

1 People are the most important aspect of life.

2 All morals should be built on respect for other people.

3 Man has certain inalienable rights.

*As the sacredness of property implies an opposite of the profanity of the person a complete scale has been added as a check upon this meaning.

Sub-scale 2   Sacredness of the person in legislation
  1 Accused people in courts should be assumed guilty and have to prove their innocence.
  2 The police should have absolute powers to deal with offenders.
Sub-scale 3   Sacredness of the person in industry
  1 Campaigns against accidents should have top priority.

	411	412	413	414	415	416	421	422	423	424	425
411											
412	.221										
413	−068	148									
414	356	405	207								
415	277	113	−010	453							
416	294	258	031	251	202						
421	000	034	−074	−260	−167	137					
422	148	111	037	−052	−068	119	525				
423	081	−044	−118	−063	−036	−088	167	162			
424	267	330	−201	174	153	071	−115	−100	−172		
425	048	−043	013	163	235	006	−364	−237	−173	234	
426	203	170	162	256	220	037	080	197	123	−012	064

Variable 2   Profession of the social ethic
Dimension 1   Belief in belongingness as a basic human need
Scale 1   Belongingness as a general value
  1 Loyalty is natural and basic in man.
  2 The ultimate need of the individual is to belong.
  3 People who are laws unto themselves have to fight a basic desire to belong.
  4 The happiness of man depends on being rooted in a stable group.
Scale 2   Belongingness in social life
  1 A man without a family is usually lonely and unbalanced.
  2 It is essential to belong to clubs or groups and share a common interest.
  3 On arrival, a new employee's biggest need is to establish himself with a group of friends.
  4 It is essential that from the earliest age children have a group of playmates.

	2111	2112	2113	2114	211T*	2121	2122	2123	2124	212T*
2111										
2112	370									
2113	164	173								
2114	056	143	209							
211T*	527	550	588	744						
2121	089	079	189	250	257					
2122	145	217	562	425	565	302				
2123	049	218	083	262	269	068	258			
2124	161	084	137	264	280	125	402	421		
212T*	163	239	390	431	515	595	725	615	650	
21TT	401	406	426	−046	352	428	524	410	473	710

*The scale totals are included to show how clear the correlations can be and also how deceptive: weak inter-item correlations can be masked by seemingly high correlation between item score and the total scale score.

Dimension 2   Belief in the group as the prime source of creativity

Scale 1   The group as a creator
  1 The best decisions are those that are the product of a team.
  2 Whereas one man puts into practice the invention takes a group.
  3 The lone inventor is a thing of the past.
  4 Science has proved that the group is superior to the individual.

Scale 2   The group as a creator in social life
  1 Every government leader should rely for decisions on a group of specialist advisers.
  2 Children should be encouraged to set up their own problem-solving groups.

Scale 3   The group as a creator in industrial life
  1 Industrial problems can only be solved by a team of men dedicated to their solution.
  2 Task-groups are the only way of tackling the problems faced by industry.

	2211	2212	2213	2214	221T	2221	2222	222T	2231	2233	2230
2211											
2212	174										
2213	176	366									
2214	252	293	311								
221T	574	598	590	834							
2221	132	139	215	089	168						
2222	−009	173	070	055	084	130					
222T	071	149	131	−092	014	814	633				
2231	062	024	001	057	040	257	112	282			
2232	256	221	347	687	643	262	202	159	248		
223T	162	058	084	039	081	401	238	481	852	486	
22TT	391	327	264	−039	217	586	362	730	534	218	761

Dimension 3   Scientism

Scale 1   Belief in scientism as a general value
  1 With the same techniques that have worked in the physical sciences we can eventually create an exact science of man.
  2 The social sciences can be employed to build an harmonious atmosphere in which the group will bring out the best in everyone.
  3 More public funds should be invested in the utilization of the social sciences to help people join the groups most suited to them.
  4 Science should be fully employed to help man achieve the belongingness he needs.

Scale 2   Scientism as a service to management
  1 Personality testing is an invaluable breakthrough in management.
  2 Personality matching of the employee with his work group is a vital management technique.
  3 Human relations training helps to overcome the adjustment difficulties of employees.

4 The more the art of management becomes a science the more it does for the employees.

	2311	2312	2313	2314	231T	2321	2322	2323	2324	232T
2311										
2312	270									
2313	326	308								
2314	216	394	381							
231T	663	660	661	728						
2321	261	365	231	264	361					
2322	164	300	294	507	421	542				
2323	048	238	258	145	214	295	297			
2324	211	259	308	123	288	266	330	439		
232T	245	400	369	358	443	733	744	660	731	
23TT	290	561	586	405	551	569	544	524	630	792

Account

These statements were given to managers in questionnaire form. The rubric was as follows.

The alternative answers are expressed as numbers; please indicate the one which comes closest to your opinion. If you feel 'it all depends . . .', then attempt an answer and note your reservations in the comments section at the end.

Circle the appropriate number from

Strongly disagree	Disagree		Agree	Strongly agree
1	2	3	4	5

To keep this questionnaire as brief as possible, just the numbers are given against the question and their meanings are given at the top of each page.

The statements were 'scrambled', shuffled like cards to a near-random order. This is done to keep a freshness for each and to try to stop cheating. A respondent may guess the themes and answer consistently – honestly or dishonestly.

The scrambling necessitates a code to unscramble the answers. All the answers have to be collated back into the design order before being punched on to cards. Invariably a computer statistical package is used that produces:

1 Means, mini-max and standard deviation: these values tell the researcher if 'the distribution is normal'.
2 Covariance and correlation matrices; these values tell the researcher if the putative scale is consistent and spot maverick items.

Having analysed for consistency – in my case by calculating alpha co-efficients (McKennel, 1970) – the researcher may puzzle over why some items did not 'work'. Eventually he must answer that 'face-validity' is not automatic and his respondents found differing meanings. He could go and ask them specifically about a few items. But in all probability he will simply continue recalculating a total score from the 'consistent' item scores and correlating it with whatever figure he has.

Appendix 2   For the record

The statistical analysis in chapter 9 is an outrage. It implies a chain of historical cause in data sampled at one time. Further, it so organizes the findings as to fit a biography. Finally, no known mode of path analysis would produce such an arrangement. Instead a hand-factor analysis – an hierarchical linkage analysis – produces the following clusters:

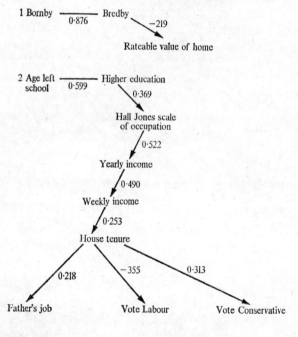

   Cluster 1 indicates the strong chance of being born in Banbury if bred in Banbury (and vice versa) and a disadvantaging effect on the rateable value of the home (or advantaging in paying less).

203

Cluster 2 is remarkably similar to the diagram drawn, apart from the omission of data from cluster 1.

Cluster 3 indicates the unlikelihood of housewives holding full-time jobs.

Appendix 3 Research units and research teams

Research units, or teams, have a team ideology: high expressivity and absent instrumentality – everyone's pals and no one is pinching ideas. The former persists long after petty feuds have been institutionalized by silence and the latter opposes discussion of others' ideas and stifles the more creative and each person's more creative moments.

Most researchers have fragile egos – they spend a lot of time apologizing for aspects of their work and are notorious for trivializing their time with bits of high-paid teaching, consultancy, university social life or just sitting anxious at a desk.

There is a very high mortality rate – people leaving before the job is finished – and people know this and pressurize each other to stay; or leave in a flock for better pastures.

The teams are not teams, they are loose affiliations between relatively weak people with special friendships/alliances and 'ideas men'. So the ethic of the team adds an additional burden. For each person, then, there can be a stylistic conflict between the interpersonality of the team and the impersonality of the containing institution. A liaison man can fulfil the role of 'bureaucrat' to neutralize this conflict.

Researchers are expected to take less than teachers and negotiate (or feel that they didn't bargain hard enough) a short-term contract salary. Every aspect is unrelated to performance.

Researchers get glory – the prestige of travelling, conferences, papers, lucrative jobs soon and light teaching loads now. Their goals are futuristic: the next paper, the next job. In tangible terms they have ambitions and aspirations or sorely feel the lack of them.

Researchers are hired because of the contribution their known expertise can make to the interdisciplinary team. Researchers are hired as 'sociologists', 'psychologists', etc. Usually they are aware that they are leaving their discipline and becoming 'applied'. They are leaving the uncommitted, sceptical pursuit of knowledge to continue the explanation of nature. Nevertheless they find it hard to describe their work as 'social engineering' – so much of the work is tidying up records.

The very occupation of researcher as a career is impossible. Sooner or later the person must realize that he cannot just research. There are always new contracts to be negotiated and there must be the planning of the next job before the present one is finished. There can only be the hope that the job will go on. In effect, the pressure upon a research team is to keep going and to get each other jobs. As there are many small tasks, more workers can be drawn in – at some times the out workers outnumber those giving them work. The researcher's family is involved because the spouse is educated. And if the spouse had only a technical training, he or she is at a loss. 'The group needs reinforcing'; the in-jokes abound. It is natural to feel unsure (even when the researcher does not know why he or she agrees to the presence of this force).

I was, and still am, a casualty myself. And yet there are moments of remembered hilarity and exhilaration. Who could deny that there are frontiers to our knowledge or that much of our knowledge is unsatisfactory? I do not condemn research units and their teams. But I suggest that all is not well with how they are run and what they have to do. Everyone knows that – everyone who knows of them.

Bibliography

ABELL, PETER (1969), 'Measurement in sociology, II measurement, structure and sociological theory', *Sociology*, vol. 3, no. 3, pp. 397–411.

ARIÈS, P. (1963), *Centuries of Childhood*, Routledge & Kegan Paul, London.

ARON, R. (1969), *Main Currents in Sociological Thought*, vol. 2, Penguin, Harmondsworth.

ATKINSON, S. M. (1971), 'Societal reactions to suicide: the role of coroners' definitions', in S. Cohen (ed.), *Images of Deviance*, Penguin, Harmondsworth, pp. 165–91.

BANDYOPADHAYAV, P. (1971), 'One sociology or many: some issues in radical sociology', *Sociological Review*, vol. 17, no. 1, 5. 29.

BECHHOFER, F. (1969), 'Occupations', in M. Stacey (ed.), *Comparability in Social Research*, Heinemann, London, pp. 112–14.

BECKER, H. S. (1963), *Outsiders: Studies in the Sociology of Deviance*, Free Press, New York.

BECKER, H. S. (1971), *Sociological Work*, Allen Lane, The Penguin Press, London.

BECKER, H. S., and HOROWITZ, IRVING L. (1972), 'Radical politics and sociological research: observations on methodology and ideology', *Amer. J. Sociol.*, vol. 75, no. 1, pp. 48–66.

BECKER, H. S. *et al.* (1961), *Boys in White*, University of Chicago Press.

BENSMAN, J., and VIDICH, A. (1960), 'Social theory in field research', in M. R. Stein and A. Vidich (eds), *Sociology on Trial*, Prentice-Hall, Englewood Cliffs, pp. 162–72, repr. from *Amer. J. Sociol.*, vol. 65, no. 6, pp. 577–84.

BERGER, J. (1967), *A Fortunate Man*, Penguin, Harmondsworth.

BERGER, PETER L. (1963), *Invitation to Sociology: A Humanistic Perspective*, Penguin, Harmondsworth.

BERGER, PETER L., and KELLNER, H. (1970), in H. P. Dreitzel (ed.), *Recent Sociology*, no. 2, Macmillan, New York.

BERGER, PETER L., and LUCKMANN, THOMAS (1967), *The Social Construction of Reality*, Allen Lane, The Penguin Press, London.

BIRNBAUM, N. (1969), *The Crisis of Industrial Society*, Oxford University Press, London.

P

BIRNBAUM, N. (1972), *Toward a Critical Sociology*, Oxford University Press, London.

BITTNER, E. (1967), 'Police discretion in emergency apprehension of mentally ill persons', *Social Problems*, 14, 4, Winter, pp. 278–92.

BLALOCK, HUBERT M., Jr (1963), 'Making causal inferences for unmeasured variables from correlations among indicators', *Amer. J. Sociol.*, vol. 69, July, pp. 53–62.

BLALOCK, HUBERT M., Jr (1964), *Causal Inferences in Non-Experimental Research*, University of North Carolina Press.

BLALOCK, HUBERT M., Jr (1965), 'Some implications of random measurement error for causal inferences', *Amer. J. Sociol.*, vol. 71, July, pp. 37–47.

BLALOCK, HUBERT M., Jr (1968), 'The measurement problem: a gap between the languages of theory and research', in Hubert M. Blalock Jr and Ann B. Blalock, *Methodology in Social Research*, McGraw-Hill, New York, pp. 5–27.

BLALOCK, HUBERT M., Jr (1969), 'Multiple indicators and the causal approach to measurement error', *Amer. J. Sociol.*, vol. 75, no. 2, pp. 264–72.

BLAU, P., DUNCAN, O. D., Jr, with TYREE, A. (1967), *The American Occupational Structure*, Wiley, New York.

BLUM, ALAN F., and MCHUGH, PETER (1971), 'The social ascription of motives', *Amer. Sociol. Rev.*, vol. 36, no. 1, pp. 98–109.

BLUMER, HERBERT (1969), 'What is wrong with social theory?' repr. in his *Symbolic Interactionism*, Prentice-Hall, Englewood Cliffs, pp. 140–52.

BONDY, F. (1970), 'Jean-Paul Sartre', in M. Cranston (ed.), *The New Left*, Bodley Head, London, pp. 51–82.

BORGER, R., and CIOFFI, F. (eds) (1970), *Explanation in the Behavioural Sciences*, Cambridge University Press.

BOTTOMORE, T. B. (1967), *Critics of Society: Radical Thought in North America*, Allen & Unwin, London.

BOUDON, RAYMOND (1965), 'A method of linear causal analysis: dependence analysis', *Amer. Sociol. Rev.*, vol. 30, June, pp. 365–74, repr. in Hubert M. Blalock Jr and Ann B. Blalock, *Methodology in Social Research*, McGraw-Hill, New York, pp. 199–235.

BRADBURY, M. (1963), *People Are Not For Eating*, Penguin, Harmondsworth.

BRAITHWAITE, R. B. (1955), *Scientific Explanation*, Cambridge University Press.

BRIDGMAN, P. W. (1961), *The Logic of Modern Physics*, Macmillan, New York.

BRUCE, L. (1966), *How to Talk Dirty and Influence People*, Peter Owen, London.

BRYAN, DEXTER (1971), 'Revisiting a reality constructionist: a reply to Heeren and Poss', *Amer. Sociologist*, vol. 6, no. 4, p. 326.

CAPLOW, T. (1968), *Two Against One: Coalitions in Triads*, Prentice-Hall, Englewood Cliffs.

CARNAP, RUDOLF (1958), 'Methodological character of theoretical concepts', in Herbert Feigl and Grover Maxwell (eds), *Minnesota Studies in the Philosophy of Science, vol. 1*, University of Minnesota Press.

CARPENTER, ROSEMARY (1969), 'That certain indestructible smile', *Radio Times*, vol. 185, no. 2396, p. 9.

CICOUREL, AARON V. (1968), *The Social Organization of Juvenile Justice*, Wiley, New York.

CICOUREL, AARON V. (1970), 'Basic and normative rules in the negotiation of status and role', in H. P. Dreitzel (ed.), *Recent Sociology*, no. 2, Macmillan, New York.

COATES, C. H., and PELLEGRIN, R. J. (1957), 'Executives and supervisors: contrasting self-conceptions and conceptions of each other', *Amer. Sociol. Rev.*, vol. 22, no. 2, pp. 217–20.

COHEN, S. (ed.) (1971), *Images of Deviance*, Penguin, Harmondsworth.

COHEN, S. (1972), *Folk Devils and Moral Panics: The Creation of Mods and Rockers*, MacGibbon & Kee, London.

COSTNER, HERBERT L. (1969a), 'Comments on Blalock', *Amer. J. Sociol.*, vol. 75, no. 2, p. 273.

COSTNER, HERBERT L. (1969b), 'Theory, deduction and rules of correspondence', *Amer. J. Sociol.*, vol. 75, no. 2, pp. 245–63.

COULSON, M. A., and RIDDELL, D. S. (1970), *Approaching Sociology: A Critical Introduction*, Routledge & Kegan Paul, London.

COXON, A. P. M. (1969), book review, *Sociology*, vol. 3, no. 2, pp. 247–50.

CROZIER, MICHEL (1964), *The Bureaucratic Phenomenon*, Tavistock, London.

CUBER, JOHN F., and HARROFF, PEGGY B. (1963), 'Relationships among men and women of the upper middle class', *Marriage and Family Living*, vol. 25, May, pp. 140–5, repr. with adaptations in Hyman Rodman (ed.), *Marriage, Family and Society*, Random House, New York, 1965, pp. 92–102.

CUZZORT, R. P. (1969), *Humanity and Modern Sociological Thought*, Holt, Rinehart & Winston, New York.

DENNIS, N. (1955), *Cards of Identity*, Weidenfeld & Nicolson, London.

DENNIS, N., HENRIQUES, F., and SLAUGHTER, C. (1956), *Coal Is Our Life: An Analysis of a Yorkshire Mining Community*, Eyre & Spottiswoode, London.

DENZIN, NORMAN K. (1969), 'Symbolic interactionism and ethnomethodology: a proposed synthesis', *Amer. Sociol. Rev.*, vol. 34, December, pp. 922–34.

DENZIN, NORMAN K. (1970), *The Research Act: A Theoretical Introduction to Sociological Methods*, Aldine, New York.

DJILAS, M. (1961), 'The new class', in A. Mendel (ed.), *Essential Works of Marxism*, Bantam Books, New York.

DJILAS, M. (1966), *The New Class*, Unwin, London.

DJILAS, M. (1969), *The Imperfect Society: Beyond the New Class*, Methuen, London.

DREITZEL, HANS PETER (ed.) (1970), *Recent Sociology*, no. 2, Macmillan, New York.

DUMONT, R. G., and WILSON, W. J. (1967), 'Aspects of concept formation, explication and theory construction', *Amer. Sociol. Rev.*, vol. 32, December, pp. 985–95.

DUNCAN, OTIS DUDLEY (1966), 'Path analysis: sociological examples', *Amer. J. Sociol.*, vol. 72, no. 1, pp. 1–16.

EMERSON, JOAN (1970), 'Behavior in private places: sustaining definitions of reality in gynaecological examinations', in H. P. Dreitzel (ed.), *Recent Sociology*, no. 2, pp. 73–97.

ENGELS, FRIEDRICH (1882), *Socialism, Utopian and Scientific*, in Karl Marx, *Selected Works*, vol. 1, ed. I. V. Adorsky, International Publishers, New York.

EVAN, W. H., and ZELDITCH, M. (1961), 'A laboratory experiment on bureaucratic authority', *Amer. Sociol. Rev.*, vol. 26, pp. 338–93.

FERRIS, PAUL (1969), 'The deadly serious business of being funny', *Observer Magazine*, 5 October, pp. 22–36; 'When the laugh's on you and me', *Observer Magazine*, 12 October, pp. 62–73.

FLETCHER, C. L. (1967), 'Organizational crises and supervision', unpublished Dip. I.A. thesis, University of Liverpool.

FLETCHER, C. L. (1969a), 'Silverman and organizations: a further comment', *Sociology*, vol. 3, no. 1, pp. 112–13.

FLETCHER, C. L. (1969b), 'On replication: notes on the notions of a replicability quotient and a generalizability quotient', *Sociology*, vol. 3, no. 1.

FLETCHER, C. L. (1972), 'Managers' stress at work', unpublished Ph.D. thesis, University of Aston in Birmingham.

FLETCHER, C. L. (1973), 'The end of management', in J. Child (ed.), *Man and Organization*, Allen & Unwin, London, pp. 135–57.

FOX, A. (1973), 'Industrial relations: a social critique of pluralist ideology', in J. Child (ed.), *Man and Organization*, Allen & Unwin, London.

FREUD, S. (1960), *Jokes and Their Relation to the Unconscious*, Routledge & Kegan Paul, London.

FRIEDRICHS, R. W. (1972), 'Dialectical sociology: toward a resolution of the current "crisis" in Western sociology', *Brit. J. Sociol.*, vol. 23, no. 3, September, pp. 263–74.

GALTUNG, JOHAN (1967), *Theory and Methods of Social Research*, Allen & Unwin, London.

GARFINKEL, HAROLD (1967), *Studies in Ethnomethodology*, Prentice-Hall, Englewood Cliffs.

GARRETT, H. E. (1947), *Statistics in Psychology and Education*, Methuen, London.

GERTH, H., and MILLS, C. W. (1954), *Character and Social Structure*, Routledge & Kegan Paul, London.

GLASER, BARNEY G., and STRAUSS, ANSELM L. (1967), *The Discovery of Grounded Theory: Strategies for Quantitative Research*, Weidenfeld & Nicolson, London.

GOFFMAN, ERVING (1959), *The Presentation of Self in Everyday Life*, Doubleday Anchor, New York.

GOFFMAN, ERVING (1961), *Asylums*, Penguin, Harmondsworth.

GOFFMAN, ERVING (1963), *Stigma: Notes on the Management of Spoiled Identity*, Penguin, Harmondsworth.

GOFFMAN, ERVING (1969), *Strategic Interaction*, Blackwell, Oxford.

GOLDTHORPE, J. H. (1959), 'Technical organization as a factor in supervisor worker conflict', *Brit. J. Sociol.*, vol. 10, no. 3, pp. 213–30.

GOLDTHORPE, J. H., and LOCKWOOD, D. (1963), 'Affluence and the British class structure', *Sociol. Rev.*, vol. 11, no. 2, pp. 133–63.

GOLDTHORPE, J. H., LOCKWOOD, D., BECHHOFER, F., and PLATT, J. (1967), 'The affluent worker and the thesis of embourgeoisement: some preliminary findings', *Sociology*, vol. 1, no. 1, pp. 11–32.

GOUGH, T. H. (1968), *Black Country Stories*, rev. and ed. Harold Parsons, A Black Country Society Publication with an introduction by Billy Russell.

GOULDNER, A. W. (1957), 'Cosmopolitans and locals: towards an analysis of latent social notes', *Administrative Science Quarterly*, vol. 2, pp. 281–306 (1), 444–80 (2).

GOULDNER, A. W. (1964), 'Anti-Minotaur: the myth of a value free sociology', in I. L. Horowitz (ed.), *The New Sociology* . . ., Oxford University Press, pp. 196–217. A presidential address delivered at the annual meeting of the society for the study of social problems, 28 August 1961, and originally published in *Social Problems*, vol. 9, no. 3, 1962.

GOULDNER, A. W. (1970), *The Coming Crisis of Western Sociology*, Heinemann, London.

GURVITCH, G. (1955), 'La vocation actuelle de sociologie', quoted in P. A. Sorokin, *Sociological Theories of Today*, Harper & Row, London, 1966, p. 474.

HEMPEL, CARL G. (1949), 'The function of general laws in history', in Herbert Feigl and Wilfred Sellers (eds), *Readings in Philosophical Analysis*, Appleton-Century-Crofts, New York.

HEMPEL, CARL G. (1952), 'Classification: fundamentals of concept formation in empirical science', *International Encyclopedia of Unified Science*, vol. 2, no. 7, University of Chicago Press, p. 9.

HEMPEL, CARL G. (1958), 'The theoretician's dilemma: a study in the logic of theory construction', in Herbert Feigl and Grover Maxwell (eds), *Minnesota Studies in the Philosophy of Science, vol. 1*, University of Minnesota Press.

HEMPEL, CARL G. (1960), 'Operationalism, observation and theoretical terms', in Arthur Danto and Sidney Morgenbesser (eds), *Philosophy of Science*, Meridian Books, Cleveland.

HEMPEL, CARL G. (1963), 'Typological methods in the social sciences', in Maurice Natanson (ed.), *Philosophy of the Social Sciences*, Random House, New York.

HEMPEL, CARL G. (1966), *Philosophy of Natural Science*, Prentice-Hall, Englewood Cliffs.

HILTON, GORDON (1971), 'Causal inference analysis: a seductive process', mimeo, Industrial Administration Research Unit, University of Aston in Birmingham.

HINDESS, BARRY (1972), 'The "phenomenological" sociology of Alfred Schutz', *Economy and Society*, vol. 1, no. 1, pp. 1–27.

HIRST, P. Q. (1972a), 'Recent tendencies in sociological theory', *Economy and Society*, vol. 1, no. 2, pp. 218–28.

211

BIBLIOGRAPHY

HIRST, P. Q. (1972b), 'Radical deviancy theory and Marxism: a reply to Taylor and Walton', *Economy and Society*, vol. 1, no. 3, pp. 351–6.

HODGES, C. (1971), *Coming of Age*, John Jones, Cardiff.

HOROWITZ, I. L. (1964), *The New Sociology: Essays in Social Science and Social Theory in Honour of C. Wright Mills*, Oxford University Press.

HUNT, A. (1969), 'Naked desperation', *New Society*, vol. 14, no. 336, p. 524.

JACKSON, BRIAN (1968), *Working Class Community: Some General Notions Raised by a Series of Studies in Northern England*, Routledge & Kegan Paul, London.

JACKSON, BRIAN, and MARSDEN, D. (1966), *Education and the Working Class: Some General Themes Raised by a Study of 88 Working-class Children in a Northern Industrial City*, Penguin, Harmondsworth.

JACOB, P. E. (1955), 'A multi-dimensional classification of atrocity stories', in Paul F. Lazarsfeld and Morris Rosenberg (eds), *The Language of Social Research*, Free Press, Chicago, pp. 54–7.

KAPLAN, ABRAHAM (1964), *The Conduct of Inquiry: Methodology for Behavioral Science*, Chandler Publishing Co., San Francisco.

KENDALL, PATRICIA L. (1950), 'A review of indicators used in *The American Soldier*', in Paul F. Lazarsfeld and Morris Rosenberg (eds), *The Language of Social Research*, Free Press, Chicago, pp. 37–9, repr. from *Problems of Survey Analysis*, pp. 183–6, in Robert K. Merton and Paul F. Lazarsfeld (eds), *Continuities in Social Research, Studies in the Scope and Method of The American Soldier*, Free Press, Chicago, 1950.

KERR, MADELINE (1958), *The People of Ship Street*, Routledge & Kegan Paul, London.

KLINE, N. S. (1969), *Depression: Its Diagnosis and Treatment*, S. Kargel, Basle.

KOESTLER, A. (1964), *The Act of Creation*, Hutchinson, London.

KOFFKA, K. (1935), *Principles of Gestalt Psychology*, Harcourt Brace, New York.

KOGAN, EUGEN (n.d.), *The Theory and Practice of Hell*, Berkley Publishing Corp., New York.

LAING, R. D., and ESTERSON, A. (1964), *Sanity, Madness and the Family*, Penguin, Harmondsworth.

LAZARSFELD, PAUL F., et al. (1948), *The People's Choice*, Columbia University Press.

LAZARSFELD, PAUL F., and ROSENBERG, MORRIS (eds) (1955), *The Language of Social Research*, Free Press, Chicago.

LEACH, EDMUND R. (1964), 'Concept models', *New Society*, no. 85, 14 May, pp. 22–3.

LEE, ALFRED MCCLUNG (1972), in *Insurgent Sociologist*, vol. 3, no. 2.

LEVY, PHILIP, and PUGH, DEREK (1969), 'Scaling and multivariate analyses in the study of organizational variables', *Sociology*, vol. 3, no. 2, pp. 193–214.

LIPSET, S. M. (1953), 'Opinion formation in a crisis situation', *Public Opinion Quarterly*, vol. 17, no. 1, pp. 20–46, repr. in Paul F. Lazarsfeld and Morris Rosenberg (eds), *The Language of Social Research*, Free Press, Chicago, pp. 125–40.

LOCKWOOD, D. (1964), 'Social integration and system integration', in

212

G. K. Zollschan and W. Hirsch (eds), *Explorations in Social Change*, Routledge & Kegan Paul, London, pp. 244–57.

LUCKMANN, THOMAS (1972), book review, *Contemporary Sociology*, vol. 1, no. 1, pp. 30–1.

LUNDBERG, G. A. (1939), *Foundations of Sociology*, Macmillan, New York.

MACCARTHY, FIONA (1969), 'In Blackpool', *Guardian*, 14 July, p. 7.

MCCORMACK, THELMA (1973), review of *The Politics of the Family and Other Essays* by R. D. Laing, *Contemporary Sociology*, vol. 2, no. 1, pp. 22–3.

MCHUGH, PETER (1969), 'A common-sense perception of deviance', in J. D. Douglas (ed.), *Deviance and Respectability*, Basic Books, New York, repr. in H. P. Dreitzel (ed.), *Recent Sociology*, no. 2, Macmillan, New York, pp. 151–80.

MCINTOSH, MARY (1972), review of *The Drugtakers*, *Brit. J. Sociol.*, vol. 23, no. 2, pp. 249–50.

MCKENNEL, A. (1970), 'Attitude measurement: use of coefficient Alpha with cluster or factor analysis', *Sociology*, vol. 4, no. 2, pp. 227–45.

MAO TSE-TUNG (1926/1956), *Analysis of the Classes in Chinese Society*, Foreign Language Press, Peking.

MARCH, J., SIMON, H. A., with the collaboration of H. Guetzhow (1958), *Organizations*, Wiley, New York.

MARTINDALE, J. (1969), *Dry Mass*, Eyre & Spottiswoode, London.

MEAD, GEORGE HERBERT (1934), *Mind, Self and Society: From the Standpoint of a Social Behaviorist*, ed. with introduction by Charles W. Morris, University of Chicago Press.

MEAD, GEORGE HERBERT (1956), *On Social Psychology*, selected papers, ed. with an introduction by Anselm Strauss, University of Chicago Press.

MELVILLE, JOY (1969), 'Down among the gag men', *Punch*, 8 October, pp. 584–5.

MERTON, ROBERT K., and LAZARSFELD, PAUL F. (1950), *Continuities in Social Research: Studies in the Scope and Method of The American Soldier*, Free Press, Chicago.

MILLS, C. W. (1956), *The Power Elite*, Oxford University Press.

MILLS, C. W. (1959a), 'On intellectual craftmanship', in *The Sociological Imagination*, Oxford University Press, pp. 195–226.

MILLS, C. W. (1959b), *The Sociological Imagination*, Oxford University Press.

NAGEL, E. (1961), *The Structure of Science: Problems in the Logic of Scientific Explanation*, Routledge & Kegan Paul, London.

NEWTON, H. (1972), interview, *Rolling Stone*, 3 September, p. 30.

O'NEILL, J. P. (1973), copy for *Making Sense Together*, quoted in Pseud's Corner, *Private Eye*, no. 299, 1 June.

OTTOWAY, R. (1966), 'The lad himself: a master of the self-inflicted wound', *Nova*, November, pp. 60–6.

PAUL, JIMMY and MUSTAFA SUPPORT COMMITTEE (1973), '20 years', The Action Centre, 134 Villa Road, Handsworth, Birmingham 19.

PHILLIPS, BERNARD S. (1966), *Social Research: Strategy and Tactics*, Collier-Macmillan, London.

POLANYI, M. (1964), *Personal Knowledge*, Harper & Row, New York.

RADCLIFFE-BROWN, W. (1945), *Structure and Function in Primitive Society*, Cohen & West, London.

RANCIÈRE, JACQUES (1971), 'The concept of critique and the "Critique of political economy"', *Theoretical Practice*, no. 2, April, pp. 45–6.

REICHENBACH, HANS (1964), *The Rise of Scientific Philosophy*, University of California Press, Berkeley.

REISMAN, D., with GLAZER, N., and DENNEY, R. (1950), *The Lonely Crowd: A Study of the Changing American Character*, Yale University Press (quotations from 2nd ed., 1961).

REX, J. A. (1961), *Key Problems in Sociological Theory*, Routledge & Kegan Paul, London.

ROCK, P. (1973), 'Phenomenalism and Essentialism in the sociology of deviance', *Sociology*, vol. 7, no. 1, January, pp. 17–30.

ROETHLISBERGER, F. J. (1943), *Management and Morale*, Harvard University Press.

ROETHLISBERGER, F. J. (1945), 'The foreman: master and victim of double-talk', *Harvard Business Review*, vol. 23, no. 4, pp. 283–98.

ROSENBERG, B., and WHITE, D. M. (1957), *Mass Culture: The Popular Arts in America*, Free Press, Chicago.

SARTRE, J.-P. (1963), *The Problem of Method*, Methuen, London.

SAYLES, STEVEN M. (1969), 'Organisational role as a risk factor in coronary disease', *Administrative Science Quarterly*, vol. 14, no. 3, pp. 325–37.

SCHUTZ, ALFRED (1967), *The Phenomenology of the Social World*, translated by George Walsh and Frederick Lehnert with an introduction by George Walsh, Northwestern University Press.

SCHWENDINGER, HERMAN, and SCHWENDINGER, JULIA (1972), 'Sociologists of the chair and the natural law tradition', *Insurgent Sociologist*, vol. 3, no. 2, pp. 2–18.

SEIGAL, S. (1956), *Non Parametric Statistics*, McGraw-Hill, New York.

SHANIN, TEODOR (1972), 'Units of sociological analysis', *Sociology*, vol. 6, no. 3, pp. 351–67.

SILVERMAN, DAVID (1972), review of Alfred Schutz, *Reflections on the Problem of Relevance*, ed., annotated, with an introduction by Richard M. Zaner, Yale University Press, *Sociology*, vol. 6, no. 1, p. 159.

SILVERMAN, DAVID, and JONES, JILL (1973), 'Getting in: the managed accomplishment of "correct" selection outcomes', in J. Child (ed.), *Man and Organization*, Allen & Unwin, London.

SIMEY, T. S. (1968), *Social Science and Social Purpose*, Constable, London.

SIMMEL, GEORG (1950), *The Sociology of Georg Simmel*, trans., ed., and with an introduction by K. H. Wolff, Free Press, Chicago.

SKLAIR, L. (1972), review of Borger and Cioffi, *Brit. J. Sociol.*, vol. 23, no. 3, pp. 368–9.

SPARKS, RICHARD F. (1973), review of Stanley Cohen (ed.), *Images of Deviance*, *Sociology*, vol. 7, no. 1, pp. 148–9.

STEIN, M. R. (1963), 'The poetic metaphors of sociology', in M. R. Stein and A. Vidich (eds), *Sociology on Trial*, Prentice-Hall, Englewood Cliffs.

STINCHCOMBE, ARTHUR (1968), *Constructing Social Theories*, Harcourt, Brace & World, New York.

STOUFFER, SAMUEL A. *et al.* (1947), *Measurement and Prediction: Studies in Social Psychology in World War II*, vol. 4, Princeton University Press.

STOUFFER, SAMUEL A. *et al.* (1949–50), *The American Soldier*, 4 vols, Princeton University Press.

STROTZ, ROBERT H., and WOLD, HERMAN (1960), 'Recursive versus non-recursive systems: an attempt at synthesis', *Econometrica*, vol. 28, April, pp. 417–27.

SUDNOW, D. (1968), 'Dead on arrival', *New Society*, vol. 11, no. 280, 8 Feb., pp. 187–9, an adaptation of part of the book, *Passing On: The Social Organization of Dying*, Prentice-Hall, Englewood Cliffs, 1967.

SWEEZY, P. M. (1953), *The Present as History: Essays and Reviews on Capitalism and Socialism*, Monthly Review Press, New York.

TAYLOR, LAURIE (1972), 'The significance and interpretation of replies to motivational questions: the case of sex offenders', *Sociology*, vol. 6, no. 1, pp. 23–40.

THOULESS, R. (1925), *General and Social Psychology*, University Tutorial Press, London.

TUNSTALL, J. (1962), *The Fishermen*, MacGibbon & Kee, London.

UPSHAW, HARRY S. (1968), 'Attitude measurement', in Hubert M. Blalock Jr and Ann B. Blalock, *Methodology in Social Research*, McGraw-Hill, New York, pp. 60–111.

WEBER, M. (1948), 'Science as a vocation', in H. H. Gerth, and C. W. Mills (trans. and eds), *From Max Weber*, Routledge & Kegan Paul, London, pp. 129–56.

WEEKS, DAVID (1972), 'Self, society and socialization', in *Social Interaction*, Open University Press, Bletchley, pp. 31–52.

WERTS, CHARLES E. (1968), 'Path analysis: testimonial of a proselyte', *Amer. J. Sociol.*, vol. 73, no. 4, pp. 509–12.

WHYTE, W. H. (1956), *The Organization Man*, Penguin, Harmondsworth.

WILLER, DAVID (1967), *Scientific Sociology*, Prentice-Hall International, London.

WILLIAMS, R. (1962), *Communications*, Penguin, Harmondsworth.

WILLMOTT, P., and YOUNG, M. (1957), *Family and Kinship in East London*, Routledge & Kegan Paul, London.

WINCH, PETER (1958), *The Idea of a Social Science and Its Relation to Philosophy*, Routledge & Kegan Paul, London.

WOLD, HERMAN O. A. (1954), 'Casuality and econometrics', *Econometrica*, vol. 22, April, pp. 162–77.

WOLD, HERMAN O. A., and JURGEN, LARS (1953), *Demand Analysis*, Wiley, New York.

WOLFE, TOM (1968), *The Electric Kool-Aid Acid Test*, Bantam Books, New York.

WOODWARD, JOAN (1958), *Management and Technology*, HMSO, London.

WORSLEY, P. (1964), *The Third World*, Weidenfeld & Nicolson, London.

WRIGHT, SEWALL (1920), 'The relative importance of heredity and environment in determining the piebald pattern of guinea pigs', *Proceedings of the National Academy of Science*, vol. 6, pp. 320–32.

WRIGHT, SEWALL (1921), 'Correlation and causation', *Journal of Agricultural Research*, vol. 20, January, pp. 557–85.

BIBLIOGRAPHY

WRIGHT, SEWALL (1925), 'Corn and hog correlations', US Department of Agriculture Bulletin 1300, Government Printing Office, Washington.

WRIGHT, SEWALL (1939), 'The method of path coefficients', *Annals of Mathematical Statistics*, vol. 5, September, pp. 161–215.

WRIGHT, SEWALL (1951), 'The genetical structure of populations', *Annals of Eugenics*, vol. 15, March, pp. 323–54.

WRIGHT, SEWALL (1954), 'The interpretation of multivariate systems', in Oscar Kempthorne, Theodore A. Bancroft, John W. Gowen, and Jay D. Lush (eds), *Statistics and Mathematics in Biology*, Iowa State University Press.

WRIGHT, SEWALL (1960a), 'The genetics of vital characters of the guinea pig', *Journal of Cellular and Comparative Physiology*, vol. 26 (suppl. 1, November).

WRIGHT, SEWALL (1960b), 'Path coefficients and path regressions: alternative or complementary concepts?' *Biometrics*, vol. 16, June, pp. 189–202.

WRIGHT, SEWALL (1960c), 'The treatment of reciprocal interaction, with or without lag, in path analysis', *Biometrics*, vol. 26, September, pp. 423–45.

WRIGHT, SEWALL (1964), 'On the nature of size factors', *Genetics*, vol. 3, pp. 367–74.

YANOUSAS, J. M. (1964), 'A comparative of work organization and supervisory behaviour', *Human Organization*, vol. 23, no. 3, pp. 245–53.

YOUNG, JOCK (1971), *The Drugtakers: The Social Meaning of Drug Use*, MacGibbon & Kee, London.

YOUNG, T. R. (1971), 'The politics of sociology: Gouldner, Goffman and Garfinkel', *Amer. Sociologist*, vol. 6, November, pp. 276–81.

ZIJDERVELD, ANTON C. (1972), 'The problem of adequacy: reflections on Alfred Schutz's contribution to the methodology of the social sciences', *Archiv. Europ. Sociol.*, vol. 13, pp. 176–90.

ZOLA, I. K. (1971), 'Medicine as an institution of social control', presented at the Medical Sociology Conference of the British Sociological Association, Weston-super-Mare, November.

Name index

Abell, P., 55–6
Ariès, P., 183
Aron, R., 98
Atkinson, J. M., 139

Bandyopadhyav, P., 175
Bechhofer, F., 5, 166
Becker, H. S., 106–7, 108, 116, 121, 122, 124, 125, 126, 127, 130, 137, 139, 140, 150, 188
Bensman, J., 180
Berger, J., 79
Berger, P. L., 105, 108, 109, 110, 119, 120, 122, 135
Birnbaum, N., 181, 185
Bittner, E., 70
Blalock, H. M., 50, 52, 54, 55, 61, 63
Blau, P., 162, 163
Blum, A. F., 134
Blumer, H., 109, 126
Bondy, F., 178
Borger, R., 63
Bottomore, T. B., 175, 182
Boudon, R., 50
Bradbury, M., 184
Bridgman, P. W., 51, 131
Bruce, L., 157
Bryan, D., 110

Caplow, T., 154
Carnap, R., 54
Carpenter, R., 150

Cicourel, A., 105, 108, 112, 139
Cioffi, F., 63
Coates, C. H., 12
Cohen, S., 137, 140
Costner, H. L., 50
Coulson, M. A., 180
Coxon, A. P. M., 55–6
Crozier, M., 5
Cuber, J. F., 124, 125, 131, 132
Cuzzort, R. P., 176

Dennis, N., 136
Dennis, N. (novelist), 74
Denzin, N. K., 108, 124, 125, 126, 127, 131
Djilas, M., 170
Dreitzel, H. P., 104, 105, 106, 113
Dumont, R. G., 61
Duncan, O. D., 50, 54, 162, 163

Emerson, J., 79, 89, 119
Engels, F., 115
Esterson, A., 181, 182
Evan, W. H., 6

Ferris, P., 147, 155, 159, 160
Fletcher, C. L., 4, 16
Fox, A., 178

Galtung, J., 37, 39, 40, 41, 44, 55, 56
Garfinkel, H., 105, 107, 116, 120, 128, 129, 130, 134

Subject index

International Library of Sociology

Edited by
John Rex
University of Warwick

Founded by
Karl Mannheim

as The International Library of Sociology
and Social Reconstruction

*This Catalogue also contains other Social Science
series published by Routledge*

Routledge & Kegan Paul   London and Boston

68-74 Carter Lane London EC4V 5EL
9 Park Street Boston Mass 02108

Contents

● *Books so marked are available in paperback*
All books are in Metric Demy 8vo format (216 × 138mm approx.)

GENERAL SOCIOLOGY

Belshaw, Cyril. The Conditions of Social Performance. *An Exploratory Theory. 144 pp.*

Brown, Robert. Explanation in Social Science. *208 pp.*

●   Rules and Laws in Sociology.

Cain, Maureen E. Society and the Policeman's Role. *About 300 pp.*

Gibson, Quentin. The Logic of Social Enquiry. *240 pp.*

Gurvitch, Georges. Sociology of Law. *Preface by Roscoe Pound. 264 pp.*

Homans, George C. Sentiments and Activities: *Essays in Social Science. 336 pp.*

Johnson, Harry M. Sociology: *a Systematic Introduction. Foreword by Robert K. Merton. 710 pp.*

Mannheim, Karl. Essays on Sociology and Social Psychology. *Edited by Paul Keckskemeti. With Editorial Note by Adolph Lowe. 344 pp.*

  Systematic Sociology: *An Introduction to the Study of Society. Edited by J. S. Erös and Professor W. A. C. Stewart. 220 pp.*

Martindale, Don. The Nature and Types of Sociological Theory. *292 pp.*

● **Maus, Heinz.** A Short History of Sociology. *234 pp.*

Mey, Harald. Field-Theory. *A Study of its Application in the Social Sciences. 352 pp.*

Myrdal, Gunnar. Value in Social Theory: *A Collection of Essays on Methodology. Edited by Paul Streeten. 332 pp.*

Ogburn, William F., and **Nimkoff, Meyer F.** A Handbook of Sociology. *Preface by Karl Mannheim. 656 pp. 46 figures. 35 tables.*

Parsons, Talcott, and **Smelser, Neil J.** Economy and Society: *A Study in the Integration of Economic and Social Theory. 362 pp.*

● **Rex, John.** Key Problems of Sociological Theory. *220 pp.*

Urry, John. Reference Groups and the Theory of Revolution.

FOREIGN CLASSICS OF SOCIOLOGY

● **Durkheim, Emile.** Suicide. *A Study in Sociology. Edited and with an Introduction by George Simpson. 404 pp.*

  Professional Ethics and Civic Morals. *Translated by Cornelia Brookfield. 288 pp.*

● **Gerth, H. H.,** and **Mills, C. Wright.** From Max Weber: *Essays in Sociology. 502 pp.*

Tönnies, Ferdinand. Community and Association. *(Gemeinschaft und Gesellschaft.) Translated and Supplemented by Charles P. Loomis. Foreword by Pitirim A. Sorokin. 334 pp.*

SOCIAL STRUCTURE

Andreski, Stanislav. Military Organization and Society. *Foreword by Professor A. R. Radcliffe-Brown. 226 pp. 1 folder.*

Coontz, Sydney H. Population Theories and the Economic Interpretation. *202 pp.*

Coser, Lewis. The Functions of Social Conflict. *204 pp.*

Dickie-Clark, H. F. Marginal Situation: *A Sociological Study of a Coloured Group. 240 pp. 11 tables.*

Glass, D. V. (Ed.). Social Mobility in Britain. *Contributions by J. Berent, T. Bottomore, R. C. Chambers, J. Floud, D. V. Glass, J. R. Hall, H. T. Himmelweit, R. K. Kelsall, F. M. Martin, C. A. Moser, R. Mukherjee, and W. Ziegel. 420 pp.*

Glaser, Barney, and **Strauss, Anselm L.** Status Passage. *A Formal Theory, 208 pp.*

Jones, Garth N. Planned Organizational Change: *An Exploratory Study Using an Empirical Approach. 268 pp.*

Kelsall, R. K. Higher Civil Servants in Britain: *From 1870 to the Present Day. 268 pp. 31 tables.*

König, René. The Community. *232 pp. Illustrated.*

● **Lawton, Denis.** Social Class, Language and Education. *192 pp.*

McLeish, John. The Theory of Social Change: *Four Views Considered. 128 pp.*

Marsh, David C. The Changing Social Structure of England and Wales, 1871-1961. *288 pp.*

Mouzelis, Nicos. Organization and Bureaucracy. *An Analysis of Modern Theories. 240 pp.*

Mulkay, M. J. Functionalism, Exchange and Theoretical Strategy. *272 pp.*

Ossowski, Stanislaw. Class Structure in the Social Consciousness. *210 pp.*

SOCIOLOGY AND POLITICS

Hertz, Frederick. Nationality in History and Politics: *A Psychology and Sociology of National Sentiment and Nationalism. 432 pp.*

Kornhauser, William. The Politics of Mass Society. *272 pp. 20 tables.*

Laidler, Harry W. History of Socialism. *Social-Economic Movements: An Historical and Comparative Survey of Socialism, Communism, Co-operation, Utopianism; and other Systems of Reform and Reconstruction. 992 pp.*

Mannheim, Karl. Freedom, Power and Democratic Planning. *Edited by Hans Gerth and Ernest K. Bramstedt. 424 pp.*

Mansur, Fatma. Process of Independence. *Foreword by A. H. Hanson. 208 pp.*

Martin, David A. Pacificism: *an Historical and Sociological Study. 262 pp.*

Myrdal, Gunnar. The Political Element in the Development of Economic Theory. *Translated from the German by Paul Streeten. 282 pp.*

Wootton, Graham. Workers, Unions and the State. *188 pp.*

FOREIGN AFFAIRS: THEIR SOCIAL, POLITICAL AND ECONOMIC FOUNDATIONS

Mayer, J. P. Political Thought in France from the Revolution to the Fifth Republic. *164 pp.*

CRIMINOLOGY

Ancel, Marc. Social Defence: *A Modern Approach to Criminal Problems. Foreword by Leon Radzinowicz. 240 pp.*

Cloward, Richard A., and **Ohlin, Lloyd E.** Delinquency and Opportunity: *A Theory of Delinquent Gangs. 248 pp.*

Downes, David M. The Delinquent Solution. *A Study in Subcultural Theory. 296 pp.*

Dunlop, A. B., and **McCabe, S.** Young Men in Detention Centres. *192 pp.*

Friedlander, Kate. The Psycho-Analytical Approach to Juvenile Delinquency: *Theory, Case Studies, Treatment. 320 pp.*

Glueck, Sheldon, and **Eleanor.** Family Environment and Delinquency. *With the statistical assistance of Rose W. Kneznek. 340 pp.*

Lopez-Rey, Manuel. Crime. *An Analytical Appraisal. 288 pp.*

Mannheim, Hermann. Comparative Criminology: *a Text Book. Two volumes. 442 pp. and 380 pp.*

Morris, Terence. The Criminal Area: *A Study in Social Ecology. Foreword by Hermann Mannheim. 232 pp. 25 tables. 4 maps.*

● **Taylor, Ian, Walton, Paul,** and **Young, Jock.** The New Criminology. *For a Social Theory of Deviance.*

SOCIAL PSYCHOLOGY

Bagley, Christopher. The Social Psychology of the Epileptic Child. *320 pp.*

Barbu, Zevedei. Problems of Historical Psychology. *248 pp.*

Blackburn, Julian. Psychology and the Social Pattern. *184 pp.*

● **Brittan, Arthur.** Meanings and Situations. *224 pp.*

● **Fleming, C. M.** Adolescence: Its Social Psychology. *With an Introduction to recent findings from the fields of Anthropology, Physiology, Medicine, Psychometrics and Sociometry. 288 pp.*

● The Social Psychology of Education: *An Introduction and Guide to Its Study. 136 pp.*

Homans, George C. The Human Group. *Foreword by Bernard DeVoto. Introduction by Robert K. Merton. 526 pp.*

Social Behaviour: *its Elementary Forms. 416 pp.*

Klein, Josephine. The Study of Groups. *226 pp. 31 figures. 5 tables.*

Linton, Ralph. The Cultural Background of Personality. *132 pp.*

Mayo, Elton. The Social Problems of an Industrial Civilization. *With an appendix on the Political Problem. 180 pp.*

Ottaway, A. K. C. Learning Through Group Experience. *176 pp.*

Ridder, J. C. de. The Personality of the Urban African in South Africa. *A Thematic Apperception Test Study. 196 pp. 12 plates.*

● **Rose, Arnold M.** (Ed.). Human Behaviour and Social Processes: *an Interactionist Approach. Contributions by Arnold M. Rose, Ralph H. Turner, Anselm Strauss, Everett C. Hughes, E. Franklin Frazier, Howard S. Becker, et al. 696 pp.*

Smelser, Neil J. Theory of Collective Behaviour. *448 pp.*
Stephenson, Geoffrey M. The Development of Conscience. *128 pp.*
Young, Kimball. Handbook of Social Psychology. *658 pp. 16 figures. 10 tables.*

SOCIOLOGY OF THE FAMILY

Banks, J. A. Prosperity and Parenthood: *A Study of Family Planning among The Victorian Middle Classes. 262 pp.*
Bell, Colin R. Middle Class Families: *Social and Geographical Mobility. 224 pp.*
Burton, Lindy. Vulnerable Children. *272 pp.*
Gavron, Hannah. The Captive Wife: *Conflicts of Household Mothers. 190 pp.*
George, Victor, and **Wilding, Paul.** Motherless Families. *220 pp.*
Klein, Josephine. Samples from English Cultures.
1. Three Preliminary Studies and Aspects of Adult Life in England. *447 pp.*
2. Child-Rearing Practices and Index. *247 pp.*
Klein, Viola. Britain's Married Women Workers. *180 pp.*
The Feminine Character. *History of an Ideology. 244 pp.*
McWhinnie, Alexina M. Adopted Children. *How They Grow Up. 304 pp.*
Myrdal, Alva, and **Klein, Viola.** Women's Two Roles: *Home and Work. 238 pp. 27 tables.*
Parsons, Talcott, and **Bales, Robert F.** Family: Socialization and Interaction Process. *In collaboration with James Olds, Morris Zelditch and Philip E. Slater. 456 pp. 50 figures and tables.*

SOCIAL SERVICES

Bastide, Roger. The Sociology of Mental Disorder. *Translated from the French by Jean McNeil. 260 pp.*
Carlebach, Julius. Caring For Children in Trouble. *266 pp.*
Forder, R. A. (Ed.). Penelope Hall's Social Services of England and Wales. *352 pp.*
George, Victor. Foster Care. *Theory and Practice. 234 pp.*
Social Security: *Beveridge and After. 258 pp.*
● **Goetschius, George W.** Working with Community Groups. *256 pp.*
Goetschius, George W., and **Tash, Joan.** Working with Unattached Youth. *416 pp.*
Hall, M. P., and **Howes, I. V.** The Church in Social Work. *A Study of Moral Welfare Work undertaken by the Church of England. 320 pp.*
Heywood, Jean S. Children in Care: *the Development of the Service for the Deprived Child. 264 pp.*
Hoenig, J., and **Hamilton, Marian W.** The De-Segration of the Mentally Ill. *284 pp.*
Jones, Kathleen. Mental Health and Social Policy, 1845-1959. *264 pp.*

King, Roy D., Raynes, Norma V., and **Tizard, Jack.** Patterns of Residential Care. *356 pp.*

Leigh, John. Young People and Leisure. *256 pp.*

Morris, Mary. Voluntary Work and the Welfare State. *300 pp.*

Morris, Pauline. Put Away: *A Sociological Study of Institutions for the Mentally Retarded. 364 pp.*

Nokes, P. L. The Professional Task in Welfare Practice. *152 pp.*

Timms, Noel. Psychiatric Social Work in Great Britain (1939-1962). *280 pp.*
● Social Casework: *Principles and Practice. 256 pp.*

Young, A. F., and **Ashton, E. T.** British Social Work in the Nineteenth Century. *288 pp.*

Young, A. F. Social Services in British Industry. *272 pp.*

SOCIOLOGY OF EDUCATION

Banks, Olive. Parity and Prestige in English Secondary Education: a Study in Educational Sociology. *272 pp.*

Bentwich, Joseph. Education in Israel. *224 pp. 8 pp. plates.*
● **Blyth, W. A. L.** English Primary Education. *A Sociological Description.*
  1. Schools. *232 pp.*
  2. Background. *168 pp.*

Collier, K. G. The Social Purposes of Education: *Personal and Social Values in Education. 268 pp.*

Dale, R. R., and **Griffith, S.** Down Stream: *Failure in the Grammar School. 108 pp.*

Dore, R. P. Education in Tokugawa Japan. *356 pp. 9 pp. plates*

Evans, K. M. Sociometry and Education. *158 pp.*

Foster, P. J. Education and Social Change in Ghana. *336 pp. 3 maps.*

Fraser, W. R. Education and Society in Modern France. *150 pp.*

Grace, Gerald R. Role Conflict and the Teacher. *About 200 pp.*

Hans, Nicholas. New Trends in Education in the Eighteenth Century. *278 pp. 19 tables.*
● Comparative Education: *A Study of Educational Factors and Traditions. 360 pp.*

Hargreaves, David. Interpersonal Relations and Education. *432 pp.*
● Social Relations in a Secondary School. *240 pp.*

Holmes, Brian. Problems in Education. *A Comparative Approach. 336 pp.*

King, Ronald. Values and Involvement in a Grammar School. *164 pp.*
School Organization and Pupil Involvement. *A Study of Secondary Schools.*
● **Mannheim, Karl,** and **Stewart, W. A. C.** An Introduction to the Sociology of Education. *206 pp.*

Morris, Raymond N. The Sixth Form and College Entrance. *231 pp.*
● **Musgrove, F.** Youth and the Social Order. *176 pp.*
● **Ottaway, A. K. C.** Education and Society: An Introduction to the Sociology of Education. *With an Introduction by W. O. Lester Smith. 212 pp.*

Peers, Robert. Adult Education: *A Comparative Study. 398 pp.*

Pritchard, D. G. Education and the Handicapped: *1760 to 1960. 258 pp.*
Richardson, Helen. Adolescent Girls in Approved Schools. *308 pp.*
Stratta, Erica. The Education of Borstal Boys. *A Study of their Educational Experiences prior to, and during Borstal Training. 256 pp.*

SOCIOLOGY OF CULTURE

Eppel, E. M., and **M.** Adolescents and Morality: *A Study of some Moral Values and Dilemmas of Working Adolescents in the Context of a changing Climate of Opinion. Foreword by W. J. H. Sprott. 268 pp. 39 tables.*
● **Fromm, Erich.** The Fear of Freedom. *286 pp.*
   The Sane Society. *400 pp.*
Mannheim, Karl. Essays on the Sociology of Culture. *Edited by Ernst Mannheim in co-operation with Paul Kecskemeti. Editorial Note by Adolph Lowe. 280 pp.*
Weber, Alfred. Farewell to European History: *or The Conquest of Nihilism Translated from the German by R. F. C. Hull. 224 pp.*

SOCIOLOGY OF RELIGION

Argyle, Michael. Religious Behaviour. *224 pp. 8 figures. 41 tables.*
Nelson, G. K. Spiritualism and Society. *313 pp.*
Stark, Werner. The Sociology of Religion. *A Study of Christendom.*
   Volume I. *Established Religion. 248 pp.*
   Volume II. *Sectarian Religion. 368 pp.*
   Volume III. *The Universal Church. 464 pp.*
   Volume IV. *Types of Religious Man. 352 pp.*
   Volume V. *Types of Religious Culture. 464 pp.*
Watt, W. Montgomery. Islam and the Integration of Society. *320 pp.*

SOCIOLOGY OF ART AND LITERATURE

Jarvie, Ian C. Towards a Sociology of the Cinema. *A Comparative Essay on the Structure and Functioning of a Major Entertainment Industry. 405 pp.*
Rust, Frances S. Dance in Society. *An Analysis of the Relationships between the Social Dance and Society in England from the Middle Ages to the Present Day. 256 pp. 8 pp. of plates.*
Schücking, L. L. The Sociology of Literary Taste. *112 pp.*

SOCIOLOGY OF KNOWLEDGE

Mannheim, Karl. Essays on the Sociology of Knowledge. *Edited by Paul Kecskemeti. Editorial Note by Adolph Lowe. 353 pp.*
Remmling, Gunter W. (Ed.). Towards the Sociology of Knowledge. *Origins and Development of a Sociological Thought Style.*
Stark, Werner. The Sociology of Knowledge: *An Essay in Aid of a Deeper Understanding of the History of Ideas. 384 pp.*

URBAN SOCIOLOGY

Ashworth, William. The Genesis of Modern British Town Planning: *A Study in Economic and Social History of the Nineteenth and Twentieth Centuries. 288 pp.*
Cullingworth, J. B. Housing Needs and Planning Policy: *A Restatement of the Problems of Housing Need and 'Overspill' in England and Wales. 232 pp. 44 tables. 8 maps.*
Dickinson, Robert E. City and Region: *A Geographical Interpretation. 608 pp. 125 figures.*
 The West European City: *A Geographical Interpretation. 600 pp. 129 maps. 29 plates.*
● The City Region in Western Europe. *320 pp. Maps.*
Humphreys, Alexander J. New Dubliners: *Urbanization and the Irish Family. Foreword by George C. Homans. 304 pp.*
Jackson, Brian. Working Class Community: *Some General Notions raised by a Series of Studies in Northern England. 192 pp.*
Jennings, Hilda. Societies in the Making: *a Study of Development and Redevelopment within a County Borough. Foreword by D. A. Clark. 286 pp.*
● **Mann, P. H.** An Approach to Urban Sociology. *240 pp.*
Morris, R. N., and **Mogey, J.** The Sociology of Housing. *Studies at Berinsfield. 232 pp. 4 pp. plates.*
Rosser, C., and **Harris, C.** The Family and Social Change. *A Study of Family and Kinship in a South Wales Town. 352 pp. 8 maps.*

RURAL SOCIOLOGY

Chambers, R. J. H. Settlement Schemes in Tropical Africa: *A Selective Study. 268 pp.*
Haswell, M. R. The Economics of Development in Village India. *120 pp.*
Littlejohn, James. Westrigg: *the Sociology of a Cheviot Parish. 172 pp. 5 figures.*
Mayer, Adrian C. Peasants in the Pacific. *A Study of Fiji Indian Rural Society. 248 pp. 20 plates.*
Williams, W. M. The Sociology of an English Village: *Gosforth. 272 pp. 12 figures. 13 tables.*

SOCIOLOGY OF INDUSTRY AND DISTRIBUTION

Anderson, Nels. Work and Leisure. *280 pp.*
● **Blau, Peter M.,** and **Scott, W. Richard.** Formal Organizations: *a Comparative approach. Introduction and Additional Bibliography by J. H. Smith. 326 pp.*
Eldridge, J. E. T. Industrial Disputes. *Essays in the Sociology of Industrial Relations. 288 pp.*
Hetzler, Stanley. Applied Measures for Promoting Technological Growth. *352 pp.*
Technological Growth and Social Change. *Achieving Modernization. 269 pp.*
Hollowell, Peter G. The Lorry Driver. *272 pp.*
Jefferys, Margot, *with the assistance of Winifred Moss.* Mobility in the Labour Market: *Employment Changes in Battersea and Dagenham. Preface by Barbara Wootton. 186 pp. 51 tables.*
Millerson, Geoffrey. The Qualifying Associations: *a Study in Professionalization. 320 pp.*
Smelser, Neil J. Social Change in the Industrial Revolution: *An Application of Theory to the Lancashire Cotton Industry, 1770-1840. 468 pp. 12 figures. 14 tables.*
Williams, Gertrude. Recruitment to Skilled Trades. *240 pp.*
Young, A. F. Industrial Injuries Insurance: *an Examination of British Policy. 192 pp.*

DOCUMENTARY

Schlesinger, Rudolf (Ed.). Changing Attitudes in Soviet Russia.
2. The Nationalities Problem and Soviet Administration. *Selected Readings on the Development of Soviet Nationalities Policies. Introduced by the editor. Translated by W. W. Gottlieb. 324 pp.*

ANTHROPOLOGY

Ammar, Hamed. Growing up in an Egyptian Village: *Silwa, Province of Aswan. 336 pp.*
Brandel-Syrier, Mia. Reeftown Elite. *A Study of Social Mobility in a Modern African Community on the Reef. 376 pp.*
Crook, David, and **Isabel.** Revolution in a Chinese Village: *Ten Mile Inn. 230 pp. 8 plates. 1 map.*
Dickie-Clark, H. F. The Marginal Situation. *A Sociological Study of a Coloured Group. 236 pp.*
Dube, S. C. Indian Village. *Foreword by Morris Edward Opler. 276 pp. 4 plates.*
India's Changing Villages: *Human Factors in Community Development. 260 pp. 8 plates. 1 map.*

Firth, Raymond. Malay Fishermen. *Their Peasant Economy. 420 pp. 17 pp. plates.*

Gulliver, P. H. Social Control in an African Society: a Study of the Arusha, Agricultural Masai of Northern Tanganyika. *320 pp. 8 plates. 10 figures.*

Ishwaran, K. Shivapur. *A South Indian Village. 216 pp.*
Tradition and Economy in Village India: *An Interactionist Approach. Foreword by Conrad Arensburg. 176 pp.*

Jarvie, Ian C. The Revolution in Anthropology. *268 pp.*

Jarvie, Ian C., and **Agassi, Joseph.** Hong Kong. *A Society in Transition. 396 pp. Illustrated with plates and maps.*

Little, Kenneth L. Mende of Sierra Leone. *308 pp. and folder.*
Negroes in Britain. *With a New Introduction and Contemporary Study by Leonard Bloom. 320 pp.*

Lowie, Robert H. Social Organization. *494 pp.*

Mayer, Adrian C. Caste and Kinship in Central India: *A Village and its Region. 328 pp. 16 plates. 15 figures. 16 tables.*

Smith, Raymond T. The Negro Family in British Guiana: *Family Structure and Social Status in the Villages. With a Foreword by Meyer Fortes. 314 pp. 8 plates. 1 figure. 4 maps.*

SOCIOLOGY AND PHILOSOPHY

Barnsley, John H. The Social Reality of Ethics. *A Comparative Analysis of Moral Codes. 448 pp.*

Diesing, Paul. Patterns of Discovery in the Social Sciences. *362 pp.*

Douglas, Jack D. (Ed.). Understanding Everyday Life. *Toward the Reconstruction of Sociological Knowledge. Contributions by Alan F. Blum. Aaron W. Cicourel, Norman K. Denzin, Jack D. Douglas, John Heeren, Peter McHugh, Peter K. Manning, Melvin Power, Matthew Speier, Roy Turner, D. Lawrence Wieder, Thomas P. Wilson and Don H. Zimmerman. 370 pp.*

Jarvie, Ian C. Concepts and Society. *216 pp.*

Roche, Maurice. Phenomenology, Language and the Social Sciences. *About 400 pp.*

Sahay, Arun. Sociological Analysis.

Sklair, Leslie. The Sociology of Progress. *320 pp.*

International Library of Anthropology
General Editor Adam Kuper

Brown, Raula. The Chimbu. *A Study of Change in the New Guinea Highlands.*
Van Den Berghe, Pierre L. Power and Privilege at an African University.

International Library of Social Policy

General Editor   Kathleen Jones

Holman, Robert. Trading in Children. *A Study of Private Fostering.*
Jones, Kathleen. History of the Mental Health Services. *428 pp.*
Thomas, J. E. The English Prison Officer since 1850: *A Study in Conflict. 258 pp.*

Primary Socialization, Language and Education

General Editor   Basil Bernstein

Bernstein, Basil. Class, Codes and Control. *2 volumes.*
   1. *Theoretical Studies Towards a Sociology of Language. 254 pp.*
   2. *Applied Studies Towards a Sociology of Language. About 400 pp.*
Brandis, Walter, and **Henderson, Dorothy.** Social Class, Language and Communication. *288 pp.*
Cook-Gumperz, Jenny. Social Control and Socialization. *A Study of Class Differences in the Language of Maternal Control.*
Gahagan, D. M., and **G. A.** Talk Reform. *Exploration in Language for Infant School Children. 160 pp.*
Robinson, W. P., and **Rackstraw, Susan, D. A.** A Question of Answers. *2 volumes. 192 pp. and 180 pp.*
Turner, Geoffrey, J., and **Mohan, Bernard, A.** A Linguistic Description and Computer Programme for Children's Speech. *208 pp.*

Reports of the Institute of Community Studies

Cartwright, Ann. Human Relations and Hospital Care. *272 pp.*
   Parents and Family Planning Services. *306 pp.*
   Patients and their Doctors. *A Study of General Practice. 304 pp.*
● **Jackson, Brian.** Streaming: *an Education System in Miniature. 168 pp.*
Jackson, Brian, and **Marsden, Dennis.** Education and the Working Class: *Some General Themes raised by a Study of 88 Working-class Children in a Northern Industrial City. 268 pp. 2 folders.*
Marris, Peter. The Experience of Higher Education. *232 pp. 27 tables.*
Marris, Peter, and **Rein, Martin.** Dilemmas of Social Reform. *Poverty and Community Action in the United States. 256 pp.*
Marris, Peter, and **Somerset, Anthony.** African Businessmen. *A Study of Entrepreneurship and Development in Kenya. 256 pp.*
Mills, Richard. Young Outsiders: *a Study in Alternative Communities.*

Runciman, W. G. Relative Deprivation and Social Justice. *A Study of Attitudes to Social Inequality in Twentieth Century England. 352 pp.*

Townsend, Peter. The Family Life of Old People: *An Inquiry in East London. Foreword by J. H. Sheldon. 300 pp. 3 figures. 63 tables.*

Willmott, Peter. Adolescent Boys in East London. *230 pp.*

The Evolution of a Community: *a study of Dagenham after forty years. 168 pp. 2 maps.*

Willmott, Peter, and **Young, Michael.** Family and Class in a London Suburb. *202 pp. 47 tables.*

Young, Michael. Innovation and Research in Education. *192 pp.*

● **Young, Michael,** and **McGeeney, Patrick.** Learning Begins at Home. *A Study of a Junior School and its Parents. 128 pp.*

Young, Michael, and **Willmott, Peter.** Family and Kinship in East London. *Foreword by Richard M. Titmuss. 252 pp. 39 tables.*

The Symmetrical Family.

Reports of the Institute for Social Studies in Medical Care

Cartwright, Ann, Hockey, Lisbeth, and **Anderson, John L.** Life Before Death.

Dunnell, Karen, and **Cartwright, Ann.** Medicine Takers, Prescribers and Hoarders. *190 pp.*

Medicine, Illness and Society

General Editor W. M. Williams

Robinson, David. The Process of Becoming Ill.

Stacey, Margaret. *et al.* Hospitals, Children and Their Families. *The Report of a Pilot Study. 202 pp.*

Monographs in Social Theory

General Editor Arthur Brittan

Bauman, Zygmunt. Culture as Praxis.

Dixon, Keith. Sociological Theory. *Pretence and Possibility.*

Smith, Anthony D. The Concept of Social Change. *A Critique of the Functionalist Theory of Social Change.*

Routledge Social Science Journals

The British Journal of Sociology. *Edited by Terence P. Morris. Vol. 1, No. 1, March 1950 and Quarterly. Roy. 8vo. Back numbers available. An international journal with articles on all aspects of sociology.*

Economy and Society. *Vol. 1, No. 1. February 1972 and Quarterly. Metric Roy. 8vo. A journal for all social scientists covering sociology, philosophy, anthropology, economics and history. Back numbers available.*

Year Book of Social Policy in Britain, The. *Edited by Kathleen Jones. 1971. Published Annually.*